I0210110

# Compassion
# Mandala

*The Odyssey of an American Charity
in Contemporary Tibet*

# Other books by Pamela Logan

Among Warriors: A Woman Martial Artist in Tibet

Tibetan Rescue: The Extraordinary Quest
to Save the Sacred Art Treasures of Tibet

# Compassion Mandala

*The Odyssey of an American Charity*

*in Contemporary Tibet*

## Pamela Logan

Published by

Copyright © 2020 by Pamela Logan

All rights reserved. No part of this publication may be reproduced, stored in a retrieval system, or transmitted in any form, by any means, electronic, mechanical, photocopying, recording, scanning, or otherwise, without the prior written permission of the author, except in brief, attributed quotations used in academic publications or embedded in critical articles and reviews.

Content is based on field notes, reports, and other documents, and on the author's imperfect recollections.

Library of Congress Control Number: 2020908682
ISBN 978-1-7350538-0-6 (pbk)
978-1-7350538-1-3 (ebook)

First paperback edition September 2020

Published by Hibiscus Books
Lakewood, Colorado
publisher@hibiscus-books.com

Cover photograph by James Whitlow Delano
Author photograph by Gregory D. Clark
Book design by Darlene Swanson • van-garde.com
The text of this book is set in Adobe Garamond Pro

www.pamela-logan.com

10 9 8 7 6 5 4 3 2 1

Library of Congress Cataloging-in-Publication Data

Names: Logan, Pamela.
Title: Compassion Mandala: The Odyssey of an
American Charity in Contemporary Tibet / Pamela Logan.
Description: Lakewood, Colorado; Hibiscus Books, [2020] |
Includes bibliographical references, maps, trilingual list of places, and index.
Subjects: Tibet, Plateau of—Social conditions—21st century | Tibet, Plateau of—Economic Conditions—21st century | Tibet, Plateau of—Rural conditions—21st century | Tibet, Plateau of—Description and travel | Ganzi Zangzu Zizhizhou | Tibetans—Education | Tibetans—Employment | Tibetans—Health and hygiene | Nomads—Tibet, Plateau of— Economic Conditions | Logan, Pamela—Travel—Tibet

Classification: LCC DS786.L DDC 951'.505

**BISAC**
SOCIAL SCIENCE / Ethnic Studies / Asian Studies
SOCIAL SCIENCE / Developing & Emerging Countries

*For Greg*

# Contents

# Part II

## [Health]

## [Environment]

## [Maternal Health]

# Part III

## [Income Generation]

## [Information]

# Part IV

### [Cultural Heritage]

# Part V

### [Governance]

### [Community Ties]

# Part VI

### [Resilience]

# Final Notes

# Maps

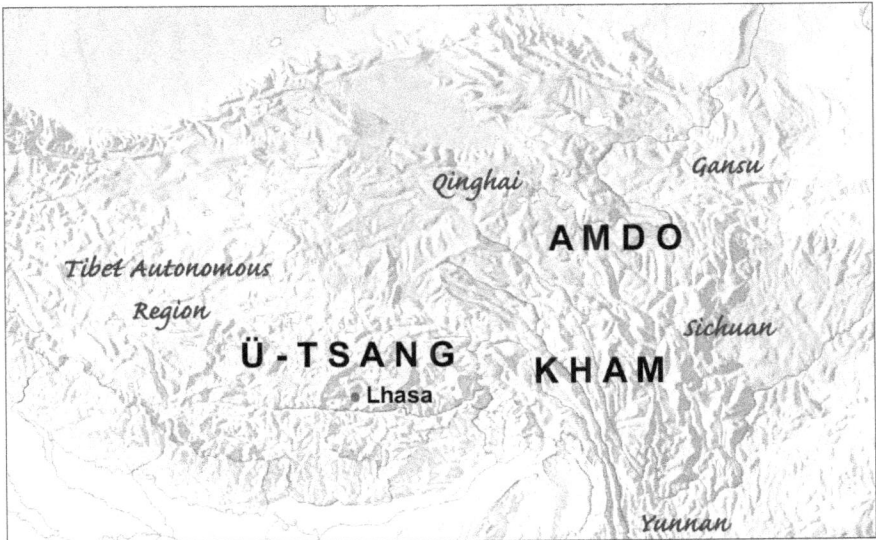

Photos and other resources may be found
at www.pamela-logan.com

# SICHUAN PROVINCE

Ngawa Tibetan & Qiang Autonomous Prefecture

Kandze Tibetan Autonomous Prefecture

Chengdu

Liangshan Yi Autonomous Prefecture

Xinjiang Uyghur Autonomous Region

Gansu

Qinghai

Tibet Autonomous Region

Yun-nan

**PEOPLE'S REPUBLIC OF CHINA**

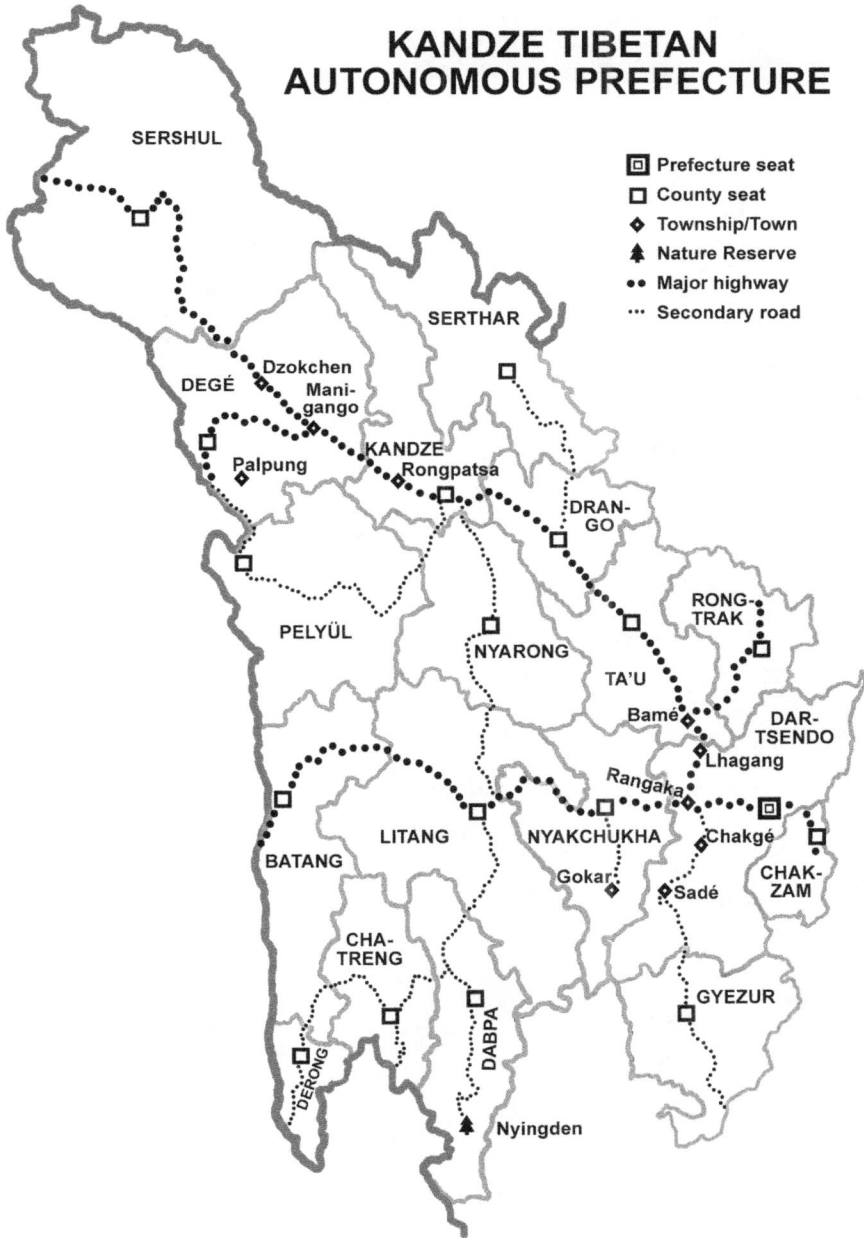

# KANDZE TIBETAN AUTONOMOUS PREFECTURE

SERSHUL

□ Prefecture seat
□ County seat
◆ Township/Town
♣ Nature Reserve
•• Major highway
··· Secondary road

SERTHAR

Dzokchen
DEGÉ   Mani-
       gango

KANDZE
Palpung   Rongpatsa

DRAN-
GO

RONG-
TRAK

PELYÜL

NYARONG

TA'U

Bamé

DAR-
TSENDO

Lhagang

Rangaka

LITANG   NYAKCHUKHA   Chakgé

BATANG   Gokar        CHAK-
                      Sadé   ZAM

CHA-
TRENG

DABPA        GYEZUR

DERONG

Nyingden

# Timeline

(External events in *italic type*)

## 1990-1991

Logan travels solo in Tibet and surrounding areas

## 1992-1997

Logan works at the China Exploration & Research Society

## 1994-1998

Logan leads Pewar Monastery repair and wall paintings conservation project

## 1997

Kham Aid Foundation is established in California

## 1998

First books delivered under KhamAid's Books for Schools program

Logan leads a fund-raising tour to Degé and meets Sögyal

Sögyal gets married

# 1999

Logan and Aldridge travel to Dzokchen

*The United States bombs China's embassy in Belgrade*

KhamAid makes a grant to Palpung Monastery for guest quarters

The Los Angeles Times publishes Logan's opinion essay

Dormitories at Chakgé School are built under a KhamAid grant

The first students enroll in middle school under KhamAid scholarships

Dana Isherwood becomes director of KhamAid's education program

A son is born to Sögyal and his wife

Logan meets the 14th Dalai Lama

*Erlangshan Tunnel opens to one-way traffic*

KhamAid's Books for Schools program publishes *Children's Fun Science* series

# 2000

Logan and others trek to Chakgé, lodging with herders en route

Sögyal passes away

KhamAid team visits clinics that employ traditional Tibetan medicine

A conservator assesses the condition of the Parkhang's wall paintings

Metok Tso enters junior middle school

KhamAid team treks in Konkaling and visits schools in Litang and Derong

KhamAid distributes wheelchairs in Dartsendo, Danba, and Ta'u

# 2001

*Erlangshan Tunnel is fully open*

*Gokar earthquake*

KhamAid plants tree seedlings above Oro Village

Wu Bangfu travels to Gokar earthquake zone

The Sichuan Archeological Institute assesses condition of the Parkhang

KhamAid cycling team assesses needs at clinics and hospitals

KhamAid funds the construction of a bridge at Gokar

Ten women from Nyakchukha complete KhamAid's midwife training

KhamAid team distributes wheelchairs in Nyakchukha, Litang, and Batang

US Consul General travels from Chengdu to inspect the Gokar Bridge

## 2002

*Western Sichuan is connected to the outside world by fiber optic cable*

KhamAid starts greenhouse program in Nyarong

Tree seedlings are planted above Oro Village in Nyakchukha

KhamAid team delivers medical supplies and equipment to clinics visited in 2001

Twenty women from Litang and Pelyul complete midwife training program

KhamAid completes renovation of Lharima primary school and clinic

KhamAid team distributes wheelchairs in Drango, Kandze, and Nyarong

## 2003

*SARS epidemic*

Nyarong greenhouses are built and owners bring in initial harvests

Books for Schools program issues books on famous people and women's health

Linda Griffin assesses the effectiveness of Books for Schools program

Metok Tso graduates from junior middle school

Twenty women from Serthar and Pelyul complete midwife training

Scholarship program grows to include senior middle school

KhamAid team renovates Bangmé school and clinic

KhamAid delivers medical equipment and supplies to monk-led charity clinics

KhamAid team distributes wheelchairs in Pelyul and Degé

## 2004

Windstorm damages Nyarong greenhouses

KhamAid team assesses midwife training program effectiveness

Eight Nyarong teachers complete certification training with KhamAid support

KhamAid team renovates Ponru School

KhamAid delivers medicines and equipment to religious-affiliated charity clinics

Kara Jenkinson becomes director of KhamAid's education program

Nineteen women from Dabpa and Sershul complete midwife training

KhamAid begins program execution under a USAID grant

KhamAid team distributes wheelchairs in Gyezur, Nyachukha, and Litang

# 2005

Kellogg Corps volunteers complete research on the handicraft market

KhamAid holds a construction skills training program at Senggé Monastery

KhamAid experts improve drainage on Senggé Monastery's main temple roof

A KhamAid volunteer gets into trouble for his liaison with a local woman

Metok Tso starts senior middle school

Twenty women from Gyezur and Nyarong complete midwife training

KhamAid builds a kitchen and guest quarters for Senggé Monastery

A KhamAid team meets residents of Wayö Village and tours their ancient houses

# 2006

KhamAid team sees the outcome of the construction skills program

Logan and Wu meet with Minyak Rinpoche

Lhamo Dolkar goes to the Gyeltang hospital for lupus treatment

Windstorm destroys the Nyarong greenhouses

KhamAid uncovers corruption at Ta'u Middle School

KhamAid holds training in the crafting of picture frames

Volunteers raise money by biking from Lijiang to Dartsendo

Metok Tso graduates from senior middle school and enters university

KhamAid surveys Wayö's ancient houses and does electrical upgrades

Lhamo Dolkar travels to Chengdu for treatment

KhamAid delivers medicines and equipment to religious-affiliated charity clinics

KhamAid repairs the damaged wall of an ancient Wayö house

KhamAid holds training in blanket weaving

## 2007

John Giszczak becomes director of KhamAid's education program

KhamAid discovers historic wall paintings in a temple in Pusarong Village

KhamAid repairs the roof of an ancient home in Wayö

KhamAid funds construction of five school greenhouses in Litang

KhamAid holds a workshop on handicraft development and marketing

KhamAid performs wall paintings conservation in Wayö Village

KhamAid repairs and helps reopen Wayö's primary school

Logan returns to Palpung Monastery

Metok Tso continues her studies at university

KhamAid team distributes wheelchairs in Degé and Sershul counties

## 2008

*Lhasa residents riot in protest of Chinese rule*

KhamAid repairs the roof of the temple in Pusarong Village

*Sichuan earthquake*

*China hosts the Summer Olympics*

KhamAid raises funds for Pusarong temple wall paintings conservation

*Global financial crisis and recession*

## 2009

KhamAid and a local NGO publish a Minyak language textbook

KhamAid gives cash and grain assistance to victims of the Sichuan earthquake

KhamAid completes repairs to the roof of the Pusarong temple

KhamAid surveys trained midwives to assess program effectiveness

The Chinese government closes Wayö School

KhamAid funds construction of five more school greenhouses in Litang

Four Dartsendo County primary schools pilot the Minyak language textbook

KhamAid's wheelchairs are delivered to Chaktreng, Dabpa, and Derong

Metok Tso applies to be an exchange student in Korea

## 2010

Metok Tso studies in Korea

*Yülshül earthquake*

Metok Tso raises funds for earthquake victims

KhamAid delivers wheelchairs to Drango, Kandze, and Sershul

Chinese art historians document the murals at Pusarong

Kham Aid Foundation ceases operations

# Compassion Mandala

# Preface

*Upstairs, in the heart of the first Buddhist temple ever built on the Tibetan plateau, sits a golden, three-dimensional mandala. Set upon a round dais about two meters wide, the mandala is square and tiered like a wedding cake: a gilded doll-house inhabited by radiant divinities paused in voluptuous mid-dance. This celestial miniature world is clasped within Samye Monastery's main temple, itself a mandala manifested as a six-story building. The main temple is, in turn, lodged at the bullseye of a circular mandala garden bejeweled with stupas, temples, and other Buddhist totems. Each nested mandala symbolizes Mount Meru, the sacred five-peaked summit that is the center of all universes.*

*"Mandala" is a chameleon concept, a shadow that can lay itself across many things. Including development. To uplift a community is a voyage with many points of departure and innumerable twists and turns. The most well-known gates are education, health care, income generation, and environment, but there are many others.*

*Most important: Entering a single gate will not solve the puzzle. One must follow every corridor simultaneously to the center, for the paths are knotted together and cannot be untangled.*

*This book is about the journey of a small American nonprofit through the development mandala in Tibet.*

# Prologue

---

I WAS WALKING WITH FIVE others, ascending into high, scrubby terrain with no sign of human life. The climb was harder than expected, and our progress was slow. I had planned for us to reach the little hamlet of Chakgé in a single day, but by mid-afternoon, it was clear that we would fall short of this goal. We debated turning around, but the local man who was our guide said that we would find houses a little way further.

The afternoon grew late, and the clouds darkened, but we kept climbing. Icy flecks of snow began drifting down. Scanning the desolate, rock-strewn landscape as I walked, I was heartened to see that the trail was gradually flattening, heralding that the pass was close.

As the last glimmers of daylight trickled away, snowflakes fell more thickly, covering the footpath and its surroundings with the same feathery white blanket. We pulled out flashlights and kept going. The trail was fading away, and I began to worry we would be lost. Bivouacking would be rough: between the six of us, we had only two small tents and three sleeping bags. But fortune smiled, for at long last, we spotted a lone black herder's tent crouched beneath the silver curtains of falling snow.

The Tibetans in our party nominated me to make the first approach. "They'll know we're not bandits," said one, "if they see you first."

Scattered around the tent entrance, a dozen hoar-frosted yaks stood mute and motionless as lawn furniture. As I drew near, a dog barked explosively, and I heard a chain's taut jangle. I stopped in my tracks and called out *"Arro! Arro!"* in my best hailing Tibetan. A moment later, a woman in a dark *chuba* (Tibetan robe) emerged to see who was there.

The woman stared at me but registered no surprise. I gestured toward my five friends standing back at a safe distance, veiled by falling snow. Her eyes quickly took in our predicament. Gripping the dog's chain with both hands to keep the dog from lunging, she beckoned me forward. I carefully skirted the snarling canine and stooped to enter the tent vestibule, where three baby yaks were tethered. Stepping over them one by one, I made my way inside.

# Part I

# The Beginning

If you ask me how I got to Tibet, in a nutshell, the answer is: I like to climb. As a tiny girl growing up in the Chicago suburbs, my earliest targets were the high-backed chairs in our dining room. My mother would come sprinting from the kitchen to pluck me from the jaws of catastrophe before the chair and I collided with the floor. As I got older, I tried climbing trees, but otherwise, Illinois was tragically devoid of verticality. We weren't the sort of family to go on ski vacations, so I was oblivious to mountains. I could only stare into the empty midwestern sky, yearning for a way up.

As a teen, I devoured science fiction and dreamed of journeying the cosmos, but my plan to be an astronaut fell apart when I found out that my bad eyes disqualified me. My father, a mathematician and ardent science-lover, packed me off to Caltech in Pasadena, California, where I started studying the subject with the most *up* in it: astronomy. When that proved difficult, I switched to the next uppest thing, aeronautical engineering. For *up* was where I was determined to go.

The convoluted version of how I got to Tibet involves a pastime I took up in college: Shotokan karate, a Japanese martial art. Throughout college, graduate school, and a postdoc, I trained relentlessly and worked my way up to third-degree black belt. This passion for Japanese *bushido*—the Way of the Warrior—led me to investigate the fighting traditions of other countries, and I learned about the warriors of a place called Kham and their role in resisting Chinese rule in Tibet. The notion of actual warriors was captivating, and Tibet had a lot of *up* in it. I sought and won a travel grant to find out more.

While I was preparing for this trip of a lifetime, an old college professor introduced me to an explorer-writer-photographer named Wong How Man. He was a Hong Kong-born Chinese and expert on

China's ethnic frontiers. Wong had a small organization called the China Exploration & Research Society (CERS). Their aim: to investigate China's little-known corners, conserve ecosystems and cultural traditions, and share knowledge about these places with the rest of the world. To Wong, I was just a wannabe with no experience or credibility. Nevertheless, he shared with me his knowledge of Kham, a region he knew well. It would be up to me to construct my own cred by completing the journey on my own.

Armed with the basics of the Tibetan and Chinese languages and Wong's precious advice, in the fall of 1990, I set out for Kham. I was by no means sure whether I could get around China's restrictions on foreigners entering the region, but I was determined to learn as much as I could. I spent more than a year on the road, probing the eastern edges of the Tibetan plateau, constantly testing the limits of the authorities' patience. Eventually, I made my way into Kham, biking, hiking, and hitchhiking to reach out-of-the-way villages and monasteries.

After that life-changing trip, instead of returning to my career in aeronautics, I decided to volunteer for CERS full-time. I was addicted to adventure, and I wanted to put "explorer-writer-photographer" in front of my name. Thanks to a modest inheritance from my father, who had passed away in 1989 of cancer, I could afford to freelance for a while. I moved into CERS's office in a village on the south side of Hong Kong island, determined to stretch my inheritance to the maximum and live the dream that CERS could make possible.

For two years, I helped put out reports, raise money, and manage CERS's collection of photos and artifacts. At times I left the office for mainland China, where I traveled far and hard and usually solo, improvising transportation, staying in tents, temples, and the homes of people I encountered. I explored Xinjiang and Inner Mongolia and saw more of Tibet. My list of published articles grew, and I started giving talks.

Then, in 1994, Wong rewarded me with a special assignment: to lead a project at a remote Tibetan monastery in Sichuan Province. The project's goal was to save precious 270-year-old Buddhist wall paintings threatened by the crumbling temple in which they were housed. At that time, Pewar Monastery was accessible only by a backcountry trail; everything we needed had to be carried in on horseback. The government was intensely suspicious of the project; it was only possible thanks to Wong's influential Tibetan friends and because officials in Degé County genuinely supported the preservation of their historic past.

During those five adventure-filled years of taking conservation teams to Pewar, I cultivated contacts of my own in Chengdu and Kham. I improved my Chinese and picked up a smattering of the Degé dialect. The knowledge and contacts were like a muscle begging to be flexed, a superpower I couldn't ignore. Now I wanted to use it to help people in Kham struggling against poverty, a great and noble reason to keep on returning to a place I loved. In the Tibetan year of the Fire-Cow (1997), I left CERS and with the help of two friends established a new nonprofit in California. I called it Kham Aid Foundation.

## A Guarded Welcome

Later that same year, on a crisp day in October, I went with my assistant, Mr. Wu, to the Foreign Affairs Office in the chief city of Kandze Prefecture. He had advised me that, instead of slinking around in the shadows as some other foreign groups were trying to do, we should seek permission from the authorities to work openly. The goal of our visit was to make official contact and get a green light to do projects in Kham.

We were in Dartsendo, a dense and bustling valley town, walking on a narrow street coursing through a forest of tall apartment buildings. The government compound rested in perpetual shadow against one of the valley walls. It was barred by a steel gate, flanked by two soldiers standing on pedestals. Mr. Wu inquired at the kiosk, where they told us to go inside, cross the courtyard, and proceed to an annex in the rear.

The annex turned out to be a concrete box covered on the outside with white ceramic tiles—a cross between a bunker and a bathhouse. Inside, it was ice cold. The two of us trudged down a long hallway to the far end where we found Zhu Changcheng, deputy director of the Foreign Affairs Office, at his desk in a small, bare room.

Zhu was a stocky, square-faced man of about forty-five, swaddled in layers of sweaters topped by a dark business suit. The suit's label was still affixed to the outside of the sleeve. His given name, *Changcheng*, meant "Great Wall," for he was born in an era when patriotic names were in vogue. Half Han and half Tibetan, Zhu was a cagey and unreadable character who avoided eye contact.[1] Although his domain was foreign affairs, Zhu spoke no English whatsoever. "Welcome! Welcome!" he spluttered in Chinese to Mr. Wu, as if I weren't there. "Have a seat," he said, motioning to a bench. "Drink tea?"

It was more of a command than a question. While Zhu was fetching tea, Mr. Wu and I sat warming our hands over an electric coil heater set into a low table. Zhu returned with two enamel mugs of fragrant jasmine tea served local style, that is, with the leaves swimming loose in hot water. I blew on the surface to push the leaves back so I could take a sip. Meanwhile, Mr. Wu explained why we had come.

"I see." Zhu cleared his throat and pulled his chair closer to the heater. "Her passport?"

---

1 Han are the dominant ethnic group in China; they comprise 91.5% of the country's population.

I pulled out my passport and handed it to Zhu. He leafed through it rapidly, pausing only on pages that had Chinese visas. Finding nothing suspicious, he handed it back. "According to the rules and regulations," he said to Mr. Wu, "you must report to us first. Then you must contact the relevant department in the county where you want to do the project and give them a detailed plan."

To make sure I understood, I asked Wu to translate Zhu's words into English. Seeing that I was taking notes, Zhu corrected himself: "No. Reverse that. First, contact the county, and then report to us. That's the procedure."

"Is this procedure written down somewhere?" I asked.

"Of course. It's the law."

"Can we get a copy of it then?"

He cleared his throat. "That's not possible." His eyes darted here and there, everywhere but to me.

"How do we register? Is there a form?"

"There's no form. Give me your name and address and a copy of your organization's certificate."

I tore a sheet out of my notebook, on which Mr. Wu and I wrote down our names and addresses, and Wu wrote down the Chinese name of our organization, *Meiguo Kangba Yuanzhu Jijinhui.* Zhu took the paper and stashed it solemnly in a desk drawer. I promised to mail him a copy of our "certificate," which I figured would be the letter we got from the State of California granting our nonprofit status. It wasn't the fancy diploma-like thing that Zhu would be expecting, but it had a stamp on it. (In China, a document is useless unless it's been stamped.)

Wu Bangfu, a.k.a. "Mr. Wu," was my nonprofit's first and, thus far, only paid employee. His starting wage was the Chinese equivalent of US$113/month. I would have preferred to hire a Tibetan, but at that time the only English-speaking Tibetans in the prefecture were a handful of India-returned monks. I had met a couple of them, and their skills were too rudimentary to be of use. My Chinese was basic and unsuitable for high-stakes parleys. I needed a good interpreter.

Over time, though, Mr. Wu would become far more than a translator. Slight of build and plain in appearance, his unassuming manner and his fluency in the local Chinese dialect had a reassuring effect on government officials. For the last couple of years, Mr. Wu had been working for me intermittently on the Pewar Monastery conservation project. His abilities had been instrumental in that project's success, and I trusted him.

The city of Dartsendo is the seat of the regional government, and it was also Mr. Wu's home. For US$23/month, he rented a two-bedroom flat to be our field office. The office was boxed in by other buildings on all sides, dark, and perpetually chilly. But it enjoyed a fine location in the center of town, across the street from a small Buddhist monastery, and within earshot of the Gyula Chu (Gyula River) hurtling through the city between concrete embankments. A few steps away were several dry goods stores and noodle shops, a vendor selling kebabs, a small bakery, and the Kangding Hotel. That little apartment would soon become our nexus of operations.

As things turned out, Mr. Wu and I would be working with Zhu Changcheng for about a decade. He was an odd bird. He didn't drink or go to banquets like most officials. He stayed at his post in the Foreign Affairs Office long after he could have retired. He wasn't exactly a champion for KhamAid, but he would keep us on the straight and narrow concerning the rest of the government. We would invite him to dinner several times but he accepted only once, an awkward evening that ended early. Zhu was not a social animal.

Our main business complete, we sipped more tea and chatted with Zhu about school projects. We wanted to hire a teacher for a small private school in a village in Degé County, and to build dormitories for a government school in Chakgé Township of Dartsendo County. Zhu asked who our donors were, and I told him they were foundations and ordinary Americans who wanted to help people in China. Zhu seemed satisfied with this answer. He didn't ask for the sponsors' names, or how much money they gave, or how the money traveled to China.

Zhu did caution us that we could not do any projects unless we followed the rules and regulations. It didn't seem to bother him that no one could tell us what they were. I could picture the report he was going to write for his bosses. The key sentence would be: *I instructed the foreigner to obey all rules and regulations.* His duty was done. After a re-fill of our mugs and more social pleasantries, we were allowed to leave.

Once safely on the street, I wanted to jump for joy, for I was on my way to achieving a marvelous objective: getting official approval to help Tibetans. It had been surprisingly easy.

Around that time two other good things happened. One was that dial-up Internet service arrived in Dartsendo, making it easy to communicate with Mr. Wu from my base in Los Angeles. The other was that the Chinese government decided to remove restrictions on foreign tourists traveling independently in Kandze Tibetan Autonomous Prefecture. I would no longer need to jump through hoops to obtain a special permit. Instead, a valid tourist visa stamped in my passport would take me anywhere I wanted to go.

The doors to Kandze Prefecture had been flung wide open. But how long could it last?

## Kham: An Introduction

Ethnographic Tibet comprises three ancient provinces: —Ü-Tsang, Amdo, and Kham. The first of these, —Ü-Tsang, is home to the holy capital, Lhasa, and the great valley of the Yarlung Tsangpo River, the cradle of Tibetan civilization. Amdo is a lesser-known territory lying on Tibet's northeastern frontier, a place of vast grasslands bordered by Chinese Muslim regions.

The place I had chosen for my new organization's focus was neither of these; it was the third province, Kham. Taking up the far east of the Tibetan plateau, Kham is a land beribboned by jagged ranges, gouged by mighty rivers, and rinsed by heavy rainfall, a land whose soil gives richly of grain and whose pastures fatten numberless livestock, a land whose secluded valleys give sanctuary to Buddhist teachings expunged and forgotten elsewhere in Tibet.

Kham and the other two ancient provinces live on in culture and dialect, but not in governance or on maps. Today's maps usually show an oval-shaped blob labeled Tibet Autonomous Region (TAR), sometimes referred to in the literature as "political Tibet." However, TAR takes up only about half the area inhabited by people of Tibetan ethnicity; four other Chinese provinces—Sichuan, Gansu, Qinghai, and Yunnan—have sizeable Tibetan populations. In this book, I will use "Tibet" to refer to this greater ethnographic area, and "TAR" to refer to the political Tibet shown on maps.

Viewed through a Tibetan lens, the region called "Kham" is home to 1.5 million Khampas, about a quarter of all Tibetans.[2] However, only once in history was the whole of Kham brought under a single govern-

---

2    To a Tibetan, the word "*Kham-pa*" refers to males, and "*Kham-mo*" refers to females. Nonetheless—and with apologies to knowledgeable speakers—here I use "*Khampa*" broadly to include all genders.

ment: in the seventh to ninth centuries, when the Tibetan Empire was at its apex. Throughout most of history, Kham was cleaved in two by a boundary that shifted with the ebb and flow of rival powers but was most often demarked by the Dri Chu (upper Yangtze River). In 1939, the Republic of China briefly joined the two halves together, redrawing borders to create a province called Xikang, and appointed Chinese warlord Liu Wenhui as governor. However, Xikang lasted only until 1955 when the victorious Communists tore it asunder once more.

So, despite their cultural similarities, Kham's western and eastern halves have charted different historical paths. The western half of Kham was an undisputed part of independent Tibet; it paid taxes to the central government in Lhasa and was defended by Tibetan troops. Meanwhile, east of the Dri Chu, Khampas rejected Lhasa's political authority, although they remained ardently devoted to the Dalai Lama as their supreme religious leader. Eastern Kham was, in effect, a buffer zone where local chieftains played Lhasa and Beijing against each other to maximize their independence.

KhamAid's turf was this eastern part of Kham, which China has placed in Sichuan Province and designated as Kandze Tibetan Autonomous Prefecture, with its headquarters at Dartsendo.[3] The eighteen counties of Kandze TAP occupy a total of 147,681 square kilometers (57,020 square miles): about the size of the nation of Croatia or the American state of Illinois. In 2010, it was home to about a million legally registered residents, of whom 78% were ethnic Tibetans.

Yet Kandze Prefecture is not a monolith; it is a mosaic of polities, each with its own language and history. Although China claimed the region, until 1950 their power was limited, for their garrisons were too

---

3   The word "autonomous" is fiction; the prefecture is subject to close oversight by provincial and national authorities.

small and widely scattered to put down a major rebellion, especially in remote areas where reinforcements could take weeks to arrive. The Chinese therefore relied heavily on Tibetan chieftains, maintaining them as puppet rulers to provide continuity and calm.

For example, the polity called Degé (now a county) was for thirteen centuries ruled by a succession of hereditary kings who conquered surrounding areas, amassed great wealth, and built large and influential monasteries. Another powerful realm, Minyak (later called Chakla) encompassed what are now Dartsendo and surrounding counties. The Minyak language is unrelated to Tibetan; between invasions by imperial China, Minyak was a flourishing center of scholarship, architecture, and art. Other enclaves included Trehor, which lay east of Degé and straddled a major east-west caravan route, Baligyesum in the southwest, Gyarong in the northeast, and Golok in the north. When the authority of China and Tibet was weak, these kingdoms frequently warred with each other for territory and power.

Thus, for centuries, the place now known as Kandze Prefecture was characterized by balkanization, fluid borders, and incessant conflict. Due to the rugged terrain, power was difficult to consolidate and hold, and many communities remained isolated. Languages and dialects are numerous and mostly unintelligible to Tibetans from outside the region and even to each other. This pugnacious and polyglot territory was where KhamAid would do virtually all of its work.

When I started the art conservation project at Pewar Monastery, Kandze Prefecture was *terra incognita* to foreign aid workers.[4] Few in-

---

4    Chöje Akong Tulku Rinpoche and his organization, Rokpa International were
     notable exceptions.

ternational NGOs (nongovernmental organizations) went there because of the transportation, travel permit, and communication challenges. By contrast, TAR—especially Lhasa—excited the imagination of outsiders and had an airport; it was therefore the earliest part of Tibet to attract international aid.

Kham's poverty was comparable to that of TAR. In Kandze Prefecture, most people lived hand to mouth and were vulnerable to extreme weather that could wipe out their crops and livestock. Government statistics showed the 1999 average annual cash income as only 721 yuan (US$89) per capita—and that includes salaried government workers living in towns. Schools and hospitals were few and far between, and people lacked the skills to work outside the agrarian economy. For KhamAid, there was much work to do.

# Education

*A child without education is like a bird without wings.*
— Tibetan proverb[5]

To develop a child's consciousness, to make it strong, is to release greatness. If we are to pass to the center of the development mandala, one indispensable gate is education of our precious children.

Tibet's academic traditions have always been laser-focused on Buddhism and a few other topics in its near orbit, and have produced many great scholars, yet historically, the average monk had only the basic literacy needed to recite prayers, and often not even that. Before 1949, secular schools were exceedingly rare. Lhasa had two small academies, together enrolling about fifty students, to prepare boys from elite families for positions in the government. British influence led to an English school being established in Gyantse in the 1920s, but it served only twenty-five students and closed after three years due to opposition from Tibet's powerful Buddhist monasteries. The rich could send children to India or have them tutored privately, but the vast majority of children had no way to get an education. Ignorance and illiteracy reigned, especially in rural areas.

In the Sichuan part of Kham, the local chieftains and Chinese magistrates who administered the region before 1950 did not establish anything resembling public schools.

---

5    Proverbs are drawn from *Tibetan Proverbs,* compiled by Lhamo Pemba, Library of Tibetan Works and Archives, 2007; and *Love Songs and Proverbs of Tibet,* by Marion H Duncan (London: The Mitre Press, 1961).

However, foreign Christians in their scattered missions defied the monasteries by giving lessons to orphans and the children of converts. As in central Tibet, monasteries taught some young novices to read and write Buddhist scripture, but regular boys and girls had no access to schooling.

When the Communists arrived, they set out to build a public education system from scratch. By the early 1950s, they had established schools in major population centers and were using them to teach children basic Chinese literacy, socialism, and to love Chairman Mao. The Party groomed the most promising young Tibetans by sending them to the Chinese interior for advanced studies. Although these students hated the brainwashing and propaganda, they still thirsted for knowledge and a chance to see the outside world.

## Schools, Children, and Books

Education was so obviously important that when KhamAid was newly formed, it was the first thing I wanted to tackle. I persuaded some officials to give me a tour of a few schools and share some statistics. In 1997, in Kandze TAP, the government was operating the following:

| Level | Number of Schools |
|---|---|
| Primary (Grades 1–6) | 1,224 |
| Junior Middle (Grades 7–9) | 22 |
| Senior Middle and Vocational (Grades 10–12) | 19 |
| Colleges and Teaching Academies | 8 |

The numbers were impressive, but many of the primary schools were little more than one-room schoolhouses, and all were badly underfunded.[6]

At about this time, 81,336 children in Kandze TAP were enrolled in the six years of primary school, and another 13,756 children in the six years of middle school up to age eighteen.[7] One official told me that the enrollment rate for primary-age children in Kandze Prefecture was 95%, but this was nonsense, for schooling was simply unavailable to many rural children because the schools were too far away and lacked boarding facilities. In fact, at that time, only three of the Kandze Prefecture's eighteen counties were able to offer a full six years of primary education to all of their children, although the Education Bureau was aiming to offer at least four years throughout the prefecture by 2005.[8]

As children advanced through the system, the schools that served them became fewer, more expensive, and located only in population centers. Tuition varied from place to place, but in the late 1990s, it generally fell between 150 and 800 yuan (US$17-$91) per year.

Because the population was so widely dispersed, some schools, mostly in the higher grades, accommodated boarding students, with the cost of food and lodging borne by parents. At the primary school in Chakgé, boarding students lived in a single-story longhouse divided into rooms, each shared by five or six students. To my Western eyes,

---

6   Nine years earlier, in 1988, Kandze Prefecture had 902 primary schools with 60,000 students, 24 junior middle schools with about 7,000 students, and 18 senior middle schools with about 3,000 students. At the secondary level, the prefecture had three teacher training academies and four other schools for specialized vocational training. A. Doak Barnett, *China's Far West: Four Decades of Change* (Taipei: SMC Publishing, Inc., 1993), p. 459.

7   Åshild Kolås and Monika P. Thowsen, *On the Margins of Tibet: Cultural Survival on the Sino-Tibetan Frontier* (University of Washington Press, 2005), Appendix 4.

8   Ibid., Chapter 3.

conditions were appalling: cold cement floors, broken windows, dis-integrating plaster, leaking roofs. There was no running water, just a pump in the yard. Heat came from a small, unventilated coal burner, and families were charged extra for the coal. The school provided three meals a day of barley flour and butter-tea; sometimes the children also got noodles, cabbage, or potatoes.

As the Tibetan year of the Earth-Tiger (1998) dawned, I was bent on raising money for education. Many Westerners I spoke to immediately assumed that we wanted to build our own school. However, building a school is not helpful unless you also operate it. Our donors liked the building idea, but not so much the idea of operation, which took real commitment. Because the Chinese government could throw us out at any moment, it seemed best to do projects that didn't require a lasting presence. Regardless, KhamAid could get more bang for the buck by leveraging existing infrastructure than by building from scratch.

In matters of education, I was guided by a Tibetan who had a doctorate in the field: Professor Palden Nyima (Ch: Badeng Nima), who was on the faculty at Sichuan Normal University, south of Chengdu. The professor was a slightly built man with curly hair, about forty years old, who looked perpetually careworn as if the world rested on his shoulders. Despite political pressures that waxed and waned, he remained at his post, where he was a tireless advocate for Tibetan education.

"We must *not* lose our traditional culture," he declared one day, as we were taking a long walk around the leafy campus. Rare among Tibetans of his generation, Palden Nyima spoke excellent English.

I asked him about monasteries and whether they might teach secular subjects in addition to Buddhism.

"Religion can help us in our work, but if we want to do big things, we need to think bigger. There is a big gap between Tibetan traditional culture and modern culture. Our children must understand both. I published some articles about this but the officials don't understand them. They think that 'development' for Tibetans means Sinicization."

Then he added: "We need to build up science in Tibetan. If we do that, then Tibetan culture will have a springtime, a flowering."

Science? This got my attention, for I was a firm believer in the power of science to help people rationally navigate their world.

The previous year, I had visited schools and spoken with many teachers and administrators. I knew that most children entered primary school understanding only their mother tongue, usually a dialect of Tibetan. At a typical primary school, therefore, the early years of instruction were in Tibetan; then instruction gradually shifted until most classes were given in Chinese.[9] Herder children from the grasslands studied Chinese history and the works of dead Chinese poets, subjects that meant nothing to them. The curriculum conveyed the message that Tibetan culture was backward and useless. As a result, it failed to engage Tibetan pupils, and many dropped out.

I enlisted the professor to help me develop a project we would call "Books for Schools." Its aims: to teach children about science, show them the greatness of Tibetan culture, and get them excited about learning. There were no science books in Tibetan suitable for children, so we would print some. Furthermore, we would buy up all of the Tibetan language books we could find to show children the panoply of Tibetan achievements.

We wrote a proposal and sent it to the Carl and Lily Pforzheimer Foundation, a staid institution that normally supported Ivy League universities and research libraries. Thanks to a California supporter

---

9 Bilingual schools also existed in Kandze TAP and elsewhere; see Kolås and Thowsen, Chapter 3.

who was connected to the Pforzheimers, we landed a US$30,000 grant.

Books were hard to get in Kham. Tibetans were devoted to the loose-leaf *chakpe* (scriptures) printed by monasteries, but these were more objects of veneration than reading material. A reader looking for a modern, bound book could find them in government bookstores where half the stock might be in Chinese and half in Tibetan, heavy on political treatises and biographies of famous communists, but also with a few Buddhist titles and a sprinkling of reference works, novels, and practical nonfiction such as farming manuals.

In practice, no one but the most erudite monks and university graduates had enough money and literacy to acquire a private library. Spoken Tibetan was everywhere, but literature was the realm of only the most educated: university graduates and monk-scholars.[10]

Palden Nyima recruited two bookish friends: Tsering, who worked for a publishing house, and Yeshi, a teacher. Together they went on a shopping spree, cleaning out all four of China's Nationality presses of everything suitable. They bought 8,929 books on myriad subjects and spent a little less than ten thousand U.S. dollars.

Tsering had recently acquired a flat near People's Road South and had not yet moved in, so he was using it as a book warehouse. I went to visit and found every room stacked with parcel towers. Yeshi opened a few packages and pulled out samples to show me. Most were cheaply made softcovers—but oh, the treasures inside: dictionaries, grammars, folktales, philosophy, history, poetry, and more. Now we just had to put them into children's hands.

---

10  Four government-run universities in China have programs in Tibetan language and literature: Tibet University, Southwest Minzu University and Northwest Minzu University (formerly Southwest and Northwest University for Nationalities, respectively), and Minzu University of China. There are also numerous research institutes.

Trusting neither the Education Bureau nor the postal system, Tsering and Yeshi were determined to hand-deliver the thousands of tomes themselves. In late autumn, the two loaded up a lorry and set out, heading for the most poverty-stricken, book-deprived schools in Kham. They were on the road for a month and delivered books to eighty-five schools with a combined enrollment of about ten thousand children.

Afterward, the pair told me about the heartbreaking difficulties facing students and teachers in remote areas. County apparatchiks were indifferent to the books (they would have preferred cash), but the teachers were excited and grateful. The two accumulated a fat envelope of hand-written thank you letters from school headmasters. "We must take care of the books and dictionaries and let the students and teachers read them," said one. "We'll never just keep the books in storage."

Now doubly energized and inspired, Palden Nyima began assembling a team of expert translators for our next project: a Tibetan-language version of a Chinese series called *Children's Fun Science*, which we would print and distribute.

## The Tea Road to Kham

The Pforzheimer grant did little for KhamAid's administrative overhead and nothing for my travel from California to Sichuan. To raise money for these expenses, I had set up an adventure tour and induced half a dozen Americans to participate. As part of the tour, we would be delivering a load of books to a rural primary school. After months of planning, I arrived in Chengdu excited to see it all come to fruition.

Chengdu was a megapolis of more than ten million people crammed under a blanket of humidity and smog. Leaving it always brought me acute happiness as the mud-brown sky annealed to purest blue. My travelers and I would take the "Tea Road to Tibet," an ancient thoroughfare named for an indispensable staple. For centuries just a footpath, the track had carried traders, soldiers, missionaries, and pilgrims westward from the Sichuan basin up into Kham's high fastnesses.

A few years previously, this first leg out of Chengdu had been a tree-shaded country lane rolling past stout farmhouses, rice paddies, and quilts of corn, rape, and sunflowers. Now, however, that venerable old road was being blasted into smithereens so it could be remade into a six-lane expressway. The bus carrying my tour group and me was propelled into Detour Hell, for construction wasn't only on the trunk roads, it was also on the side roads. Even the detours had detours, and those detours were torn up, too.

Having my own hired bus was a great luxury, for I usually traveled on public transit. As we bumped along, I explained to the tour group that for two years the Sichuan Transportation Bureau had been diverting traffic to a mountain pass far to the south, and the journeys were epic. You boarded a sleeper bus at three in the afternoon, reclined on a narrow, accordion-shaped bed in close contact with the stranger next to you, and lurched away the hours. If your luck was good, you would reach the other end before noon the next day, but sometimes the voyage stretched to twenty-four hours or longer.

In early afternoon, we reached the tea capital, Ya'an, the last truly Chinese city. After lunch, we set out on a slender artery slithering up into the mountain jungle. Rain began to fall, the last hurrah of the summer monsoon. Here, too, work was underway, to shore up unstable slopes that often dropped rocks onto the pavement or snatched away roadbed from underneath. We passed mile after mile of road crews: scrawny, ill-clad wretches who toiled with picks and shovels to connect China to its far west.

Many miles later, a concrete wall with a gaping black hole in it sprang out of the jungle, like a gateway to the underworld. This was the Erlang Shan Tunnel, an engineering wonder at that time, especially in Tibet. Drilled laser-like through a vast barricade of rock, it was a tesseract from Sichuan tea country to the beginnings of the high plateau.

I explained to my travelers what this futuristic marvel was replacing—a crooked, six-times-longer track throttled by rain-filled runnels and jungly overgrowth. As yet, only one tunnel lane was open: eastbound traffic on even days, westbound on odd. I had planned carefully to swim with the current. We plunged in, and after 4.2 kilometers (2.6 miles) in tubular *bardo*, we burst out into the immense canyon of the Tatu Chu.

It was getting dark, but we still had many miles ahead. Navigating by headlights and a constellation of faintly flickering farmhouses arrayed on the opposite side, we descended on a series of crazy switchbacks, drove three more hours on the river's eastern bank, then crossed to the west side and commenced to climb. An hour later we emerged from blackness to see a line of low-slung chow-houses and automotive repair shops, all shuttered at this hour. There followed the dim lights of the Dartsendo bus station, then the beginnings of the town proper.

Dartsendo Town sits on the threshold of the Roof of the World and serves as its gateway. In all, we had driven fourteen hours to get here—the same journey taken by every book, notepad, and pencil used by every schoolchild in Kandze TAP. And we still had far to go.

## Guardian of the Future: Gyalten Rinpoche

We took a day in Dartsendo for sightseeing, then set out on the road again, westward ho. The monsoon had snagged on the foothills behind us, and we enjoyed a dry, sunny ascent. Crossing a pass, the first of many, brought us to a landscape that was purely Tibetan: stone houses set between fields of barley; rangelands and grazing livestock; Buddhist temples, stupas, and strings of red-white-blue-green-yellow prayer flags snapping in the wind.

Two days later, we reached the township of Rongpatsa, a broad valley delineated on the south by a rake of snaggled-tooth summits and on the north by swelling hills. Now, close to harvest time, the valley was an amber carpet of barley almost ready to reap.

The passage of trading caravans since time immemorial had made Rongpatsa prosperous, as we could see from the spacious rammed-earth homes. Nevertheless, the valley was book-poor. The next day we were received by a local school, set on a broad plain. They had pitched a gaily decorated canvas tent, roomy enough for a dozen people to sit on carpet-covered benches. Outside the tent, visible through its one open side, were some 260 pupils garbed in festival finery. The sunstruck tent fabric glowed incandescently, and the sky was peppermint blue.

The books, still wrapped in brown paper, were the first order of business. The school headmaster made a brief speech about the importance of literacy and education, and I replied with my own speech on how glad we were to help. Ceremoniously, I presented the head teacher with a written inventory of the books they were getting. Then everyone pitched in to open the packages. The children fell on them like hungry wolves.

A short time later, food arrived, a repast of *momo* (dumplings), and *droju* (fried bread), served with tea and bottled drinks. Teachers set up an ancient loudspeaker and began pushing music through it. Then the show began: groups of children danced in pin-perfect routines, girls in blouses of blazing magenta and sunflower yellow, boys sporting headdresses crowned with fur.

Sitting with us was the school founder, a man called Gyalten Rinpoche. Aged about fifty-three, and tall for his generation, he wore dark trousers and a slate-gray windbreaker, and said very little. Nevertheless, the local people's eyes were on him and him alone. Whenever he uttered a word or made even the smallest gesture, they leaped to respond.

I quietly explained to my group the meaning of the word "Rinpoche" in the man's name—it is an honorific meaning "precious one," for he was a *tulku,* a sacred personage whom Tibetans believe is the reincarnation of a great enlightened teacher of the past. Discovered as a small boy in an ordinary village in the hills above Rongpatsa, he had been brought to nearby Dargye Monastery to be lovingly educated by monks.

Gyalten Rinpoche's life was meant to be devoted to the teachings of Sakyamuni Buddha, but in 1950, when he was still a boy, his fate had been changed forever when Mao Zedong's armies took control of Kandze Prefecture.

Soon after, the victorious Communists set out to remake the economy in Kham, destroying the power enjoyed by the monasteries and transferring resources from rich to poor. Tibetans bitterly hated these changes and the brutal tactics the Chinese used to accomplish them. In 1956, across the region, Tibetan insurgents took up arms against the Chinese in a revolt that became known as the Khampa Rebellion. At first, the rebels enjoyed the advantage of surprise, but they were outgunned and outmanned, and eventually many had to seek shelter within the walls of monasteries. Dargye Monastery became a battleground as Chinese forces sought to kill the rebels holed up inside.[11]

---

11  Melvyn C. Goldstein, *A History of Modern Tibet,* 4 vols. (University of California Press, 2014), Vol. 3, *The Storm Clouds Descend: 1955-57,* p. 193.

Ultimately, a few dozen insurgents escaped and left Rongpatsa to join Khampa forces amassing in TAR.[12] The Chinese then emptied Gyalten Rinpoche's monastery of its remaining monks, leaving only twenty behind as caretakers. Those twenty stayed until 1966 when the so-called "Cultural Revolution" began. It was during this awful decade that Tibet's traditional way of life suffered the most violent attacks. Young, brain-washed zealots known as "Red Guards" smashed everything in China that represented ancient traditions: scriptures, paintings, statuary, and all other emblems of scholarship and faith. They attempted, with some success, to destroy places of worship, shuttering Dargye Monastery and leaving it to rot.

His monastic education halted, Gyalten Rinpoche was compelled to return to his village, to do farm work by day and join in political studies at night. People who had been utterly devoted to him were now forbidden to look on him as a tulku or accord him any special privileges. It was a time of hunger, violence, and pervasive fear; those who resisted Communist orders were publicly ostracized, tortured, or executed, and some were sent to labor camps from which they never returned.

After Mao died and the Cultural Revolution ended, Deng Xiaoping emerged as China's new leader. In 1982, Deng's policies of reform allowed monks to return to Dargye Monastery. The government supplied 530,000 yuan (US$77,000) for rebuilding. It was a pittance compared to the real cost of replacing Dargye's ruined temples, but it was a start. The monastery invited Gyalten Rinpoche to return to his traditional seat, but at first, he refused because he didn't see how he could support himself as a monk.

---

12 Tibet Oral History Project, Interview #48D – Norga, 5/18/2012, and Interview #52D – Gyendun Tashi, 5/18/2012. https//www.tibetoralhistory.org (accessed 4/7/2020).

As the years passed, the climate of fear receded, and the economy revived, so that ordinary Tibetans could once again afford to give offerings. Dargye Monastery's finances improved, and one by one buildings were repaired and repopulated. Gyalten Rinpoche's monastic training was incomplete, and he was ill-prepared to fulfill his traditional religious role. Nevertheless, the people wanted their monastery made whole, and they wanted him in it. So, he returned.

The government recognized his potential and offered him an official post, which he accepted. I never asked him about his decision to join China's government. I never asked him about the Khampa Rebellion or his monastery's role. I was always careful to censor myself when speaking with him and other Tibetans. If they brought up sensitive topics, I listened, but I didn't go digging. What would be the point? The world already had thousands of activists campaigning for an end to Chinese rule in Tibet. Joining them would put KhamAid's work in jeopardy—work that I was in a unique position to do. That work was much too important to risk.

From the 1980s on, Gyalten Rinpoche wore many hats: Abbot of Dargye Monastery, Deputy Director of the Sichuan Buddhist Association, and Member of the National People's Congress, China's rubber-stamp parliament. That last job sounds important but had little real influence; it required him to dress in lama's robes and travel to Beijing to take part in an annual convocation each March. The man I knew never put on robes while at home.

As I told my tour group Gyalten Rinpoche's life story, from time to time I turned to glance at him as he sat in the place of honor. A stream of local people, drawn by the news of his visit, lined up to see him. One by one, they approached him with tears in their eyes and white *khata* (offering scarves) in their hands. Gyalten Rinpoche heard what each had to say and offered a few wise or comforting words.

After a time, the stream of visitors ebbed and I saw him enjoy a rare moment of repose, just watching the children dance. In that brief moment, the man's veneer cracked open to reveal pure joy. Oh, how he loved these kids! Getting permission to start a school had been difficult, but he never gave up. He obtained a plot of land a few kilometers from the monastery and built a walled compound enclosing two long-houses partitioned into classrooms, offices, and dorms. He poured his personal savings into the project, sold his family's horses, and when that wasn't enough, he took out loans. He hired teachers, staff, and an experienced administrator. "I opened a school because I think culture and literacy are extremely important," he once told me. "In my family, everyone but me was illiterate."

An outsider might wonder if a high position in the Chinese government tarnishes a tulku's reputation, or if his speeches advancing Party policies might diminish the people's trust in him. They did not. Gyalten Rinpoche had planned to accommodate eighty children, targeting the poor, orphaned, and disabled, totally free of charge. When word got out, there were so many applicants that, in the end, they took 138 students and still had a long waiting list. Many people didn't trust government schools, but they trusted him.

By now the school had been operating for four years. Conditions were austere. The children sat on hard benches at plain wooden worktables. The classrooms were unheated and poorly lit. The only teaching aids were blackboards, chalk, copybooks, and a collection of tattered texts. The school had no toilet; children and teachers relieved themselves in the open. Yet most government schools out here were no better than this, and often worse.

Seeing these beautiful children now dancing under the afternoon sun fired me with purpose, but it would take time, money, and much more work to make a difference here. First, I had a tour to lead.

## Guardian of the Past: Sögyal

The next morning, we motored west to Manigango, an outpost of mud streets on a broad, grassy plain. After lunch, we left the grasslands and began the ascent of Tro La, which would be the highest pass of our journey.

We followed the dirt road up onto scrubland too desolate to support even itinerant herders. Crawling up Tro La's flanks, the scrub gave way to a hardscape of lichen-splattered stone. The sun's light edged toward the ultraviolet, cranking up the sharpness and contrast filters. We bumped up rocky inclines, slid around hairpin turns, lurched over potholes, and slashed through ice-skinned streams. And still we climbed, ascending into realms ever more blazing and tenuous, squinting against the cerulean glare as the sky hollowed out and the earth fell away. At last, we reached the dominion of clouds, a pass at 5,019 meters (16,500 feet), an abode so dazzling I could scarcely open my eyes.

Height is exhilarating, but the wise traveler does not linger, lest the pinch of tweezers at the outermost lobes becomes the hammering of an anvil that turns one's brain to paste. We stopped for photos, then quickly moved on, and after a rumbling, four-hour descent, we reached the seat of Degé County.

The county seat was a jewel of a town swathed in a toga of mountain greenery, nestled where a tumbling stream pours into the larger Ser Chu. We had come to see the region's leading cultural site: the Degé *Parkhang*, or Printing House, a big workshop that printed traditional Tibetan texts by hand.

The next morning Mr. Wu went off to arrange horses for our next day's travel while I took the group to the Parkhang. I asked at the office for someone to guide us and was told he would come soon. Presently, the "someone" appeared: a man who introduced himself as *yuanzhang,* the Director. His name was Sögyal.

I had met some Parkhang staff before, but Director Sögyal was new to me. He was short and stocky, and a scar sliced his right cheekbone—the relic of a childhood brawl, I would later learn. I noted with bemusement his long black leather coat, like the one worn by the character Neo in *The Matrix*. Such a zippy fashion statement was a bit startling in this remote Tibetan town.

He led us into a long, high-ceilinged chamber where workers sat in pairs facing each other, tools arranged between them. No one looked up when we entered. Moving in mechanical synchrony and at superhuman speed, one of each pair would apply ink to a carved wooden block, then the other would press paper on the ink to transfer the lines of text.

We watched for a while, marveling at the workers' unwavering focus and the fast-growing stacks of product, while Sögyal spoke about the materials used in the printing process. His speech was crisp, fluent Mandarin, not the gentle cadences of Sichuan-*hua* (dialect) that I was used to hearing from Tibetans in Kham.

Then he led us out of the printing room and into the first of two chanting halls, meanwhile relating Degé history from the earliest recorded beginnings in the seventh century. The Parkhang, he said, had been established in 1729 by the twelfth Degé king. That period marked the kingdom's apex when Degé ruled twenty-five tribes—one of the mightiest empires ever to arise in eastern Tibet. My adventure travelers gazed around the ornately decorated chanting hall and its high ceiling held up by wooden columns. The darkened room smelled of the smoke from butter lamps. Motes of dust danced in a column of sun falling from a skylight, but the place seemed otherwise frozen in time.

As our eyes adjusted, clay statues dressed in rich brocades, immobilized in regal expressions of bliss or wrath or lordly power, peered back at us from the perimeter. Gradually, we could also make out painted deities peering over the heads of the statues: a solemn line of Buddhas and bodhisattvas encircling us.

Sögyal explained, "During the Cultural Revolution, Degé's monastery was badly damaged, and the king's palace was destroyed, but Zhou Enlai ordered the Red Guards to protect this place." Gesturing with his open hand at the images painted on the wall, he said, "Nearly everything in the Parkhang survived, except these murals."

I translated his words, adding that the bright-colored artworks they were looking at were replacements for lost originals. During the Cultural Revolution, all printing ceased; the local government took over the Parkhang and used it as a hospital and warehouse. The roof wasn't adequately maintained, allowing moisture to invade the rammed earth walls, making them crack and also dissolving the binder that fixed the paintings to the underlying clay. The paintings separated from the wall and fell to the floor in flakes. Following significant repairs to the building in 1991 in which many timbers were replaced, artists were hired to paint new murals. Nevertheless, moisture continued to be a problem, and the new paintings were already showing signs of deterioration.

Sögyal then led us to the West Hall. Here most of the original murals had survived: exquisitely detailed images painted in blue-green Karma Gadri style, now browned with age, but still glittering with gold-painted highlights that time had not diminished. No inch was undecorated: the lotus-throned deities were suspended in a cosmos crowded with flames, mountains, clouds, multitudes of smaller Buddhas floating in air, and tiny human figures cavorting among courtly pavilions with gilded roofs. The room's beams were carved and painted, and the pillars were wrapped in sumptuous brocade.

Looking closely at the paintings, however, one could see that some portions were discolored—possibly due to fumes from stored chemicals—or had been gouged and pitted, perhaps by careless workers. Moisture had stained some areas and caused others to flake away. Painters had unskillfully repaired the lost areas with cheap plaster and inferior pigments, which gleamed like scars across the patina of the majestic original.

Switching to Chinese, I turned to Sögyal and pitched my ability to bring skilled foreign conservators who could take proper care of the Parkhang's paintings, for it had long been my ambition to replicate our success at Pewar at this far more important site. However, Sögyal only nodded. The Parkhang had been designated a national-level historic site, on a par with the Forbidden City and the Potala Palace. I would later come to understand that, although the Kandze Prefecture Cultural Relics Administration could develop conservation plans in coordination with Degé County, officials in Beijing had sole authority to greenlight any actual work.

Sögyal led us up a wooden staircase to the Parkhang's vast library: aisle after aisle of shelves stretching from floor to ceiling, each packed with wooden plates. Sögyal explained that the Parkhang's collection of printing blocks included the *Kangyur,* the original teachings of Sakyamuni Buddha, the *Tengyur,* which was the earliest set of commentaries. It also held teachings produced by all four major Tibetan Buddhist orders and Bön, Tibet's indigenous animist faith. "Eighty percent of Tibetan literary culture is stored here," he said. "Lhasa is the center of Tibetan religion, but this" —a broad sweep of his arm across the many rows— "*this* is the heart of Tibetan culture."

The archive held some 270,000 plates, which were made from knotless red birch, fire-cured, water-soaked, then baked, planed, carved, and meticulously checked for calligraphic and textual correctness. The printers constantly needed new plates as old ones wore out. As we walked the long corridors, Sögyal pointed out treatises on art, science, medicine, and history. He had an unruly thatch of thick, black hair, and his face seemed young and old at the same time. His words poured out in a torrent: facts, dates, names—as if a literary encyclopedia lived in his head.

After the tour, as we were walking back to town, he asked whether I was married, a question I often heard. I gave him my standard reply: that constant travel made it difficult to find a husband.

"Me, too," he said. "After I graduated from university, I stayed in Qinghai and did some business there. Conditions weren't right for starting a family."

He looked to be ten years younger than me, so I ignored this information and the hint it contained. Anyway, I had seen enough to know that I didn't want to marry a man from Kham, for I didn't care for their customs regarding gender roles. Among farmers and herders in Kham, it seemed to be a man's prerogative to smoke, drink, gamble, and play billiards, while the women did nothing but work. Such a life was not for me.

Tomorrow I would take my group on a horseback ride to Palpung Monastery in Degé's backcountry. Getting ready for that was uppermost on my mind. I quickly forgot about Sögyal.

One member of the tour group was Dr. Dana Isherwood, a retired scientist and avid adventurer whom I had met through the Explorers Club. She was petite but very strong, almost old enough to be my mother, and so packed with energy that I often could not keep up with her. She was an accomplished mountaineer and had climbed many challenging peaks, including Denali, the highest in North America.

She loved exploration and had endless stories of adventures at the earth's far corners. We didn't know it yet, but this trip would be the start of her many years of involvement in Kham.

The ride to Palpung didn't go as planned. First, the horses arrived late, delaying our start. Then Mr. Wu's horse bolted while he was dismounting, throwing him to the ground and shaking him up badly. After that, part of the group lost the trail in the dark. Nevertheless, in the end, we all got there and had a magnificent time.

I paid the monks well for hosting us. And I thought: if they can host us, why not others? Why not make a business of it? Quietly, I began plotting.

When we returned to Degé, Mr. Wu and I found that news of our visit had reached several locals who had been involved with our work at Pewar Monastery, work we had completed just the previous year. They wanted to invite Mr. Wu and me to a reunion dinner. I couldn't abandon my group, so Mr. Wu booked two tables at the local stir-fry joint: one for the Americans and one for the local crowd.

I don't know who invited Sögyal, but he arrived with the others. The room was packed and the mood was convivial. After we had eaten our fill, it was time for songs. The locals opened with a few rounds of Tibetan and Chinese standards, then begged us Americans to sing one of our own. My adventure-travelers insisted they could not sing, so I warbled "Bicycle Built for Two," a ditty I often hauled out on such occasions.

Then Sögyal rose for a solo. With eyes gazing at some invisible horizon, he began singing a soulful old melody. It was a Chinese-language song, but I had heard it so many times, belted with such operatic ardor, that it seemed like a virtual anthem of Tibet. It translates as follows:

*Who brought the ancient call?*
*Who offers one thousand years of prayers?*
*Who passes on wordless songs*
*Of ancient unforgettable yearning?*
*Oh…*
*I see it: a mountain, a row of mountains,*
*A mountain range.*
*Ya lha so…*
*Is it the high Tibetan plateau?*

*Who sees the blue sky day and night?*
*Who yearns for an eternal dream?*
*Who offers songs of praise*
*With immutable solemnity?*
*Oh…*
*I see it: a mountain, a row of mountains,*
*A mountain range.*
*Ya lha so…*
*It is the high Tibetan plateau*
*Ya lha so…*
*It is the high Tibetan plateau!*

On the last line, Sögyal's liquid tenor vaulted to a high note and held it until I thought his lungs might burst. The sound was a volcanic explosion of love and praise for his stunning homeland, the wave upon wave of snow-capped ranges held so dearly and adored so fiercely by every Tibetan ever born. It sent shivers down my spine. More than a decade later, Dana Isherwood still vividly recalled Sögyal's singing that night.

After dinner, as we were all getting up to leave, Sögyal sidled up to me. "So, you're leaving tomorrow for Chengdu?" he asked.

Yes, I said, wondering what he was up to.

"And you've got a bus?"

Sure.

"Do you have an extra seat?"

Of course. Public transit was abysmal, so cadging rides was an endless preoccupation. I consulted with my group and they agreed that he could come along.

We had our first kiss a day later, on a secluded bit of riverbank. After reaching Chengdu and seeing off my travelers, I stayed in town, as I was worn out from my just-finished trip and I had plenty of networking and report-writing to do. Over the next three weeks, I saw Sögyal often. He was busy with one of his radical innovations: opening a retail shop that would sell Parkhang books to local buyers and by mail. My Tibetan was lousy, and he had no English at all, so we conversed in Mandarin. He was patient and a good communicator. I learned much about him in a short time.

His full name was Sönam Gyaltsen. He was born in a hamlet on the slopes of a sacred mountain in the year 1972—the middle of the Cultural Revolution. Because Sögyal's parents were well off, the local Communist Party labeled them as "rich peasants." The government had confiscated their home and taken everything but the barest essentials for survival. During this time, his father died. Sögyal never shared the details, but if his father's death was like so many others, then the cause could have been famine, or torture, or suicide wrought by pressure to betray others, or by the crushing shame of being persecuted and dispossessed.

Sögyal's mother, a schoolteacher, was left to raise three children by herself in a hut allocated to them by the government. Sögyal did well in school and eventually was admitted to university from which he graduated with excellent grades. After a few more years away from home, he returned to Degé when the government offered him the Parkhang directorship.

As a Westerner falling for a Tibetan, I had plenty of company; I've known many such pairs.[13] This begs the question: why would an educated person from a rich country want to pair up with someone from Tibet?

For one thing, many westerners find Tibetan faces exotic and lovely to look upon. Khampas are taller, have more aquiline noses, and a reputation for ferocity and courage that is legendary in the Himalayas. An old Tibetan saying has it that the best religion is found in Lhasa; the best horses in Amdo; and in Kham, the best men.

Some Khampa men are quite attentive to their appearance. Once, after a week of backcountry travel, I went into a Degé salon to have my hair washed. In a chair across the room was a strapping young gentleman decked out in full regalia: high felt boots, a spotless chuba, and a colorful sash around his hips from which a foot-long knife dangled. His long locks were already clean, but the stylist was still working on them, putting his hair in rollers. I detected a familiar chemical aroma and realized the Khampa was getting a perm.

Tibetans can be sublimely spiritual, too, inspiring outsiders with their Olympic acts of faith and their ordinary devotions: turning a prayer wheel, circumambulating a stupa, lifting an insect from the path and setting it safely to one side.

Yet the most bewitching elixir Tibetans can offer is entrée to their magical kingdom, the chance to become an adopted child of snowy peaks and monumental temples, to throw off our dismal industrial burdens and disappear into the mists of Shangri-La. Remarkably, some Tibetan-Western couples I've known did not, when they tied the knot, have sufficient language skills to carry on a complicated conversation. Those Westerners did not wed only individuals; they married *Tibet*.

---

13  Marriages between Tibetans and Han are extremely common in China.

As I got to know Sögyal, the mythic mirage of the Khampa warrior was quickly replaced by a real, three-dimensional person. Yet because of the closeness of the Degé community, our affair was cloaked in secrecy. Whenever I stopped by the Parkhang's little bookshop in Chengdu, he and I carried on a masquerade of being mere acquaintances. At other times, though, the city's anonymous crowds allowed us to eat in restaurants and take long walks together, always observant of Asian decorum, which required at least an arm's length between us.

As far as I could tell, Sögyal had no interest in politics, though he did passionately believe that Tibetans should develop their economy and modernize their way of life. One evening, we strolled down a long boulevard that was, like so many in that fast-growing metropolis, a forest of enormous steel skeletons overhung by cranes, and he suddenly spat out: "Look at all these tall buildings they're putting up!"

His vehemence startled me, and I stared at him in surprise, but then his tone became despairing as he added, "Why don't we Tibetans have these?"

Yet Sögyal was just as fierce in his conviction that traditional culture had a vital place in modern Tibet. He was, after all, literally the guardian of Tibet's religious and literary traditions—traditions embodied in the words of great philosophers carved letter by letter into tens of thousands of blocks in the Parkhang archive. Sögyal did not want to emigrate to the United States, India, or anywhere else. "Of course, I would like to visit America someday," he once said, "but my work is here."

We never discussed the future, until one evening as we sat on a park bench staring at the green slime of the Nanpu River sliding between concrete banks. Suddenly he blurted out, "*Women liangge shi bukenengde!*" We two are impossible.

I asked him what he meant, and he revealed that he was engaged to marry a young woman in Degé chosen by his mother. "I met this girl only twice," he explained. "I don't feel anything for her. But she is the daughter of my mother's best friend. Our mothers very much want us to marry."

Although it pained me, I understood his position. Sögyal had two siblings: a brother and a sister. His brother had gone into a monastery and would never marry. His sister had married into another family, a love match, freely chosen. Sögyal was his mother's sole heir, and he would be the one to support and care for her when she grew old. Whom he married was a matter of great concern to her. Naturally, she preferred not to leave it to whim.

"After all the sacrifices my mother made to bring us up," Sögyal said, "I must show gratitude and respect by doing as she asks."

Sögyal told me that, despite his marriage, he hoped we would continue to see each other. Perhaps he desired the status-enhancing effect of an American mistress. However, I broke off our relationship. Shortly afterward, Sögyal went back to Degé and married his fiancée. Yet there was no bitterness between us. We needed to be friends so we could work together on the conservation of the Degé Parkhang.

By January, Sögyal and his young wife were expecting their first child.

# Openness

*However wide the blue waters may be, a sound boat
crosses to and fro with ease.*

— Tibetan proverb

For centuries, Tibet's defining feature has been isolation. Isolation is why the world fêted the rare European who reached Tibet's holy capital. Isolation is why a plumber from Devonshire, self-named "Tuesday Lobsang Rampa," could masquerade as a Tibetan lama and publish a series of entirely made-up books about Tibet, one of which became a bestseller. Isolation is why people believe that Tibetan remedies are effective, Tibetan society is utopian, and Tibetan lamas are infallibly wise. Isolation is why a trip to Lhasa earns top bragging rights for tourists, and it's why people from all over the globe flock there.

Isolation is why Tibet is poor.

For it takes more than a village to uplift citizens and unearth their talents; it takes the whole world. Therefore, one gate of the development mandala is a passage between one's home and places outside.

For most of history, Kham was difficult to leave. In 1950, a mounted party traveling from Batang to Chengdu—479 kilometers (298 miles) away as the crow flies—needed twenty-four days to complete the journey. After gaining control of the region, the Chinese Communists set about widening the caravan paths into motorable roads. They blasted away prodigious volumes of rock to allow automobiles, trucks, and military convoys to squeeze around mountains. By the early 1990s, one could complete the same journey in thirty-three hours, in the comfort of a motorized vehicle. Fifteen years later, the time had shrunk again by one-third.

Although the new roads had secured China's occupation of Tibet and opened the floodgates to Han immigrants, virtually everyone I met in Kham liked living near a road and regarded isolation as undesirable. Isolated places suffer from a myriad of wants. The food is monotonous and lacks nutrients. A simple toothache or broken bone can be disabling. Farmers do not know the value of their crops to markets outside. Basics like toothpaste, toilet paper, and menstrual products are hard to find and even harder to afford.

Equally important, an isolated person is kept colorblind to a rainbow of ideas. And where facts are in short supply, superstition flourishes.

## Journey to Dzokchen Monastery

In spring of the year of the female Earth-Rabbit (1999), I was back in Sichuan with Stephen Aldridge, a member of KhamAid's board. The two of us were setting out to lessen the isolation of a place called Dzokchen by the simple expedient of visiting it. Aldridge, a scholar-pilgrim, had long yearned to see Dzokchen Monastery, a venerated bastion of the Nyingma School, Tibet's most ancient Buddhist order. I wanted to find out if Dzokchen had any historic buildings or paintings of note, and if I should include it in future fundraising tours.

Well before dawn, in the grubby chaos of the Dartsendo bus station, we boarded a Leshan bus. It was overfull, and Aldridge and I sat in the back row, behind a mountain of baggage and standees.

At that time, the Leshan "Joy Mountain" model was the long-haul standard in Kham: a boxy, low-tech, thirty-four-seat contraption with lots of ground clearance to negotiate the punishing dirt roads. I thought it a tremendous advance over the older buses with their hard, bench-style seats. Not that the Leshan was very durable. Its chief virtues, in a developing nation like China, were that it was cheap to build, inexpensive to operate, and easy to repair. That was how a ticket to a place 526 kilometers (327 miles) away could be priced at a mere US$13.67.

Snow had recently fallen in the mountains, and we quickly came to an obstruction caused by another bus mired ahead of us. After a seven-hour wait, the way was finally cleared. Stephen Aldridge, taller than most Asians, was uncomfortably jackknifed into the tiny space next to me. Rolling down from the first pass on the uneven dirt road, we were thrown around and slammed from side to side. Several other passengers, evidently unused to motor travel, opened windows so they could be ill. After a descent lasting two hours, we pulled into the transit yard in the town of Rangaka ("Rah ngah kah") for a brief stop.

After lunch, the road west became a stripe of construction that coiled snakelike across the prefecture. On it was a line of laborers toiling in the mud to level the roadbed and dig ditches and culverts. Each culvert was a slash across our path that forced our bus to take a detour, swimming through the knee-deep mire. Six hours and two towns later, the driver stopped to have a blown tire repaired. By the time we reached the town after that, it was getting late, so we stopped for the night.

After a short sleep at the transit hostel, everyone re-boarded, and we set out again well before sunrise. Just outside of town, we came to a truck stuck in the mud. After we got clear of it, we had to stop for an hour in the next town for a shop to repair our already-repaired tire again.

Thanks to a spell of dry weather, a pall of dust followed every vehicle; it swirled in through the windows, coating us and everything inside. It was wretched, but at least we were moving; at every turn, we passed less fortunate folk standing on the shoulder, forlornly trying to flag down a ride.

By the end of the second day, Aldridge and I should have been in Dzokchen already, but we were still 143 kilometers (90 miles) away—a long distance in a Leshan bus. As we pulled into a transit yard, famished, dust-choked, and woozy, the bus driver announced we would leave at five the next morning. We unfolded our aching joints and scrambled out the door to another traveler's hostel for the night.

The next morning, at the appointed hour, a shivering mob stood in the yard waiting to board. Half of them were our fellow-sufferers from the past two days. The other half were local boarders hoping for an empty seat.

Faces looked drawn and tight in the glare of the single bulb that illuminated the yard. There were many more people than spaces. As the clock ticked twenty, then thirty minutes past the scheduled departure time with still no sign of the driver, tension mounted. Young men drifted toward the passenger door, positioning themselves for the scrum that would ensue when it opened. Stephen Aldridge and I hung back, pinning our hopes on the theory that passengers who boarded in Dartsendo would get priority, and that people would be kind to the two hapless foreigners in the rear.

At last, the driver appeared. He climbed through his driver-side door, and a moment later the passenger door hissed open. The mob surged in. In seconds, every seat was full, and the aisle, too. Aldridge and I were still outside, as were many others, especially women, children, and seniors.

The folks hunkered down in the seats wore expressions of dogged determination. An old monk clad in fraying, butter-stained robes had grabbed a prime seat at the front. He settled down solidly and stared straight ahead, ignoring the turmoil churning around him.

My heart sank. If we lost our seats, we'd have to wait three days for the next bus, then fight this battle again.

Standing in the cold by the idling bus, Stephen Aldridge and I eyed the squatters. None of us displaced riders seemed willing to confront them. Would we be stranded? A standoff ensued for some twenty minutes, until a transit company employee, a tall Han man, emerged from the ticket office to break the deadlock. He ordered everyone off. His authoritative tone, coupled with the certainty that the bus would not move until ticket-holders had regained their rightful seats, convinced most of the squatters to give up. Sheepish and dejected, they filed off the bus.

Unlike the others, the lama in the front row stayed put. The official shouted at him and tugged at his robes, but he sat stonelike, immoveable. When the bus was nearly empty, we ticket-holders squeezed on board. Every inch of space was instantly full. The old monk was among a handful of new passengers. A couple dozen more were out of luck.

Motoring west, we climbed through velvety foothills peppered with fly-speck yaks. The rest of the journey passed without incident. When we reached Dzokchen, I yelled down the length of the bus at the driver to stop. We dropped our backpacks from the rear window, then climbed down after them. With parting waves from our fellow passengers, the bus pulled away.

## A Monastery Business Plan

Dzokchen Monastery stands at the mouth of a sylvan valley: a gateway to turquoise lakes, misted groves of evergreens, and meadows clotted in wildflowers. Stephen Aldridge and I settled into rooms of an earthen lodge used to house monastery guests. The next day we hiked up the valley to visit meditation caves that had sheltered famous ascetics and a rock said to bear the footprint of an eighth-century sage.

Upon our return, we were met by one of my Degé friends, an official who had accompanied my conservation team in years past. He told us that the United States had just bombed the Chinese embassy in Belgrade, Yugoslavia. Anti-American protests were erupting all over China, and police had been ordered to protect foreigners from the mobs.

The next day, my friend arranged for us to ride in a truck over the mountains to the seat of Degé County. As we walked through town, I was alert for anything unusual; but nothing seemed out of place. We headed over to a local tulku's home where I usually stayed when not with a large group.

In the morning, I went with Aldridge to buy his bus ticket. Then we headed over to the Public Security Bureau to register as we were required to do. There we met the head of the Degé County foreign affairs police, a sallow, potbellied, 40-something Tibetan fellow named Bu Ge ("Boo Guh").

I was not glad to see him, for we had history, Bu Ge and I. Three years earlier, at Pewar Monastery, he and I crossed swords over photos I had taken inside the temple, where he insisted that photography was not allowed. Ever since then, I had pegged him as a dim, plodding bureaucrat, an impediment to be overcome.

Bu Ge asked where I would be going in Degé. I told him that Aldridge was leaving tomorrow, but I wanted to visit a village school that KhamAid was supporting and check on conservation work and repairs at two monasteries where KhamAid had been involved.

"There has been some, er, little problem with foreigners," Bu Ge said, measuring his words with care. "You shouldn't go to the countryside alone."

What I didn't tell him was that I had a secret plan to help monks launch a tourism business catering to foreign backpackers. The plan had to be secret because foreigners were usually prohibited from staying at Tibetan monasteries. If you tried it in Lhasa, the police would be there instantly to remove you. Yet I had learned over my years in China that legal and illegal were not always black-or-white matters. You can do all sorts of technically illegal things if you bring skill to the effort. Taking a policeman along with me, however, would *not* be skillful, not at all.

I was expecting to hitchhike and trek to the monasteries as I had done in the past, but Officer Bu Ge said that, for safety's sake, he would arrange a vehicle and escort. I argued, but he was utterly unmovable. It would have looked suspicious if I canceled the trip, so I agreed.

The next morning, I came to the police station to meet my escort and learned it would be Bu Ge himself. He looked glum, for he would have to leave the lazy comforts of police headquarters and accompany me into the mountains and their assorted inconveniences.

An old jeep soon appeared, with a driver. I would be paying for gas, but they were otherwise free of charge, a bonus to be sure, but one that hardly made up for the nuisance of lugging around a chubby, interfering cop.

One of the two monasteries I wanted to visit, Pewar Gonpa, possessed a set of historic Buddhist wall paintings: appealing to art historians but perhaps not so much to tourists. The other, Palpung Gonpa, was the superstar: both a power center of the Karma Kagyu tradition and an architectural wonder. Palpung's colossal main temple was the second-largest traditional Tibetan building in the world; some called it "the Little Potala Palace." The timber and rammed-earth edifice was nearly 300 years old and had a footprint the size of a football field. The temple sat on a high promontory, center stage in a natural amphitheater of steep walls carpeted in ancient pine.

I was sure that adventure travelers would adore Palpung if only they could get there. However, the monastery was not just off the beaten track, it was lost in space as far as tourism was concerned. A 1999 Footprint guide wrongly put it on the road to Mesho District. Another book gave no location at all, just saying you could get there "by hitching a lift." None said how long the journey would take, how a visitor might subsist at Palpung, or why it was worth the trouble. Thanks to misinformation and neglect, nobody went there. Travelers missed out on a transformational adventure, and the monks missed out on some extra income.

So, I was aiming to bootstrap a tourism business at Palpung Monastery—if only my unwanted bodyguard would stay out of the way.

We set off early, motoring through a valley of farms and picturesque log houses. Barley, Tibet's staple grain, had been sowed the previous month and was bursting from the soil; the fields were a checkerboard of green.

The jeep sputtered west for 28 kilometers to where the highway plunged into the immense chasm of the Dri Chu, or Female Yak River, known downstream by the more famous name, Yangtze. A bridge crossed over into Tibetan Autonomous Region, but that was off-limits to me without a permit. Hugging the Sichuan side of the river, our jeep turned south on an ill-kept road tracing the canyon wall next to the silt-laden torrent. This road would become unreliable during the summer monsoon, but for now no landslides blocked our path, and we made good time.

After 34 kilometers in the gorge, we turned onto a logging road that followed a stream back into the interior of Sichuan. Despite heavy spring runoff, the road gods favored us that day; three hours later, we reached the seat of Palpung Township.

Beside the river was a line of timber houses, one of which contained the offices of the local Party Secretary and assorted other bureaucrats. We saw a schoolhouse and a small clinic. Around this little enclave, the mountains rose steeply. The forest in this valley was protected from logging by tradition and by law, so there was little land available to cultivate and few inhabitants.

Ever mindful of the regulations, Bu Ge asked for my passport, which he took inside to show someone in the township government. When that was done, we set out climbing a twisted dirt road with many hairpin turns until we emerged from valley shadow into the electric sunblaze of the highlands. At last, we reached Palpung Gonpa, stunning and fortress-like on its high perch.

"*Ga-ah ti!*" were the words I heard as I alighted—hard journey? My old friend Shongshong was grinning as he came down the monastery's stone steps. He was an old man by Tibetan reckoning, about fifty-five. Short and unimposing, he was dressed in an olive green chuba that wrapped around his torso and was bound to his hips by a precisely tied sash. His skull bore the gray stubble of a recent monkish haircut. He took my hand and gripped it warmly.

"*Ga muh-ti!*" I answered, grinning also. Not hard.

Shongshong was a well-known builder in Degé. Humble and hardworking, he lived a monkish existence in service of the Buddhist faith. Now he was at Palpung directing ongoing restoration of the main temple. Although KhamAid hadn't commissioned this work, we were paying Shongshong's monthly wage of 950 yuan (US$115) as our contribution toward the preservation of this historic site.

A couple of young monks took our bags from the jeep and hauled them upstairs. They led Bu Ge, our driver, and me through Palpung's labyrinth of hallways to the temple's south wing. We were shown to a suite of rooms once used by Tai Situ Rinpoche, the highest religious authority of Palpung. His Eminence now resided in Bhutan, but he had come here in 1984 and 1991 for brief stays. The monastery had renovated the audience hall and Rinpoche's sleeping chamber, but the rest of the suite looked ancient. We were shown into a pair of small compartments that had probably once housed servants.

In terms of housekeeping, Palpung Monastery at that time could be compared to rooms used by any collection of young, unmarried males. Dirt was swept under beds. Castoff junk sat on shelves and in corners, rendered anonymous and untouchable by a thick coat of dust. On warm days, one might detect a rising ripeness from the centuries of tea-bowl and butter lamp spills.

Although many parts of Palpung were being made new, it would be some time before these servant quarters would be touched. The walls were rough-split logs and the windows covered in cotton fabric that admitted little daylight. My room had basic Tibetan furnishings: a low, boxlike table and a flat couch that served as seating in the daytime and a bed at night.

After we had eaten and drunk, I wanted to ditch Bu Ge and speak privately to the monastery leaders about opening a hostel, but Shongshong, who was my preferred Chinese-Tibetan translator, had gone down to the village and no one knew when he would return. None of Palpung's handful of Chinese-speaking monks were currently in residence.

This was a setback. My Degé dialect was limited to survival essentials. If I had to use it for this discussion, the project would bomb, because most people I met in Kham didn't understand why non-Buddhists would want to travel to places as undeveloped as Palpung. To them, a person who was inexhaustibly rich (as we foreigners surely were) would want to go to futuristic dreamscapes like Hollywood and New York City, not remote mountain villages with poor transportation and no running water or electricity.

To convince the monks to trust in, and gamble on, the inexplicable peccadillos of foreigners was far beyond my meager Degé-ke. There was no choice: I would have to use Bu Ge as my translator or admit defeat.

"No problem," said the policeman, genial but unknowing. "What do you want to say?"

There wasn't much to do but to lay my cards down. Meekly, I murmured something about tourists staying at Palpung. As the words were passing my lips I braced for a sharp rebuke and a lengthy sermon about obeying regulations.

Bu Ge looked doubtful. "*Foreign* tourists?" he asked.

Um…possibly.

Bu Ge pondered this. "According to the relevant laws and regulations," he intoned, "Degé County is now open. If the purpose is tourism, foreigners can come here. But—" he added sharply, "if they come here to do work, for example, do wall paintings conservation, then they must contact the Foreign Affairs Office."

I was astonished that Bu Ge didn't instantly shoot down my idea. But the devil is in the details: China had a multitude of ways to keep foreigners under tight control. One of these was to house us only in hotels with special licenses. Could Palpung ever get licensed? I doubted it, but I wasn't going to bring that up.

Through Bu Ge, I explained to the monks why Palpung appealed to adventurous foreigners. I said that KhamAid would like to help them attract such foreigners by giving the monastery a small grant to convert some space to guest rooms. The business would hardly be a bonanza, but it would bring in a bit of spare change to help with repairing the temple or whatever else the monks wanted to do.

The discussion needed a higher authority, so one of the monks went to fetch Khenpo Tsering, the monastery abbot.[14] He arrived an hour later, a slender and fine-boned man of about 60, with a dignified bearing and a finely wrought face shrink-wrapped over high cheekbones. I knew him as a man of few words, sphinxlike and unpredictable. Bu Ge and I quickly moved over to give him the seat next to the brazier.

Speaking slowly in Chinese, one sentence at a time so that Bu Ge would translate exactly, I explained my vision for Palpung's guest house. I told Khenpo Tsering that it offered foreign tourists unequaled authenticity and adventure. KhamAid would give them a grant to cover the initial investment, so they would have minimal risk.

Throughout my speech, Khenpo Tsering sat silent, straight-backed, and poker-faced.

The biggest stumbling block, I continued, would be communication. I proposed to create a poster showing services and rates in Tibetan, Chinese, and English that could be tacked to the wall; visitors could just point to what they wanted. I told them I would do some publicity for the monastery to get the word out.

When I was done speaking, I looked at the old monk for some sign of approval, but he didn't move a whisker. After a long, pregnant pause, he opened his mouth to speak.

---

14  Usually, monasteries are led by a tulku, if there is an adult one in residence. Palpung had only a child tulku at that time.

"Before he answers," Bu Ge translated, "Khenpo Tsering wants to know what you plan to do about the paintings in the temple?"

The question made me squirm. A year previously, my Pewar team had started some conservation work on a set of small wall paintings at Palpung. They dated from the 1980s—not very long ago—and would have been lost in the course of the structural repairs now underway. We had detached the paintings from the wall to save them and had then run out of money and done no more. To bring a team back to finish the job would cost twenty or thirty thousand dollars. I had no idea where I would get this money, for the people who had supported my work at Pewar were tapped out.

Palpung Monastery, I knew, had resources, modest though they might be. For one thing, it owned a truck. A compromise was in order. I told the lama that if he could send the paintings to Dartsendo in their truck, then I would find a way to finish the job.

As Bu Ge translated my answer, Khenpo Tsering's frown deepened. He muttered a few words, then stood to go.

"He said, he will answer you later," Bu Ge said.

"Did he like the tourism idea?"

"I'm not too clear."

"Will he send the paintings to Dartsendo?"

"I'm not clear about that either. Wait a while. Maybe he'll answer tomorrow."

The next day there was no sign of Khenpo Tsering, but Shongshong returned and took me on a tour of the new construction. Above the monastery, a new *shedra,* or Buddhist institute, had just been completed, monks had moved in, and classes started. Elsewhere workers were rebuilding a *labrang* (residence) belonging to an incarnate lama who traditionally resided at Palpung but now lived in exile.

Palpung was critically dependent on distant donors for its income, especially on Tai Situ Rinpoche, whose global following included many affluent Westerners. Otherwise, Palpung's income was modest. Tibetans tithed butter and grain and gave cash offerings, a total annual take estimated in 1991 at 5,000 yuan (US$610) per year.[15] In that same year, Palpung also earned up to 20,000 yuan (US$2,400) from the books produced by its small press. Palpung earned a bit more when its monks itinerated to perform ceremonies in private homes, although the monks kept most of these offerings themselves.

Only wealthy monasteries could afford to house and feed their monks, and Palpung was not wealthy. Monks lived on cash from their itinerant services and on support provided by their families, who generally gave food and bought or constructed small houses nearby. Until recently, the local population had prospered thanks to jobs in the timber industry. However, because of catastrophic flooding along the Yangtze River, in 1998, the government had banned commercial logging throughout the Yangtze watershed. If the money from Situ Rinpoche ever stopped flowing, Palpung surely would not be able to maintain and operate, let alone rebuild the enormous temple and the rest of the complex. They needed to diversify.

KhamAid's policy was that we didn't support religion, but we *did* support the preservation of historic architecture. It was for that reason that I wanted to help Palpung make ends meet. After years of neglect during the Cultural Revolution, and the costly repairs afterward, it would be tragic if the monks could not maintain their spectacular temple.

---

15  Wong How Man et al., "Buddhist Monasteries of Ganzi Tibetan Autonomous Prefecture, Western Sichuan, China: A Project for Architectural Conservation Funded by the Getty Grant Program," China Exploration & Research Society, (1992), p. 65.

In the afternoon, I went to pay my respects to Urgyen Rinpoche, the monastery's ten-year-old tulku. Then I returned to my lodgings to write and study. Just before dinner, Khenpo Tsering appeared, a significant gesture that could only mean he was ready to talk.

He wanted more details, so I explained that the guest house could offer bed-and-breakfast style lodgings in dormitory rooms. The monastery had no washing facilities, but monks could provide hot water in thermoses—the same standard offered at many Chinese guest houses. There would be a menu of foods available at different prices, and guests could have all the *tsampa* and butter-tea they could eat.

(Tsampa is the Tibetan staple, made with roasted barley kernels that are ground to a nutty, whole-grain flour. The flour is mixed with butter and tea to a soft dough that is eaten by hand. In my experience, Westerners almost invariably find it vile, so I knew that tourists would hardly bankrupt the monastery with their appetite for this item.)

The monastery might also offer hiking tours and hire out horses. To prevent misunderstandings, the monastery would post the fees on the wall for everyone to see.

"He wants to know about the grant for the monastery." Bu Ge translated.

I had already inspected likely rooms and drawn up a budget for window glass, bedding, washbasins, and thermoses. Cleanliness was a concern, but with customer feedback, I hoped the monks would figure it out.

Bu Ge asked, "How much money will they make?"

I pulled out a sheet of paper on which I had drafted proposed fees. The basic price was seventy yuan (US$8.40) per person per night for shared accommodations. I thought this was more than fair considering the intangibles of the Palpung experience: waking to a moan of horns calling monks to prayer, the sacred incantations and pounding of drums that went on all day long, the jaw-dropping view outside every window.

In most parts of Tibet, the government forbade foreigners from spending the night in monasteries, especially in Lhasa, where even talking to a foreigner could be risky for a Tibetan. Palpung offered a singular experience.

Khenpo Tsering stared at the numbers on my sheet, frowning, seemingly lost in thought. He made no reply, so I asked him in the Degé language: "*Di yakpo a-re?*" Is it good?

He looked up. "*Re,*" he said shortly. It is.

This was as ringing an endorsement as I could hope to get. I glanced at Bu Ge to see if he was on board or if he had suddenly remembered a reason to kibosh the deal. Lo and behold, Bu Ge looked impassive. Game on.

But there was one matter still outstanding: the paintings.

Bu Ge consulted with the khenpo. At last, he said, "They're not going to send the paintings to Dartsendo. You need to bring the experts here."

Bringing a team to Palpung would add thousands of dollars to the cost. I told him I couldn't do that, but if he changed his mind, he should let me know.

We requisitioned a sheet of poster paper from Palpung's printing operation and set about writing up the menu of services. A monk inked the Tibetan script, which he did with painstaking care using a paintbrush, fine calligraphy being much valued in Tibet as a sign of scholarship. I wrote the English, and Bu Ge wrote the Chinese. The poster went on the wall, where it became Palpung's Rosetta Stone. It would remain there for a very long time.

The budget for improvements worked out to US$297.27, which became the amount of KhamAid's grant. In hindsight, it was naïve of me to give a grant to a monastery. It's not that monks are dishonest; they just see things differently. To them, an NGO grant is an offering like any other; they might change the plan without notice and spend the money on something else. Later, I would see a partnership with a different monastery come horribly unraveled. But the Palpung monks did just as I asked: they fixed broken windows, purchased new bedding, and swept the flotsam and jetsam from the guest room floors.

Now the pressure was on me to conjure up some visitors. When I got back to town, I dashed out a handwritten opus titled *The Quick and Dirty Guide to Trekking in Degé* and left photocopies in a few shops and with friends. It provided directions to Palpung and Pewar Monasteries, phone numbers of Bu Ge and others who could help travelers with matters such as car hire, and a list of words and phrases in Degé-ke.

Some may be astonished that the police wanted to help—not arrest—foreign visitors, but these were heady days when Degé was newly opened, and anything seemed possible. Bu Ge, like many local officials, wanted to display their kingdom's proud history to the world.

Later, I uploaded the typed materials to KhamAid's website and sent them to our modest emailing list. It was a shot in the dark, and I had no idea if it would work.

## Our Scholarship Program Starts

Litang County is a chilly and blustery place, a land of wind-scoured prairies rimmed by dark, formless serrations. Mostly over 4,000 meters (13,000 feet) in elevation, the county is roughly the size of Connecticut, but with fewer people per square mile than North Dakota. In 1999, approximately 94% of the 47,500 registered Litang residents were Tibetan, most of them herders.[16] Yaks were the economic mainstay, for the county had little arable land and no industry apart from the government and thirty-eight Buddhist monasteries.

In hindsight, Litang was an ambitious choice to establish KhamAid's scholarship program. Litang-pa had played a leading role in the Khampa Rebellion and were known as some of the most intractable people in Kham.

Outside of the monasteries, the pinnacle of scholastic achievement in Litang was a graduation certificate from the county's junior middle school, which served grades 6-9. My contacts in Dartsendo introduced me to the Litang headmaster, Gelek. He was thirty-nine years old, a thin and wiry man with longish hair, wire-rimmed glasses, and a light beard—a Bohemian look that would have been perfect in SoHo or West Hollywood, but which was uncommon among government officials.

Gelek had been born in the backcountry, to illiterate parents. He was one of eight children, a not-unusual number for a rural family, especially in those days. (Before China implemented the One Child policy in 1979, birth control was unheard of.) Gelek was among the earliest Litang children to enroll in the schools built by the new Communist government in the years following their takeover of Kham.

I had come here to meet Gelek and to find out what KhamAid could do for education in his county. Mr. Wu had come with me as translator. Dana Isherwood had come, too; she was no longer a tourist but a KhamAid volunteer. Gelek showed us around the bare-bones, three-story concrete structure that housed the classrooms for his students. It resembled a prison block. It had no heat, but it did have big windows to let in the natural light, which was often needed thanks to Litang's unreliable

---

16  2001 figures. The unregistered population, i.e., migrant workers, would have added hundreds or thousands of Han to the total.

electricity. We walked from classroom to classroom, where red-cheeked, bundled-up children sat two to a desk, focused intently on their lessons.

That evening, we enjoyed what passed for fine dining in Litang: an unheated, windowless restaurant where we sat inhaling cigarette smoke around a banquet table covered with an orange, grease-spotted tablecloth. There were no vegetables, eggs, or tofu to be had, so Gelek ordered potatoes and several meat dishes. "When I was in primary school," he said, as platters of gristle began to arrive, "there was only one class at each grade. In my class, I was the *only* one from the countryside; all the rest were from town."

Despite this handicap and many other obstacles, Gelek got enough schooling to become a certified teacher. Like many officials I would meet over the years, he was a smooth-talking wheeler-dealer who was always looking for angles. Nevertheless, beneath the slick sales patter was a true believer in the central importance of education in advancing individuals as well as society.

Many parents in Litang did not share Gelek's views and did not send their youngsters even to primary school. Gelek admitted that, in 1999, only about half of the county's school-age children were enrolled in government schools. Some of the missing children had become monks—Gelek estimated that about six hundred dropouts could be accounted for in this way.[17] Monasteries taught Buddhism and the Tibetan language, although not all of them did a good job, and over the years, I met many illiterate monks. Monasteries did *not* teach real-world skills like math, science, Chinese, or English.

---

17  Litang County had no registered nunneries. Even if there had been, girls in Tibet do not usually join nunneries until well into their teens, an age at which they would have already completed primary school.

"Monastery education is good," Gelek said, "but our schools are better."

One barrier to education was distance. In rural areas, tykes might trudge for an hour or more just to reach a village primary school that could take them only as far as grade 2 or 3. Understandably, parents didn't like to send their children to distant schools where the parents couldn't check that they were being properly cared for. And children who were away at school did not learn how to grow crops or herd livestock, essential survival skills. Parents rightly worried that their educated child would be unable to support himself or herself as an adult.

Another barrier to education was poverty. Herder families lived mainly outside the cash economy, and so did many farmers.[18] In the late 1990s, the annual per capita cash income in Litang County was 590 yuan (US$71), an amount that was barely enough to send one child to board at a primary school, let alone middle school, much less multiple children. A family's other expenditures (such as health care) put education utterly out of reach.

I struck a deal with Headmaster Gelek to match needy Litang youngsters with KhamAid donors who would pay tuition and boarding fees at his school. The next day I wrote a simple contract with Gelek, knowing that, at that time in China, contracts were not worth the paper they were written on. The *real* contracts were not written, but social: the people who had introduced me to Gelek and who stood as unnamed guarantors of our agreements. If those relationships did not protect us, as outsiders, KhamAid would have no recourse.

Of the many contracts that KhamAid entered into over the years, most worked out. Some did not. One bombed spectacularly.

---

18   This began to change a few years later as rural people began earning significant income from collecting caterpillar fungus, as described in the chapter titled "Earthquake!"

Gelek contacted primary schools around the county, and they recommended children who would soon be finishing grade 6 but could go no further without help. All but one were girls. Gelek's list in hand, I canvassed a few friends back in the United States, and several stepped forward to help. Our scholarship program was born.

## A Major Misstep

As I worked on raising money for books and scholarships, people in Los Angeles and elsewhere asked many questions. *Do the schools teach Chinese?* they wanted to know. And when I told them that yes, they do, they replied: *Isn't that part of the Communist plot to destroy Tibetan culture?* I tried to explain that not knowing Chinese is a big handicap when you live in China, at which point they would advise me archly that Tibetans don't live in China; they live in *Tibet.*

To vent my growing frustration, I wrote an essay about Tibetans' rights to enjoy cultural exchange with people outside Tibet. I sent it to the *Los Angeles Times,* which published it on its editorial page, where it drew modest attention.

After that success, my hubris grew, and I resolved to speak out about something else that bothered me a great deal: the way the Western media always casts Tibet in the role of victim nation, making Chinese oppression the theme of every story. The idea resonated with Americans, reared as we are on our nation's give-me-liberty-or-give-me-death founding credo, while also plucking the strings of our national guilt over annihilating our own natives. Many people had come to believe that nothing whatsoever was happening in Tibet except an epic struggle for human rights and religious freedom.

I also noted that many Western observers—and indeed some exiled Tibetans—were uncomfortable with the idea of fighting poverty in Tibet. Poverty-fighting contradicted one key tenet of the Tibet independence movement: that China refused to allow advancement of Tibetans and their culture, that it sought only to crush them. Poverty-fighting clashed with the movement's unspoken rationale that Tibet was a lost paradise that could only be recovered under self-rule.

Yet the cold-water reality was this: the campaign for Tibetan freedom had been going on for decades, had been championed by influential people, and had spent millions of dollars, yet had shown no sign of progress whatsoever. Meanwhile, I was learning that I could advance the cause of Tibetan education fairly easily and with modest resources.

Every day I met potential donors who loved Tibet but didn't believe KhamAid could do what we were doing. One day I had had enough and dashed off another essay to the *Los Angeles Times*. In it, I castigated the media for uncritically accepting information gathered from flawed and biased sources such as exiled Tibetans and tourists. I stated that the media had become a virtual mouthpiece of the Tibetan government-in-exile and were ignoring other complex and nuanced stories unfolding in Tibet— stories that I experienced every day while doing KhamAid's programs.

My words were a direct attack on the Tibetan independence movement, and their reaction was swift. "I wonder what the motives behind the writing of the article were?" wrote one netizen on a public forum. "Obviously, Beijing will be pleased with the article's point of view."

Other people, only a few of them Chinese, wrote supportive letters to the newspapers where the article appeared.[19] But the damage was done: I was now a pariah among the community of people who should have cared most about my cause. But I ignored the flak and pressed forward, for there was much to do.

---

19　It was reprinted in *The Boston Globe*, Tokyo's *Daily Yomiuri*, and the Hong Kong *Standard*.

## Encounter with the Dalai Lama

Usually, my fieldwork ran well into the fall, but this year I headed home early because His Holiness the 14th Dalai Lama was coming to southern California. I wanted to meet him, first, to tell him about KhamAid's programs, and second, to explain myself and make amends for what I had written in the press a couple of months earlier. Whether it was because of my work or my notoriety, I wasn't sure, but a series of emails with the Central Tibetan Administration landed me a fifteen-minute audience.

On a sunny October afternoon at the appointed hour, I arrived at the Huntington Ritz-Carlton Hotel, a lush Spanish-style mansion surrounded by gardens and sequestered among multi-million-dollar estates. His Holiness had been teaching all day at the Pasadena Convention Center. A factotum in the hotel lobby told me that when the day's program was finished, he would come back to the hotel, give a press conference, and then see me. The efficient and gracious machinery of his staff brought me through metal detectors and past armed guards, depositing me in the temporary office of His Holiness's secretary.

They all seemed to know who I was and what I had written. The secretary, a well-dressed and articulate man in his late 40s, wanted to talk about it. "When the people in His Holiness's office read your article," he said, "they were very . . ."

He was hunting for a word, so I suggested "upset?"

"Yes."

He wanted to argue their side of it, and he had a lot to say. I took care to listen well without interrupting or contradicting. No informed person could disagree with the view that Tibetans had suffered terrible losses under Chinese rule, including loss of life as well as cultural and economic devastation. He wanted to tell me about the achievements of Tibet's government-in-exile, of which he seemed very proud. He also felt that not enough people knew about Tibet and her plight.

The secretary expressed the view that Chinese rule was destroying Tibet's culture. Citing a dance troupe from Tibet Autonomous Region he had seen, he said, "They were very Sinicized. The dresses were *much* shorter than real, traditional Tibetan clothes."

Although I had no opinion about the correct length of Tibetan dresses, I could easily imagine what he was talking about: the 'happy dancing ethnic' act that must be hideously offensive to people who regarded themselves as an occupied nation.

Still, I couldn't resist asking, when he paused long enough for me to get a word in, why so many people who considered themselves well-informed about Tibet were surprised when I told them that monasteries were being revived and rebuilt and that schools were teaching the Tibetan language? Why was this news to everyone?

Our conversation was interrupted by the news that His Holiness's press conference was almost over. I was led down the hall to a suite and directed to sit down. I was utterly unprepared for what happened next.

When the Dalai Lama entered the room, he was not the gentle and saintly character I had seen on TV; instead, he seemed very angry. Not a stooped and ancient sage at all, to me he looked seven feet tall, a wrathful Mahakala with bulging eyes, flaming eyebrows, hooks for hair, and wearing a crown of skulls. My heart dropped through the floor, and my mouth went dry.

My fright must have shown, for His Holiness took pity on me, dialed back the fireballs a bit, invited me to sit on the sofa, and asked about my work in Kham. I brought out a package of reports, and he thumbed through them while I choked out a couple of sentences about our programs. Then he, too, came around to the topic of the newspaper article. His approach was oblique, and he was impeccably polite, but his meaning was clear. "It's good that you have a skeptical mind," he said. "You should keep on being critical. That's very healthy."

"In the meantime," he added, with a gentle but meaningful look, "I invite you to come to India to check the situation."

As a gift for His Holiness, I had brought some Tibetan language books purchased in Sichuan: a science dictionary, a math textbook, and a couple of others whose titles I couldn't decipher. When I presented them, he remarked, "Some amazingly good books are coming out of there these days."

When my fifteen minutes were up, the Dalai Lama stood up, took me warmly by the hand, and then pulled me ever-so-gently out of my chair and pointed me toward the door.

As I was leaving, he asked, "Have you learned any Kham-*ke*?" (Khampa dialect)

I started spinning out some earthy Khampa phrases—plain and robust language, nothing like the high honorifics one is supposed to use to Tibet's supreme religious leader—eliciting gales of laughter.

As I left, I gave him the Khampa farewell, "*Yammo deh.*"

"*Demmo, demmo!*" he said, replying in kind.

That audience notwithstanding, I had committed a serious error by publishing an essay offensive to Tibet supporters. It would take years to repair my reputation, yet I had work to do in Kham, and no time to waste.

## Gaining Momentum

As the year of the Iron-Dragon (2000) approached, I labored in California to raise money and develop KhamAid's website. One section was dedicated to travelers, and there I posted details on Palpung

Monastery's guest house. Soon after, a journalist named Peter Hessler contacted me. He was going to Degé to research an article for the *New York Times* and wanted to know more about Palpung.

Meanwhile, Sögyal and Mr. Wu were emailing back and forth about the preservation of the Degé Parkhang. Sögyal said they averaged only about fourteen hundred visitors a year, so ticket sales could not possibly bring in enough money for a full-scale conservation project.[20] The central government would not or could not help. The county leaders wanted money from KhamAid. I wanted KhamAid to be more than just a cash machine. Still, given the political sensitivity of Tibetan cultural heritage, any communication at all from the county leaders was an encouraging sign.

While this was going on, our Books for Schools team was working hard. They completed the Tibetan translation of the *Children's Fun Science* series and had 3,000 four-volume sets printed by the Sichuan Nationality Press. Tsering and Yeshi were not up to another road trip, so this time they shipped the books by mail.

Out in Litang, our first cohort of scholarship children were doing well under Gelek's care. He collected their letters, which he sent to Mr. Wu to be translated and forwarded to the sponsors overseas. The letters related the heart-rending circumstances of children struggling against overwhelming odds. Sponsors loved these letters, for each handwritten page connected them to a real Tibetan child, who personified Tibet with all its splendor and struggle. Dana Isherwood was enthusiastic about the program, so I asked her to lead it, and she agreed. We also decided that, henceforth, we would focus exclusively on girls.

---

20  At that time, the Parkhang did not keep official records of visitation. However, they estimated that two hundred of the visitors were foreign or Han Chinese, two hundred were Tibetans from other parts of Tibet, and a thousand were local people coming for special events.

The journalist Peter Hessler made his trip to Degé, and his story about it appeared on the front page of the *New York Times* Sunday travel section.[21] It included an interview of Sögyal about the Parkhang, and it described the trek to Palpung Monastery. Shortly after the story came out, I headed back to Kham for the spring field season.

These days, although Sögyal had access to email, I did not write to him directly. Using Mr. Wu as an intermediary was much easier than wrestling with a clumsy Chinese language plug-in and slogging through the tedious process of looking up unfamiliar characters. And it was better to keep my distance.

So, after I returned to Dartsendo in April, an unexpected knock came on the office door, and I opened it to see Sögyal. The sight of him was a jolt, but I quickly squelched my emotions, for all that was behind us now. I invited him in. He didn't mention the past; instead, he talked about his infant son, of whom he was very proud. He confided that he believed the boy would someday be recognized as a tulku.

When the conversation ran out of steam, I shooed him out the door, saying, "See you in Degé," for I would be following him there in about a week.

Little did I realize this would be our last meeting.

## Rescued by Herders

Before going to Degé to meet with Parkhang officials, I had planned to spend a few days trekking in the backcountry with a couple of American friends. Poring over my collection of paper maps in search of a route in Dartsendo County, I selected a dashed line that led from the main east-west highway up into the mountains, then over a pass to the township of Chakgé. To accompany us three foreigners, I invited a couple of Tibetan

---

21  March 19, 2000.

friends who were learning English, one of whom was a native of the area.

The day dawned gray and cold as we boarded a local bus to take us to the starting point for our trek. There we found a local man who said he knew the trail and agreed to be our guide. Carrying various backpacks and duffles, we six set out walking.

The walk took much longer than expected. Assured by our guide that houses were not far away, we kept climbing long after we should have turned around. The day grew late, snow began to fall, and still, there was no sign of human life. The six of us were ill-equipped to bivouac, and it was too late to go back, so we kept trudging forward, climbing toward a pass that we hoped would lead us to safety. Darkness fell, and even with flashlights, it became difficult to make out our path against the obliterating whiteness.

At last, we spotted a nomad's black tent a few dozen yards from the trail, barely visible behind curtains of falling white. Responding to my shouts, a herder woman in a dark chuba emerged. She took pity on us and invited us to take shelter inside. One by one, we came into her tent, carefully skirting their snarling guard dog and stepping over three baby yaks tethered at the entrance.

We offloaded our burdens and sat down, me cautioning the Americans to aim the soles of their feet away from the altar and our hosts. We introduced ourselves and asked their names. The woman was Dolma Tso, eighteen years of age. The man sitting cross-legged by the fire was her bachelor uncle Nyima, age fifty.

The shallow fire-pit had only a few glowing embers, but the loosely woven tent fabric kept the heat in well enough. Once I had stopped shivering, I began to look around. The tent was of typical herder design, made of strips of woven yak hair sewn together to make dark fabric. It was square, about five meters (16 feet) on a side and almost tall enough to stand up in. The floor was hard-packed dirt, and the perimeter lined with sacks holding down the tent edges. At the center was a small open firepit beside a stack of branches and twigs. In the back was a low, decorated table of the sort that usually serves as an altar but now held a motley assortment of bowls. From the tent poles hung ladles, bundles of coiled rope, rags, and other articles of daily life.

In my travels around Asia, I had experienced a variety of less-than-sanitary conditions, but this dwelling obliterated all previous records, for the fusion of dirt, ash, and butter, and the shortage of hot water, had handicapped their housekeeping. The inhabitants' clothes and belongings were grubby all over.

"*Ja tung?*" Nyima offered. Tea sounded mighty fine to us cold, soggy travelers. Dolma Tso put a few sticks onto the fire and began pumping hand-held bellows to fan the flames. A few minutes later, the kettle was boiling.

Dolma Tso opened up a sack to expose a ball of butter. She cut off a hunk and was about to drop it into the kettle when my American friends hurriedly broke in, an edge in their voices, "No, thank you! Can we please have plain hot water?"

Dolma Tso looked puzzled when I translated the request, but she willingly poured hot water into our mugs and instant noodle bowls. Then she asked if we wanted tsampa, indicating a sack of roasted barley flour and pantomiming the act of kneading it. The Tibetans in our party accepted her offer but we Americans demurred. I usually enjoyed tsampa but was put off by the many black specks in the butter that would be an essential ingredient.

After I had eaten and drunk, my curiosity awoke, and I began to ask questions about Nyima and Dolma Tso's life here in the mountains.

"We have about fifty yaks and three horses," Nyima said, answering my first query. "We used to have more, but recently some were stolen." He added that during the previous year, they hadn't slaughtered any yaks at all because their herd was simply too small.

Assuming that the meat could be preserved by drying, slaughtering one yak a year would give them a daily ration of about 0.4 kilograms of meat, here shared by two people.[22] Without meat protein, the two would need to consume more milk products such as cheese and yogurt, yet *dri* (female yaks) give far less milk than dairy cows. They also lactate only six months a year, and a portion of their milk must go to their young. Given the difficulty of transportation, Dolma Tso and Nyima's diet could not include many fruits or vegetables.

"Our health is good," Nyima replied to my next question, "but sometimes our yaks get sick." Their biggest problems, he said, were snow and bandits. The former could prevent yaks from finding food, and the latter threatened a herd's very existence.

While Nyima answered our questions, Dolma Tso set a cauldron of water on the fire. Into it, she threw chili pods and dark tea leaves. She pumped hard on the bellows until the cauldron was hot, then she opened a bottle of grain alcohol and poured a dollop into the stew.

"What is that for?" asked one of my companions.

"The yaks," she replied. "To warm them up. This time of year, they are very weak." Protecting her hands with a rag, she lifted the heavy cauldron and hauled it outside.

Nyima told us that his brother was a farmer. "Farming is a hard life—harder than mine," he said. "They have three children, and they are always working."

---

22  One adult yak yields 150-200 kg of meat, depending on the quality of forage. The pasture around Nyima and Dolma Tso's camp was poor, and their yaks were likely at the low end of the scale.

Watching Dolma Tso at her tasks, it seemed to me that she worked much harder than Nyima. As she grew older, the constant bending, stooping, and hauling would take a toll, and the poor sanitation would likely affect her health more than his.

"In the last ten years, has your life gotten better, worse, or stayed the same?" one of my companions asked Nyima.

"It hasn't changed much. A little harder, I guess. But it's better than my father's."

"Would you prefer to live in a house?"

"I *have* a house," he said. "It's being used by relatives."

The next day we would reach the valley, where we would see the farms that belonged to the relatives of Nyima and other highland herders. It was advantageous to have agricultural and grazing lands close together so that farmers could jointly manage their herds. When Nyima grew too old for life on the grasslands, he could return to his village home.

We chatted about their household expenses: the cost of vaccines for his yaks and the taxes he paid to the government, which amounted to 800 yuan's worth of butter, grain, and cash annually.[23] Like most people I met out here, Nyima was very candid about his finances.

While we were conversing, Dolma Tso came back into the tent. She had said very little since we arrived. Wanting to draw her out, I asked her which she preferred to live in, a house or a tent?

"A house," she replied as she set down the empty cookpot. She then went to the vestibule and came back with a baby yak, a skittish creature with dark curly hair, only a week or two old. She picked up a baby bottle that was sitting by the fire and, holding the calf tenderly, she fed it.

"Can't it get milk from its mother?" asked one of my companions.

---

23  In 2004, the government would cancel all taxes on rural Tibetans.

"It's sick," she said. She let the calf suck until the bottle was empty. Then she took a bucket, poured tsampa and water into it, mixed it into a dough, and took it to the other calves tethered at the tent entrance.

"Dolma Tso, have you ever attended school?" I asked when she returned.

"No, never," she said.

By now, the fire was down to a few smoldering embers. Nyima helped us find places to sleep, giving the best spots to us foreigners. I filled my mug with water from the kettle and went outside to brush my teeth. A foot of snow lay on the ground. There was no latrine, but the darkness provided plenty of privacy. Returning to the tent, I wriggled into my sleeping bag and curled my body to fit the mat, which was rock hard and several inches too short. Soon the tent was silent but for the gentle sighs of creatures in slumber.

## Sögyal's Circle

After I returned to Dartsendo, I saw off the two Americans, then set about planning for work I intended to do in Degé. I tried to reach Sögyal on his mobile phone several times, but he didn't answer. Finally, I asked Mr. Wu to call Sögyal's office and tell them we would arrive soon.

The landlines to Degé were unreliable, and Mr. Wu had to dial half a dozen times before he was able to connect. There followed an eruption of rapid Sichuan dialect, and I heard Sögyal's name mentioned. Then Mr. Wu hung up the phone.

"Sögyal died," he said shortly.

Died?

That can't be. He was here just a week ago. I saw him.

*Died???*

Mr. Wu shared what little he knew. After Sögyal left Dartsendo, he traveled the usual two days to reach Degé, arriving on May 3rd. The next day he was ill with abdominal pain. They took him to Degé County Hospital, a place I remembered well, as I had been treated there for a dog bite five years before.

Degé's hospital was very basic, but the nearest better facilities were two days and several mountain passes away. Sögyal's condition made travel inadvisable, so the attending physician took his best guess and diagnosed a blocked intestine, which needed immediate surgery.

During the operation, the doctor realized that his diagnosis was wrong; the pain was caused by something else. But it was too late. Sögyal died in the early hours of May 5th—a mere four days after I had seen him alive and well in Dartsendo.

Sögyal . . . *died?*

The awful tragedy notwithstanding, Mr. Wu and I had work to do and left for Degé the next morning. For two long days, I rode the bus in a fog of hidden grief. I replayed my memories of the Degé hospital: the dungeon-like rooms, sickly green walls, battered furniture, and blood-stained sheets. I vividly remembered the steel instruments soaking in a jar of iodine on the doctor's desk, and the antiquated paraphernalia that made that hospital look more like Frankenstein's laboratory than a place of healing.

The physician I had seen in Degé was competent enough to treat my minor wounds, but the notion of him wheeling Sögyal into their primitive operating theater and cutting open his abdomen was a horror.

We arrived to learn that Sögyal's funeral had occurred that very morning. The line of mourners had stretched from the burial grounds, past half a dozen farms, the enormous main temple of Gönchen Monastery, the even bigger Parkhang, and into the town's business district. Three chiefs of neighboring counties made long journeys on short notice to attend. Two hundred monks made a procession to the cemetery. They formed a circle around Sögyal's grave and chanted from the *bardo thodol,* a religious text on death, so that Sögyal's consciousness would be released from his lifeless body and find safe passage to its eventual rebirth.

On the second morning, I rose at dawn and made the trek alone up to Sögyal's grave. Because of his position, Sögyal had been honored with a burial plot in Degé's small hillside cemetery. Reflecting Han funerary practices, a hole had been dug in the hill; one end of his coffin was pushed into it while the other was covered with an earthen mound and fronted by a headstone.[24] Sögyal's grave was too new to have a marker, but I identified it by the piles of freshly dug earth.

As I sat by his grave, I could see fields nearby where ranks of barley shoots were jutting out of the earth. The air was crowded with scents of spring. I could hear men and women calling to each other as they came out of their houses, and the roar of tractors plying the trail to town. From Sögyal's resting place, I could see the Parkhang below; I could also see, far across the valley in the distance, the flanks of the sacred mountain where he had grown up. His brief life's journey had brought him full circle.

---

24 Tibetan funerary practices vary by region. In one common form, "sky burial," the body is brought to a high place, cut up, and fed to vultures and other carrion. Interment in the ground may be used when illness is the cause of death. "Water burial," in which the corpse is placed in a river, can also be used in cases of illness. The remains of high lamas are cremated or preserved as objects of veneration within stupas.

# Part II

# Health

*Cure the illness that is not yet an illness.*
— Tibetan proverb

Caring for the sick is the purest expression of compassion, and because it protects precious human capital, health care is a critical gate of the development mandala. Historically, Buddhist monks provided virtually all health care in Tibet. Although the monks were well-schooled in compassion, their technical knowledge was inadequate, and they had few tools apart from their senses and things they took from the natural world to use as medicine. Records left by missionaries and other outsiders suggest that cholera, dysentery, parasites, and venereal disease were widespread. People also died from accidents and wounds received in armed conflict. Sanitation was poor, and people rarely bathed. No one knows for sure, but life expectancy must have been very low.

In 1948, just before the start of the Communist era, Kandze Prefecture had only two hospitals: a larger one in Chakzam operated by foreign missionaries, and a small one in Batang, likely the legacy of missionaries who had left Batang sixteen years earlier.[25] The vast majority of residents could not access them because they were too far away. Otherwise, the region had no doctors who understood even the fundamental elements of science-based medicine, such as the germ theory of disease.

---

25  Barnett, p. 460.

After the Communists arrived in 1949, they set out to create a new health care system based on modern principles, although they had few resources. Besides treatment centers staffed by trained professionals, the system included rural practitioners ("barefoot doctors") who received six months of training, then gave free primary care to members of the communes where they lived. By 1988, the Party had abolished communes and incorporated most rural practitioners into the formal public health system. In Kandze Prefecture, this consisted of four hospitals, nineteen clinics, and nineteen maternity and birth control stations.[26]

The system continued to grow, and by 2001, it included 350 hospitals and clinics, and thirty-eight health care stations, all together providing 2,773 beds for a population of 900,000.[27] Many of these offered both Western and traditional (Chinese or Tibetan) medicine. The region had a medical training academy, Kandze Health School (*Sichuan Ganzi Zhou Weisheng Xuexiao*), located in the Tatu Chu valley, enrolling about seventeen hundred students. Talented (or well-connected) Tibetans could also study medicine at various universities around Tibet and China.

Although health care in Kham had massively improved, services remained decades behind the standard found in Chinese cities. Throughout the system, doctors were woefully underpaid, feeding corruption and driving talent away. Perverse economic incentives caused doctors

---

26  Barnett, pp. 460–461.

27  *Supporting Sustainable Development, Environment Conservation and Cultural Preservation in Tibetan Areas of China,* Winrock International, (internal research report), ca. 2005, p. 9.

to prescribe more drugs than patients needed and to keep them in the hospital for too long. The low level of education meant that people made unhealthy choices such as smoking. In the Tibetan countryside, many illnesses went untreated because health care was too far away and unaffordable. Distrust was exacerbated when patients and their doctors belonged to different ethnic groups.

## Searching for a Health Care Path

That someone so young, so vigorous, and so promising as Sögyal could die was unacceptable. Had he been in Chengdu or even Dartsendo when the pain started, he might have been seen by better doctors and been saved. It's one thing to read statistics on short life expectancy; it's quite another when the short life happens to someone close.

Health care was much on my mind as we left Degé for an already-planned trip to the grassland region of Sershul. People in that sparsely populated county had many needs, but perhaps the most acute was health care. In the county seat, we toured a teaching hospital dedicated to transmitting the wisdom of Mipham, a philosopher who had penned books on medicine and other topics a hundred years earlier. An hour further up the road was a monastery where a tulku told us he was planning to build a small clinic. Both organizations emphasized traditional remedies.

Traditional Tibetan medicine was taught at state-run schools and was well accepted—even promoted—by the government. The medicines are made from herbs, fungi, animal products, and minerals ground into powder and then formed into spherical brown pills. Many Tibetans—especially herders—preferred them to western pharmaceuticals. They were also much cheaper than Western drugs.

During my travels, acquaintances occasionally gave me envelopes of such pills—not to treat any particular illness, but for general health purposes. People believe they are especially powerful if blessed by a high lama. A tulku's excrement is regarded as very potent and is much desired as an ingredient. Once, a friend suggested that if I put some medicine away in a dark, quiet place, the pills would spontaneously multiply.

As we drove back to Dartsendo, one of the three local people traveling with me lay prostrate across the back seat, suffering from acute abdominal pain. He agreed that it was probably caused by eating parasite-infected meat. Despite the many positives of traditional Tibetan medicine, I doubted its ability to treat this chronic ailment or, indeed, most illnesses suffered by Kandze residents. I decided not to pursue a partnership with either of the traditional medicine clinics we had just seen.

Heading back to California in early summer, I stopped in Chengdu and Hong Kong. There, I met with several people from other NGOs, but they brought me no closer to solving the problem of how KhamAid could improve health. It would take many more months before I would find a way into the mandala's healthcare gate.

We were, however, making progress in other areas. Our base of supporters was growing. Most donors gave amounts less than a thousand dollars, but we got a few larger grants. Thanks to my being unpaid, our overhead remained low, so that ninety percent of monies donated could go directly into programs.

KhamAid's scholarship program was doing well under its new director, Dana Isherwood, the traveler I'd recruited from the Degé tour group. Thanks to her relentless efforts, we signed up a score of new sponsors for the coming school year.

Recently, we had been introduced to the leaders of the Kandze

Prefecture Women's Federation. This was the local arm of a sprawling national organization charged with advancing the interests of female citizens. The leaders were much interested in getting more girls in school and wanted to help us expand our scholarship program. They introduced us to their counterparts in Ta'u and Derong Counties. These women then contacted primary school headmasters, who drew up lists of academically gifted girls, but whose families could not afford middle school. There were plenty of these, and we quickly found a girl for every sponsor.

In the autumn, after school started, I crossed the ocean and traveled to Sichuan again, where Dana Isherwood joined me. With two others, we set out on a road trip to visit our sponsored children, both old and new.

## Encounter with a Prostrating Pilgrim

After two years of construction, at last, upgrades on Kandze Prefecture's two trunk highways were complete. Travel was easier now than ever before, especially because, for this field trip, we splurged on a hired car and driver. The car would be needed to reach our new program site in Derong County, which had infrequent bus service.

Our first stop was Litang. Now, in early October, the pastures were wilting, and the morning air crackled. At the Litang Middle School we had ten girls and one boy on scholarship. We spent all day visiting with the children, met several of their families, and joined school officials for the usual greasefest in the usual restaurant.

After that long day, we needed some time off, so the next morning we slept late, then set out for some sightseeing. Leaving the business district, we labored uphill along a road lined with traditional Tibetan homes until we reached the gate of Litang Monastery. There we would meet a young man who embodied two vital truths about Tibet: first, Tibetans' total and unwavering faith in Buddhism, and second, the miraculous power that their faith engenders.

The monastery was a tilted campus of fortress-like stone temples set in a web of footpaths and enclosed by a high stone wall. Ripples of pasture poured from the highlands and flowed around the monastery, making it seem like a lone raft bobbing on an ocean of prairie. Within such lofty Rivendells of the high plateau, the external world fades away, leaving only red-robed monks and their gentle cycles of ritual and contemplation.

We came to two large chanting halls where we stopped to see if anything was going on, but the giant doors were padlocked shut. Panting from the thin air, we resumed a slow trudge toward the highest part of the complex.

At the pinnacle of the campus stood a U-shaped wing of monk residences attached to the front façade of a temple. Passing through an opening into a flagstone courtyard, I emerged from the shadows to face Litang's oldest and most sacred sanctuary: the Tse Phodrang, or Summit Palace. I crossed the flagstones to the far side, where ten broad steps led up to the temple portico.

Above me, I heard a scraping sound and saw a figure moving in the shadow of the colonnaded roof, but I paid no attention. Gathering several more lungfuls of air, I began to climb toward the entrance.

By the fifth step, my pupils had dilated to the darkness above, and I could see a lone monk standing with his back to me, his face aimed toward the great doors and the unseen sacred image beyond. A lean and sinewy figure beneath his robes, the monk stooped, then stretched out flat to press his body onto the floorboards, hands overhead, palms joined together in prayer. He was reciting a mantra, but I couldn't make out the words.

Having completed this profound obeisance, the monk pushed himself up to stand fully vertical. Then he repeated the whole exercise again and again.

Unlike many traveler-seekers in the Himalaya, I have never taken up a serious study of Tibetan Buddhism. I am sympathetic and respectful, but I am not a believer. My own spiritual practice is drawn from *bushido,* the path of Japanese *karate-do* that I had doggedly pursued since college, and in which I had recently been honored with the rank of fourth-degree black belt.

To me, *bushido* and Buddhism didn't seem far apart. As a martial artist, I sought to transcend my ego and face my fears through the practice of simulated combat, passing through a veil of fire into a place of joyous release. Zen practitioners might compare that to *satori,* imperfectly translated as "enlightenment" or "liberation." Followers of Tibetan Buddhism seek to overcome mental obscurations, leading to an understanding of emptiness and the true nature of reality, a state of continuous bliss sometimes expressed with the same words: "enlightenment" and "liberation."

In Tibet and other places that practice the Mahayana Buddhist tradition, practitioners seek liberation not for themselves, but for the sake of helping others. A *Bodhisattva* is a revered being who has achieved Buddhahood; however, rather than disappear into the radiance of eternal transcendence, the Bodhisattva instead chooses to remain in this imperfect world to serve others seeking the path to liberation. The Dalai Lama is held to be the Bodhisattva of Compassion, representing the highest ideal of selflessness and sacrifice.

I had been headed to the temple doors, but now I was frozen in my tracks staring at the prostrating monk. The deftness of his movements told me he was a serious devotee of the practice. On his hands, he wore wooden paddles that clapped loudly when they hit the floor and had rubbed two blond tracks into the wood. His much-stained shirt of gold-colored fabric was rolled up at the sleeves. His red quilted monk's skirt was in shreds, exposing knees shielded by leather pads.

Not wanting to interrupt, I stood back to admire the consummate smoothness with which his body folded and unfolded, the humility and devotion that shined from every pore. My companions had climbed more slowly, but presently they caught up and were standing beside me as I watched transfixed.

The Buddhism of Tibet traces its origins to the teachings of a mystic philosopher whom legend holds emerged from the plains of the Indian subcontinent, six centuries before the birth of Christ. Born into a life of privilege, at the age of twenty-nine, Siddartha Gautama renounced wealth and pleasure to become a wandering ascetic, a rootless seeker looking for answers to fundamental questions of death, suffering, and the nature of existence.

After years of homelessness, self-denial, and starvation, the story goes, Siddartha came upon a giant fig tree, sat beneath it, and plunged into deep absorption, not moving for days. After this extended period of reflection, at last, he found understanding that released him from his restless searching. In a torrent of blazing insight, he realized that human suffering, which is inseparable from our existence, arises from our attachment to external things. Want, he realized, and we shall suffer. Cease wanting, and we shall experience bliss.

As this powerful idea crept from the Indian subcontinent west along the Silk Road and over the Himalaya, the spare framework of Buddha's teaching clothed itself in the garb of the native beliefs it met. When it arrived in Tibet eleven centuries after its birth, Buddhism fused with Tibet's indigenous animist religion, Bön, adopting shamanistic and nature-worshipping Bönpo practices.[28] Tibetans projected their newly adopted beliefs upon a pantheon of supernatural beings that look to the uninitiated like gods. These are the paintings and statues one sees in Buddhist temples.

My martial arts practice pulled me toward Zen Buddhism, but I never had much use for the intricate embellishments of the Tibetan interpretation. Yet there was one place where my warrior's Zen intersected with the Buddhism of Tibet, and that is the act of prostration. Not genuflecting out of reverence or supplication, but the physical movement of prostration itself, the actual *movement*—and the mindfulness, humility, and awakening it invokes.

I had first seen it nineteen years earlier when I met a group of prostrating pilgrims traveling from western Sichuan to the holy city of Lhasa, about the same distance as from Amsterdam to Rome. After each prostration, a pilgrim would walk to the farthest place reached with his fingertips, then prostrate again, over and over, measuring the miles of longitude with his very flesh.

Now here at Litang Monastery, I stood mesmerized by the prostrating monk. One member of my team, a young man named Tsering Perlo, noticed my interest. He murmured something in Tibetan to the monk, which made the latter leave off prostrating.

I was momentarily embarrassed to have disrupted the man's prayers, but just then, another monk arrived carrying a tea kettle. The prostrating monk pulled the paddles from his hands and sat down, folding his legs beneath him on a triangle of sun-warmed floor. Reaching for his satchel, the monk pulled out a bowl, and the kettle-bearer filled it with steaming broth.

---

28  Bön is still actively practiced in Kham, especially in the counties of Zungchu, Nyarong, Degé, and Rongtrak.

For nearly ten years, I had wondered many things about prostrators. Now, at last, I had a chance to ask.

Sitting cross-legged on the floor sipping his tea, the monk looked oddly ordinary, like any farmer resting from his labors. His skin was the color of mahogany, and he had thick but close-cropped hair. At the center of his forehead was a quarter-sized red callus, badge of the thousands of times his face had touched the earth.

I sat down a few feet away on the temple steps. Wanting to know if the monk understood Chinese, I asked him in that language if he belonged to Litang Monastery. No, he replied, he was from Rasha Monastery. I had to ask him to repeat the name, for I had never heard of the place. "It's in Bamé Township," he explained, naming a place 266 kilometers (165 miles) to the east. "Rasha belongs to the Nyingma School," he said.

By asking more questions, I learned that his name was Tenzin Dendrup and that he was twenty-eight years old. But something was nagging at me. If he was from Rasha, a Nyingma monastery, what was he doing at this place, which belongs to the Gelug order?

But before I could shape my lips around the question, the answer was suddenly as plain as the callus on his forehead and the mitts he had just taken off his hands: Tenzin Dendrup had left his home and become a prostrating pilgrim. Like the pilgrims who had so amazed me years before, he was measuring each step of his sacred journey with his own tender body striping the earth.

And where did the journey lead? There was only one possible place. "Are you going to Lhasa?"

"Yes."

"That is very far," was my lame response.

"Yes," he said, and added with breathtaking understatement: "It's far." And the route is far from straight: it's a jagged path that creeps up ranges, crawls into gorges, spans mighty torrents.

"You're prostrating there?"

"Yes."

"You started in Bamé?"

"Lhagang," he said, naming a town in Kandze Prefecture where they have the twin of Tibet's holiest of holies, the *Jo* statue of Lhasa's Jokhang Temple. The two statues stand like bookends to frame a pilgrim's journey. "From Lhagang to Lhasa is 2,000 kilometers," he said.[29]

"That's far," I said again, wishing that my modest Chinese would allow me a more intelligent response.

"I do five hundred prostrations for each kilometer," he offered. "That's *yi bai wan* prostrations."

I had to blink a couple of times while I replayed the words in my head. *Yi bai wan.* One hundred ten-thousands. One million? Even taken with the grain of salt I always applied to numbers given to me in Tibet, this boggled my mind. If each prostration took ten seconds, and Tenzin prostrated for eight hours a day, every day—a fantastic feat of endurance—it would be almost a year before he reached his goal.

With practices like these, it's not hard to see why many Han found the Tibetan religion to be utterly impractical. Tibetan parents offered their precious sons into monasteries, leaving families short of workers and women short of husbands. Poor Tibetans gave money to already-lavish temples where it supported an idle priestly class. In the name of religion, Tibetans devoted their time to carving prayers into rocks, painting mantras on cliff faces, and manufacturing clay totems by hand. Some abstained from eggs, poultry, and fish—fine sources of

---

29  Actual (road) distance: 1,714 kilometers (1,071 miles), Google Maps.

protein—because they believe that no creature's soul should be sacrificed for such a measly harvest of edible food. Quite ridiculous, some would say. And yet, the beliefs persisted and flourished.

"How long are you staying here in Litang?" I asked.

"Twenty days."

"You don't travel straight through?"

"Sometimes I stop along the way to worship at a temple, or at a sacred lake or mountain," he said. "Sometimes, I have to stop because I'm sick or hungry. Sometimes I stop because I'm just too tired to go on."

Tenzin explained that his family consisted of his father and a married sister. His mother had died when he was a year old. Because his family was illiterate, he did not write letters to them, nor did they send any kind of support. He was on his own, utterly cut off, a lone man laying his body on the road as trucks rumbled past, mammoth and indifferent, burying him in dust. How did he survive?

"People I meet on the road give me alms," he explained. "When people are kind, I can eat three bowls of tsampa, three times a day. When people aren't so generous, I eat only once a day."

I enjoyed a bowl of tsampa dough for breakfast, especially if the butter was fresh and there was a bit of sugar to put in it. But to eat tsampa three meals a day and *for months on end?* Even worse: tsampa only *once* a day, and nothing else? That was an inconceivable hardship, an austerity beyond conception. No wonder he sometimes felt too weak to continue. The miracle was that he'd gotten this far.

"Where do you sleep?"

"Anywhere. Sometimes in a cave. Sometimes in the open on the ground."

"Do you have a tent?"

By now, a member of my team, a young man named Tsering

Perlo, was helping to translate the conversation. Tenzing turned to him and said in Tibetan, "Why does she ask so many questions?" Not with irritation, just gentle curiosity.

"Because," Tsering Perlo replied, "they don't have this kind of pilgrim in America."

Tenzin nodded and turned back to me. "Just a blanket," he said. His eyes were luminous, the light of Siddartha Gautama pouring like fireflies from their black depths.

"Why are you doing this?" I asked at last, wondering if he could possibly communicate across the language barrier something I could not myself describe and of which I was only dimly aware.

He answered without hesitation. "Before this journey," he said, "I felt I never did anything worthwhile with my life. I feel regret for past bad actions, for example, insects I've killed. I feel regret that, when my mother died, I couldn't help her."

Guilt about insects? About his mother's death? He was only a year old at the time! How profoundly tender he must be to feel this way.

Tenzin continued: "During this pilgrimage, these feelings of guilt and regret are gradually lessening. I feel cleaner now and have greater peace of mind than at any time before in my life. Sometimes I have weak moments, such as when I'm hungry and have to beg for food. But compared to before, I have a much cleaner spirit, and I'm much happier."

Such was Tenzin's incredible equanimity, his supernatural calm, that I had not a shred of doubt he spoke the truth.

"While I'm prostrating, I feel very grateful that I'm alive to make this pilgrimage. As long as I don't die from robbery or sickness or some other cause during this journey, I'm truly a fortunate person."

# Environment

*A plain with one tree standing*
*is a grief to a boundless forest.*
— Tibetan proverb

If Tibet is known for one thing besides isolation, it's the purity of its mountain spaces. For centuries, people in Kham had free access to the mandala's environmental gate, for their environment was protected by its remoteness, sparse population, and strictly agrarian economy. Although Tibetans cleared forests for crops and grazing and collected firewood and cut timber for building houses, they lacked the mechanized tools needed for broader exploitation. Also, they held certain trees, groves, and mountains to be sacred, and placed a high value on living harmoniously with nature.

When China's Communist government moved into western Sichuan, they could not, at first, exploit the natural resources they found there. Transportation was difficult, people were consumed by the endless political movements, and the People's Liberation Army was busy fighting the Khampa rebels. Also, China was still very poor.

However, after Deng Xiaoping loosened the shackles of China's command-driven economy, the race began in earnest to extract Kham's wealth. Gold miners arrived in the early 1980s and began ripping up pasture and poisoning water. Hunters came seeking meat, fur, and wild animal parts used in Chinese medicine. Engineers dynamited mountains, redirected streams, flattened hills, and dammed rivers. Growing material wealth and rapid population growth unleashed a colossal waste management problem.

Yet since the start of the Deng era, the most visible injury to Kham's environment has been the slaughter of its ancient forests. In 1975, western Sichuan was 30% covered in spruce, fir, juniper, pine, and other noble species.[30] As roads improved and the region's seclusion waned, chain saws spread like a plague ever deeper into the mountains. Timber was vital for the developing Chinese nation, and it was profitable for the workers who cut it and the counties that taxed it, so logging became the impetus for more roads, and clear-cutting expanded until half of the slopes in western Sichuan were shorn of life.[31] Every day, hundreds of lorries descended to the Sichuan basin, swaying and groaning under a crush of logs.

By 1998, forest cover in western Sichuan had plummeted to a mere 6.5%—and these were mostly trees that were too remote to extract. That same year, deadly floods on the lower Yangtze River aimed a spotlight at deforestation on the eastern Tibetan plateau. In response, China's government established the National Forestry Conservation Program, comprising three major efforts: a ban on commercial logging throughout the Yangtze watershed, an expansion of work to plant new trees on denuded slopes, and a

30 Rudy van Bruggen, "Forest values of Khampa people in Ganzi Tibetan Autonomous Prefecture, Peoples' Republic of China," (M.S. diss., Wageningen University, 2003).

31 The 50% loss of forest cover occurred over forty years to the mid-1990s. Daniel Winkler. "Forests, forest ecology and deforestation in the Tibetan prefectures of western Sichuan." *Commonwealth Forestry Review* 75(4) (1996): 296-301.

program called *Tuigeng Huanlin* ("Grain for Green") aimed at returning agricultural land to forest.

Chinese law limited the rights of citizens over their land; ultimate control was reserved to the government, which rarely involved ordinary people in its decision-making. Residents had to wait for officials to arrive in their jeeps and Land Cruisers to learn how *Tuigeng Huanlin* would impact land they had used for generations. Implementation was inconsistent because it depended on how local officials interpreted their instructions. Some residents could choose whether or not to participate in the new programs; others were obliged to take part, even if it meant sacrificing land used for grazing or growing food.

Already, since 1979, the Chinese government had been directing tree-planting on a national scale, especially in the country's arid northwest. Each March, on the designated day, millions of workers, students, and farmers headed to the outskirts of their communities to plant trees, an effort mainly aimed at halting soil erosion and desertification. More than a hundred million trees were planted, but the survival rate was low due to a lack of continued care for the fragile seedlings. The Forestry Bureau had already been doing limited reforestation in Kandze Prefecture; now, they were poised to expand that effort significantly. The work was meeting resistance from some herders, who preferred to see the clear-cut slopes remain available to their livestock.

## Trees and Mountains

Reforestation was on my mind because people in a village called Oro, in Nyakchukha County, had asked KhamAid for help replanting a bare mountain slope above their community. Once smothered in spruce and pine, in 1994 a wildfire had burned the slope to a stubble of charcoal fingers.

At this time, to combat damage caused by logging, the Kandze Prefecture Forestry Bureau was getting ready for a massive reforestation effort and had set up tree nurseries in Dartsendo, Drango, Litang, and other locations to grow seedlings. Livestock owners often opposed reforestation because the cleared areas made excellent pasture. However, Oro Village relied mainly on farming; they missed their 130 *mu* (8.7 hectares) of wooded enchantment and the wildlife it sheltered. Oro leaders had asked for government help, but the Forestry Bureau refused because fire, not logging, had caused Oro's loss. The community thereupon appealed to KhamAid.

In KhamAid's early years, we chose projects that appealed to donors and us; we had no overarching strategy. Although we were inexperienced in environmental work, I liked the idea of planting trees, so I recruited an American volunteer to lead the effort; he was accompanying Dana Isherwood and me on the current trip. A few days previously, we had stopped in Oro for a planning meeting.

To get an idea of what undisturbed old-growth forest looked like, we were now heading into a nature reserve called Nyingden (Ch: Yading). The reserve was also known as Konkaling, a name used by explorer Joseph Rock who had written about the place in *National Geographic* magazine in 1931. Established in 1996, the reserve enclosed three great mountains held sacred by Buddhists. I wanted to know more about China's environmental policies and how they were playing out at Konkaling.

Then, too, was my encounter with the prostrating pilgrim at Litang Monastery. Tenzin Dendrup had awakened a visceral craving to hit the pilgrim's trail myself. For many reasons, I could not undertake a journey of prostrations, but walking a *korra* (circumambulation) around a sacred mountain would do very nicely. Konkaling's three holy mountains had an ineluctable appeal to me and my fellow travelers, who were also Buddhist.

From Litang, we drove for two days to reach the Reserve entrance. On the way, we learned that a convoy of cars had gone in ahead of us, carrying eight Americans and a bevy of guides. We had a good idea of who the Americans were, for Dana Isherwood had heard through her mountaineering grapevine that an entertainment attorney and a filmmaker from California were headed to Konkaling, one of a series of visits. The two Americans were making a film about a place described in the book *Lost Horizon*.

*Lost Horizon*, a novel published in 1933 by James Hilton, is about an airplane that falls into a remote, snowy land somewhere on the Tibetan plateau. Local inhabitants rescue the travelers and take them blindfolded to a secret stronghold called Shangri-La, where the inhabitants enjoy perfect harmony and live to fantastic ages. *Lost Horizon* was made into a Frank Capra movie of the same name, and the story quickly infused into the sprawling, iridescent, bewitching mythology that the world has constructed around Tibet. Several towns on the southeast Tibetan plateau have attempted to lure visitors by advertising themselves as the Shangri-La of Hilton's book.

Reality check: history offers no evidence that Hilton ever went anywhere near Tibet, so Shangri-La cannot be based on his personal experience of a real place. Nevertheless, when I later spoke to the attorney myself, he insisted that not only was it real, but he and his filmmaker buddy had found it in Konkaling. "We have twenty-two points of proof, so it's conclusive in my mind," he said. "We saw some people who claimed to be very old. One person called 'Day-Star' claimed to be born in the year of Halley's Comet and has seen it twice since. That's at least 152 years!"

He would not tell me the location of the valley he believed was Shangri-La, saying, "We don't want people to rush to this place and ruin it like so many places have been ruined."

Like many Western eccentrics I had met since starting KhamAid, this one seemed harmless, but there was a disturbing twist to this tale. Dana Isherwood had heard that this time, the pair were bringing with them a noted mountain-climber, Pete Athans. Athans was rumored to be scouting a first ascent of one of Konkaling's three sacred summits.

Just outside the Reserve entrance, several dozen locals were gathered, awaiting visitors who might hire them as guides. Nearby, tied to a fence were their horses, saddled and ready to take us in. Business was slow; before we were even out of the car, the people were swarming, vying for our business. We had already hired one guide in the Dabpa County seat; he now helped us hire five more people, each with a horse, for we were required to have one horse and wrangler for each entrance ticket we purchased.

On the drive here, we had seen lots of open space, as many hillsides had been cleared of trees so that residents could graze their animals and farm. However, as soon as we passed through the Reserve gate, we tunneled into a dusky fairytale forest that showed no signs of ever having been cut. The tree-shaded trail brought us past walls and towers of *mani* stones etched with the Sanskrit mantra, *om mani padme hum,* loosely translated as "hail the jewel in the lotus"—a ubiquitous phrase in Tibet that venerates the Buddha's teaching.

After a short hike, we came to a clearing. At one end stood two large tents, operated by Han, that provided food and lodging to visitors who lacked camping gear. It was already late afternoon, so we pitched our small tents amid the yak patties and stones, then wandered off to look around.

We soon found Tronggu Monastery, a small dilapidated temple set in a field of stone rubble. There was no one in sight, and the door was unlocked, so we went inside. With neither electricity nor butter lamps, the place seemed more tomb than temple. On the second floor, we found a gray-haired monk sitting alone in the shadows. He was Abbot Losang Drakpo, age fifty-three, and he had been a monk since he was thirteen. He said that even during the Cultural Revolution, he had kept his vows and continued to study Buddhism as best he could. We asked him if any foreigners had passed by.

"Yes, a few days ago, some Americans came through."

"Did they say anything about climbing?"

"Climbing?" he said uncertainly.

"To the summit," I said, "of Jambeyang." Mount Jambeyang, named after the Bodhisattva of Wisdom, was one of Konkaling's three sacred peaks.

"It can't be done," said the monk shortly.

"What if it can? What if someone tried?"

He was visibly appalled. "They can't. They shouldn't. It's prohibited."

"We know," said Dana Isherwood, nodding emphatically. "You're right!"

"But what if someone was going to do it?" I persisted.

"Then I would try to stop them," said the abbot, his eyes filling with tears. "But I haven't seen such people here. And it's impossible to climb."

We returned to our camp, feeling uneasy. Above the canopy loomed the immense massif of Chenresig, Bodhisattva of Compassion, haloed by shimmering twilight. At 6,030 meters (19,900 feet), Chenresig was the tallest of the three Konkaling peaks. Its avalanche-scarred, ice-crusted central summit was flanked by the humped shoulders of two lesser spires, shoulders that cascaded into arm-like ridges wrapping around the north face and coming together in a rocky *mudra* on the mountain's lap. Chenresig was both the magnet and axis of our journey; we planned to circumambulate this lordly figure hewn from stone.

At sunup the next morning, the Tibetans in our party boiled black tea over the campfire. We breakfasted in local style on tsampa and butter carried from a farm belonging to Andri, the guide we had hired in town. Thus fortified, we packed up and set out walking south on the well-worn *korra* trail, horses carrying our bags. Mount Chenresig hung on our right shoulder, as it would for the next two days while we circled it.

Our guide, Andri, about forty-five, was a self-made man. One income stream came from his family farm, another from producing wooden bowls turned from knotty hardwoods. Some of his bowls, he told us, sold for 1,000 yuan each. Andri had two wives and six children. However, unlike polygamous Tibetan noblemen of times past, Andri's two spouses were not sisters and did not live in one household. Wife Number One lived in Andri's village farmhouse; she was the mother of five children, most of them grown. Number Two, who was much younger, lived in the county seat where Andri kept his wood-shop; they had an infant.

Dabpa County had just completed a master tourism plan for the Nyingden Reserve, modeling it on Zitsa Degu (Ch: Jiuzhaigou), a wildly popular scenic area in northern Sichuan. (From the moment I first set foot in Sichuan, people were perpetually asking me whether I had been there.) Dabpa County's plan was aimed squarely at maximizing tourism income; it addressed the logistics of hosting visitors, including feeding and housing them and managing their waste, with only a passing mention of alleviating poverty for local people.

During 1999, about 5,000 visitors had come to Konkaling, but the plan set a target of 350,000 visitors annually by 2010, a shockingly large number. [32,33] It seemed that Chinese policy-makers did not want to limit profit-making activities—not for the sake of fragile ecosystems and the needs of indigenous people, and not just at Konkaling, but at dozens of other reserves, where similar stories were unfolding.

At the moment, I was blissfully unaware of the county's plans. I was loving this holy walk: the fresh air and mountain scenery, and the company of happy fellow pilgrims. Our wranglers laughed and sang as they walked. For them, the trip was a double blessing: they were earning wages and benefitting all sentient beings at the same time.

As we walked, Andri shared his storehouse of Konkaling lore, pointing out a cave whose waters enable the mute to speak, where one can find chalk with healing power and a dark stone wall that is a manifestation of the underworld. At other times, Dana Isherwood and I traded theories about the intentions of Pete Athans and the other Americans now somewhere in the reserve. I wondered if they were planning an illicit climb—pretending to be tourists, sidling up to a mountain, then dashing to the top. A few intrepid Western climbers

---

32   Yuan Li, "Konkaling – One Man's Shangri-La," *Asian Geographic*, Sept.-Nov. 2000.

33   Travis Klingberg, "A Routine Discovery: The Practice of Plan and the Opening of the Yading Nature Reserve," p. 14; found in *Mapping Shangrila: Contested Landscapes in the Sino-Tibetan Borderlands,* Emily T. Yeh, Chris Coggins, ed. (University of Washington Press, 2014).

had reached lesser summits that way. No one could stop them, for who would be crazy enough to follow?

Our journey along Chenresig's eastern flanks took us into an alpine valley where a meandering brook had carved out sinuous half-moons of marshy pasture. The valley walls were an amber-and-avocado abstract of evergreen and larch. There were no houses—permanent settlements were prohibited within the reserve—but the government had put up boardwalks over the marshiest spots to make walking easier. From time to time, our guides stopped to pick up discarded Fujichrome boxes and instant noodle wrappers, the first time I had ever seen people in Tibet take direct action against litter. Indeed, the place was pristine, perhaps like California's Yosemite Valley before Euro-Americans arrived seeking conquest and gold.

Our initial heading took us in the direction of Mount Chanadorje, named for Buddha's fierce protector and guide. Striped with vertical slashes of snow, the mountain crouched like a tiger over the valley. As we moved along, we leapfrogged over several parties of Han Chinese travelers on horseback. Tripods lashed to their saddles and long-snouted cameras on their chests told why they had come. Each pony was led by a Tibetan from Nyingden Village.

By midmorning, we came around a bend, and our jaws dropped, for Mount Jambeyang was suddenly uncurtained. While the two other Konkaling spires are prodigious and extravagant, Jambeyang takes top prize: a splendid three-sided pyramid, a geologic dagger cracking open the vast liquid sapphire above.

Curving around Chenresig's southern foothills brought us up against Jambeyang's stunning northern face: a vertical ice slab thousands of feet high. Here we paused to catch our breath and squint up at the blinding heights. Savage easterlies were clawing snow from

Jambeyang's summit, creating immense silvery maelstroms. We pulled out our cameras.

Mountaineer Dana Isherwood studied Jambeyang through her telephoto lens, looking for a way up. "The face is too steep," she said at last, "and that ridge is very exposed."

At length, she put down her camera and shook her head. "That is a difficult climb!"

We stopped for lunch at Drongropo Pasture, a rare flat spot in a borough of steep falls. Our wranglers eased the loads from the horses, which quickly scattered to munch the rich green turf. Lazing on the meadow under the noonday sun, lulled by the gentle dinging of horse bells, I got out my camera and longest lens to scan Jambeyang again. Amid the jumbled rock and ice, I spotted a small, high eyrie of green. "Is that a pasture?" I asked, hoping that someone else had better eyes than mine.

Everyone stopped eating and stared upward. *That could be a base camp!* I thought. *And those dark dots—could those be horses?* Was I imagining things? Or were Athans' guides there even now, grazing their mounts while waiting for their client to come down?

None of us could make out what was happening on that spit of green, and there were no herders around to ask, only tourists.

We resumed our march. The trail steepened as we threaded into the slender defile that knifes between Chenresig and Jambeyang. An hour later, we reached a pass, where our guides stopped to straighten a tangle of prayer flags strung from poles. The place was surprisingly crowded: a dozen or more travelers were resting there before they would turn back and retrace their steps to the tent camp at Tronggu Monastery. Not us. We would continue to circle the mountain.

A little way farther, Andri, our guide from town, made an abrupt right turn away from the trail, motioning me to follow. Not sure where we were going, I chased his white shirt as it receded up a rocky hill. It was a hellish little climb. I gasped for breath and wondered if my karma needed this much help. Eventually, I made it to the top of a ridge, where Andri sat waiting.

"Look," he said, gesturing to a valley laid out beneath us, invisible from the *korra* trail and hidden from other trekkers. At the bottom was a slate-colored lake, shaped like a teardrop, imprinted with a shimmering reflection of Chenresig's lower slopes and a cloud-strewn sky. "This lake can tell the future," he said. "Stay quiet and watch."

I watched, and to my astonishment, a bright green flower spread across the surface, suddenly changing to lapis, then cobalt. Black shadows winked at me from the depths; then, in a twinkling, they were gone, and I saw only wind-ruffled surface.

"Wait," said Andri. "When it's clear as glass, that's when your future will appear."

I waited. Suddenly the spectral silence was broken by a gigantic C-R-R-ACK from somewhere high on Chenresig. Could it be one of those giant ice sheets hanging from the face? Fear tightened my chest, but then, with an effort of will, I let it go and was rewarded with a bloom of Buddha-like calm. What a splash it will make if it falls!

At once, the wind ceased, and a black hole appeared in the lake. I had a vision, one so sudden and potent that it took my breath away: According to Chinese law and Tibetan belief, these mountains should be protected. But will the laws be enforced? The lake said *yes*. Or was it only my naive optimism?

With the sun skating downward, we crossed the highest pass of the day, some 4,400 meters (14,850 feet) above sea level. An hour later, we stopped at a small stone hut used by passing herders. While we pitched tents, our escorts swept out the hut and made it habitable. Soon they had a kettle boiling over a sprightly fire. After dinner, I watched clouds churn in the valleys beneath us. The sunlight faded to magenta, kindling a crimson radiance on the ice dagger of Jambeyang's summit. The sky slowly darkened to ignite unimaginable billions of stars.

The next morning, groaning from the aches of yesterday's march, we made a late start. The day began with a brutal climb of two and a half hours. As I dragged my weary bones up the trail, I wondered if Athans was hauling himself up a Jambeyang glacier even now. At last, we crossed Pute La, the highest pass of the *korra* at about 4900 meters (16,200 feet). There, a thoughtful voyager had left a cache of walking sticks, attesting that Chenresig was indeed a compassionate mountain after all. We grabbed some for the descent.

Quickly we dropped below the tree line, past looming cliffs, into the shade of an ancient forest layered in lichen and moss. Our wranglers often stopped to make prostrations: here at a spring, there at a grove of trees, and again at the center of a clearing.

I realized that, for the local inhabitants, protecting Konkaling's environment was not just a matter of regulation or economics or appearances, but a spiritual practice of venerating the principles embodied in the three holy summits. I wished that the practice could be extended to the rest of Tibet, where most every inhabited place I had visited smelled of open toilets and was festooned with trash. The problem was one of resources and governance: people could not, by themselves, create the infrastructure needed to keep up with the fast-rising volume of waste, and the government was not even trying.

Despite frequent pauses, we made good time to our lunch stop at another hut. The last lap brought us into a forest of larch, yellow as daffodils in the biting autumn air. At last, we reached Tronggu Monastery, the starting place for our *korra*.

Months later, Dana Isherwood would solve the mystery of the Konkaling mountaineers: there was not one, but two teams scouting Mount Jambeyang. In one group, the leader Pete Athans studied the conditions and declared there was *no way* they would climb that mountain. He then went to have a look at the south side of Mount Chanadorje. There, conditions were also bad, and he wisely gave up. The second team was composed of two other climbers; they, too, did not succeed. Reportedly, none were planning to return.

Even so, protecting Konkaling was like trying to stop a tsunami. Everyone wanted a piece of it: tourists, the local people who guided them, operators of the tent camp, the two Americans making their film about Shangri-La, and the county government with its mega-tourism plan. I hoped, at least, that Athans' visit would not be the starting gun for a stampede of climbers who would transform Konkaling into a garbage dump like so many Himalayan peaks.

All that was out of my control, but the forests of Konkaling had given me a hazy vision of what we might accomplish by planting trees on the fire-ravaged mountainside above Oro.

## A Prodigal Child

Our holiday was over, and now it was time to meet our newest sponsored students. From Konkaling, we wound our way among oxblood hills forested with long-needled pines, to the seat of Derong County, a pleasant, low-lying town straddling a river. The school headmaster and Women's Federation ladies were waiting for us, as well as thirteen newly enrolled girls.

We spent two days meeting the kids, visiting classrooms and

dorms. Dana Isherwood took portraits of every girl, and we collected their biographical data. Our hosts arranged for the students to perform traditional Tibetan singing and dancing. Their grateful parents layered us in garlands of feather-light khata.

This was the year a child named Metok Tso entered KhamAid's orbit. She had been born in a low-lying farming village. Her name means *flower lake*. Her father had been the village accountant, but when she was little, he had left her mother and run off with another woman, never to return.

A poor rural woman in Derong County had no realistic means to extract child support from a runaway husband. Metok Tso and her two siblings subsisted on their mom's meager earnings from doing unskilled labor, often in construction—low-paid, dirty, dangerous work. They lived in a one-room, mud-walled shack divided by a tarpaulin into living and sleeping areas. When it rained, water leaked through the roof and dripped on the floor just inches from Metok Tso's bed.

Neighbors ostracized the family because they were poor. That was a bitter pill to swallow for a young girl.

Metok Tso had completed up to grade 6 at a village schoolhouse, but her mother could not afford the tuition and boarding fees to send her to the middle school in the county seat.[34] Without help, the girl's prospects were bleak.

Metok Tso had a round face, pink cheeks, and straight black hair like all of the other girls who joined our program that year, and she did not stand out. To this day, when I look at the group photo we took on that first visit, I am not sure which one was her.

When we left Derong and headed back to Chengdu, my thoughts

---

34  The school charged us 2,000 yuan per semester per student.

were on other programs—especially a new effort to assist people with disabilities that would start in less than a month. I quickly forgot about Metok Tso and her twelve classmates now being sponsored by KhamAid donors.

I had no idea that we had a prodigy on our hands.

## The Disabled

Once back in Chengdu, I leaped into last-minute preparations for the launch of a new program, one that would bring donated wheelchairs to people with disabilities in Kham. The Foreign Affairs Office liked the concept—probably because it did not involve any risky business like books or monasteries. Also, the existence of disabled Tibetans was not a concern to Tibet freedom activists abroad. Even so, the last week was a nail-biter, for our shipping container of American-made donated wheelchairs was stuck at Chengdu's customs office. Meanwhile, three American volunteers who would be the linchpin of the program would shortly board a flight for Chengdu on nonreturnable, unchangeable tickets. Without the chairs, their trip would be for nothing.

This program was complicated because we had three partners: Wheelchairs for the World (an American charity that supplied the wheelchairs), China Disabled Persons' Federation, and a Chinese non-profit called the Holy Love School that provided logistical support and administrative lubricant.

That last ingredient was vital, for cooperation among the parties would require a frenzy of letters, emails, faxes, certificates, contracts, applications, forms, carbon copies, translations, lists, receipts, and official chops. Mr. Wu was adept in these matters, but KhamAid was a backdoor organization—we had no legal existence in China, and our bank account was not in our name, but in Mr. Wu's.[35] The Holy Love School, which had been founded by a Chinese Christian to care for people with disabilities, believed in our project's mission. Better yet, they were a legitimate Chinese nonprofit with an energetic staff and a place in Chengdu big enough to store 240 boxed wheelchairs.

The deal we had made was this: the Disabled Persons' Federation would be the receiver of the chairs—which meant that import taxes would be waived—and they would negotiate the gnarly import process. In consideration of this contribution, we would give them 120 chairs to distribute to needy disabled people in Chengdu and other parts of Sichuan.[36]

Customs released our wheelchairs just one day before the three American volunteers landed. Thirty were allocated to Chengdu residents who had been identified by the Holy Love School. We ran a distribution event there so that our expert volunteers could match and adjust the motley assortment of chairs to the needs of individuals who would use them. That evening we loaded the ninety remaining chairs onto a truck bound for Kham, with Mr. Wu riding shotgun.

Two days of travel brought the team and chairs to Rangaka, a crossroads town where the highway forked. There the local Civil Affairs Bureau had arranged for our first delivery to a man named Denba Namgyal, age twenty-five. Our little caravan, consisting of a minibus and a chair-laden Dongfeng truck, squeezed through a narrow alley as far as it could, then we all got out and walked to the two-room shanty where Denba Namgyal and his mother lived.

---

35  Some NGOs registered as Chinese nonprofits, but that process was prohibitively difficult and costly for a small organization like KhamAid.

36  Ngawa Tibetan Qiang Autonomous Prefecture and Liangshan Yi Autonomous Prefecture received thirty wheelchairs each. A few years later, we began purchasing Chinese-made chairs so we could take them all to Kandze Prefecture.

Part II · 105

We found the young man lying flat on his back in a dark chamber hardly bigger than a closet. His moonlike face was terribly pale, and he was sucking on one finger. His mother told us that he had contracted a fever when he was four days old; as a result, he was severely developmentally disabled and unable to move his legs or speak. Over time, he had become too heavy to lift, so she could only tend him as he lay in bed. He had not been outdoors for years.

Denba Namgyal's mother asked us to wait in the alley so that she could put pants on him. One of our volunteers went to help her and noticed that his bedding was wet. We all waited in the alley while the volunteer cleaned him.

At last, two of our team hoisted the bundle of bones that was Denba Namgyal out of bed and lowered him into a wheelchair. When they rolled him outside into the daylight, his eyes went round with wonder. Two team members showed his mother how to lock and unlock the brakes and maneuver the chair over uneven terrain. When they tipped the chair backward to pull it over a bump, he broke into a huge grin.

"Thank you, thank you!" Denba Namgyal's mother said, tears streaming. "I never knew such people could exist!" She knelt to the ground to prostrate, but we gently lifted her back to her feet.

In the days that followed, we met more disabled people and had many more such moments. Some of them had injuries from car wrecks and other accidents. Others had advanced arthritis, one had contracted polio as a child, and one was a stroke victim. One heartrending story came from an older woman who had received a savage beating at the hands of her brother when she was still a girl. One man, a Tibetan, was a combat veteran of China's People's Liberation Army; he had lost a leg to a land mine during action in Viet Nam.

The Federation maintained a registry of disabled people. For those without families, the Federation assigned caregivers and paid them fifteen yuan (US$2) per day, which was far too little to assure adequate quality of care. Even those who received excellent care had no access to any sort of therapy, for no one in the region had the requisite training. Although Chengdu had a wheelchair factory, the chairs did not reach Sichuan's far west.

Most of the people who received our ninety chairs were ethnic Tibetan, but not all of them. We refused no one on the Federation's list. Aside from the importance of honoring our partnership, morally I could not bear to withhold a wheelchair from someone who needed it, no matter what their race.

## Earthquake!

The Tibetan year of the female Iron-Snake (2001) brought terrible news that interrupted everything:

> February 23
> Dear Friends of the Kham Aid Foundation,
>
> I just received word that an earthquake struck eastern Kandze Prefecture at about 7 PM (Beijing time) last night, that is, about six hours ago.
>
> Official Chinese sources are reporting that the epicenter was somewhere near the place where Kangding [Dartsendo], Jiulong [Gyezur], and Yajiang [Nyakchukha] counties meet, and the magnitude was 6.0. They also report three dead and "45,000 missing."

To get more complete information, I phoned the Kham Aid Foundation office, which is located in Kangding town. Our field office director, Wu Bangfu, lives on the ground floor of an old building, and so I was extremely concerned about his safety, not to mention all of the other friends and coworkers we have in the town.

Mr. Wu reports that in Kangding town, the tremors were "very slight." His building and family are completely okay. It appears that the main force of the earthquake struck in a relatively unpopulated area.

The most urgent matter now facing us is the immediate needs of Tibetans whose homes and livelihoods were destroyed by yesterday's quake. If anyone would like to send money to those people, I will ensure that it is properly directed.

The initial reports came from the Nyakchukha County seat, a town of several thousand people located 50 kilometers north of the epicenter. There, several buildings collapsed, and many others—reportedly 40% of the total—had some degree of damage. A five-kilometer-long fissure opened in the ground in nearby southwest Dartsendo County, cutting off one of the two routes leading to the worst-hit townships.

In the week following the earthquake, there were some six hundred aftershocks, the largest of which was magnitude 4.5, wreaking terror among traumatized residents and throwing down more stones from the high slopes. Government reports said the earthquake had affected about twenty thousand people spread over 5,000 square kilometers (1,930 square miles). Three people had died, seven were missing, and 119 were injured. Damage to dwellings was tallied in *jian*, which is the unit of space defined by four neighboring columns in a traditional building. The government reported that 20,757 *jian* were damaged to some degree, including 16,518 *jian* that had collapsed altogether.

The Chinese government has many shortcomings, but during natural disasters, they are masters of mass mobilization. They have a massive standing army spread all over the country with no wars to fight and a top-down command structure that can make decisions in a hurry.

Nevertheless, even the People's Liberation Army had trouble getting through the craggy terrain that lay in the way of the worst-hit villages. After the biggest landslides had been cleared, lorries traveling beside the twisted Nyak Chu could go only halfway before the road became too narrow, and cargo had to be transferred to *tuolaji* tractors. The government took a month and a half to deliver tents to all four affected townships. The tents were far short of the number needed, but they were better than nothing.

KhamAid was the only foreign NGO with resources already in the region. My initial report, sent to several hundred supporters by email, brought a welter of donations, about US$2,000. Thanks to our wheelchair program, Mr. Wu already knew many Civil Affairs officials. He learned from them that victims needed shoes and food, so he used the money to buy a load of rubber-soled canvas shoes and three thousand kilograms (6,600 pounds) of rice. They arranged for our goods to be part of a relief convoy headed into the disaster zone.

On this occasion, we found the government quite willing to cooperate. This earthquake did not make international headlines. The area was so remote that even the most intrepid reporters couldn't get there. Political sensitivity was zero. Later we would respond to much more public quakes—disasters that drew in observers from around the world who scrutinized China's relief effort and sniped at every misstep. For those later quakes, the proud Chinese would not want international help, accepting it only with reluctance, and only from large, well-established organizations like the Red Cross. For those later quakes, KhamAid would have to sneak in assistance undercover. But for this one, we worked openly.

The government was sending coats, cotton quilts, blankets, cloth, medicine, and food to the affected townships. Office workers around the region were asked to donate to the relief effort. Schoolchildren were exhorted to pitch in with cash and goods. I was not satisfied with shoes and rice; I wanted to do more. Mr. Wu agreed and volunteered to go out there to take a look.

As Mr. Wu set out on the dangerous journey into the earthquake zone, he was perhaps an unlikely looking hero. He was small of stature, slight of build, and brainy in appearance, with thick glasses. Beneath an oversized red nylon jacket, his clothing was more suitable for an office meeting than a foray into the wilderness. Nevertheless, he set out on the damaged highway toward the Nyakchukha County seat. There, a Civil Affairs official offered to accompany him through the Nyak Chu gorge toward the epicenter.

They rode on a cart pulled by a *tuolaji* tractor, for the earlier clearing operation had been undone by fresh rockfall. The road was littered with rocks of all sizes, making the cart buck and shimmy with such violence it was impossible to sit down. The two men rode standing, hanging onto the cart's grab bar for dear life.

Indeed, the bumpy ride was of less concern to Mr. Wu than the stones that sporadically shot down the mountain and smacked the roadway. The cart had no roof and offered no protection whatsoever.

As they made their way south, Mr. Wu lost count of the narrow misses.

About an hour into the journey, when the driver suddenly swerved to avoid a boulder, Mr. Wu almost lost his grip. Looking out the left side, he saw the wheels heading toward the drop-off. Just when disaster seemed certain, the driver swerved back to the center, jerking the cart away from the abyss.

"Be careful!" Wu shouted over the roar of the engine.

"Don't worry," replied the driver, a cheerful farmer who lived up-valley. "I know this road so well I can drive it with my feet alone!"

A few minutes later, the driver slowed and stopped. In front of them was a heap of stones—debris from a landslide. The only way forward was the narrow, rock-strewn shoulder.

"Get down," said the county official who was escorting Mr. Wu. "This section is a little dangerous. We'll walk through."

"Take your bag," added the driver.

Mr. Wu picked up his small satchel, and the two men climbed down. As soon as they hit the ground, the driver gunned the engine and took off. Mr. Wu watched the cart tilt sideways and bounce so hard that he thought it might flip over. If it did, the whole thing would roll over the side and fall a hundred feet into the Nyak Chu.

Luckily, the cart didn't flip. The driver cleared the rock pile, then kept going. Looking ahead, Mr. Wu saw there was not just one pile of stones on the road, but a series of piles, one after the other, like an obstacle course. And more rocks raining down.

"Hurry!" said the official. Not waiting for Mr. Wu, he took off at a run. Mr. Wu shouldered his bag and followed. He got around the first pile and started trotting toward the second, threading a path between fallen stones and missing surface where soil had plummeted to the river. The other two were already far ahead.

Mr. Wu never saw it coming: a falling rock that smacked him in the face. He didn't know whether it was large or small, only that it fell on him like a guillotine. Reflexively he shut his eyes at the moment of impact. When he opened them, the world had gone blurry. Cautiously, he put his hands to his face expecting to find a bleeding gash, but when he checked his hands, they were clean.

Then he looked down and saw the twisted wreck of his spectacles lying at his feet. His glasses, not his face, had taken the brunt of the impact. He was blind without his shattered specs but otherwise uninjured. It was a near-death experience, but Mr. Wu was not a man to whine about such things. In his report, he hardly mentioned it.

"The transportation situation is bad and has impeded the relief work," he wrote. "The relief goods can't be sent to the victims of the earthquake because of the great distance and rugged terrain. Basic building materials such as cement can't reach the area. I couldn't visit the epicenter partly because of strong aftershocks and the bad condition of the bridges, road, and many loose rocks still cascading down the steep slopes."

Thanks to drenching monsoons and brawny rivers, Kham has some spectacular gorges, but gorges are unfriendly to both agriculture and livestock, and few people live in them. During Mr. Wu's fifty-nine-kilometer journey down the Nyak Chu, he passed by just one tiny village before reaching the first severely affected township, Gokar. The heart of Gokar was several dozen stone houses arrayed over a steep hillside among sliver-shaped fields. The houses were shabby, and the fields were small, telling a story of pre-existing poverty. Among the houses were a few bright blue tents provided by the government relief effort.

Beyond Gokar lay three other devastated townships, but there was no more road, only a footpath. Wu saw a train of pack animals heading south, laden with relief supplies. The closest of the three townships, Benyukrong, was eight kilometers south of Gokar. The other two, Posershö and Nyayűlzhab, lay even farther, beyond a mountain pass more than 4,500 meters in elevation. Those who dared to walk these paths were beset continuously by falling rocks.

The Tibetan plateau—especially its eastern flanks—is alive with movement because of an ongoing tectonic invasion by the Indian plate, a continent-sized slab of the earth's crust. The Indian plate travels northeast toward Tibet at an average speed of 2 inches (5 cm) per year, crashing into the Eurasian plate, which underlies the Sichuan basin and the rest of China. The collision is pushing up the Himalayas, and it has raised what was once ancient seabed to an average elevation over 5,000 meters (nearly three miles), forming what is now the Tibetan plateau.

With so much lifting, pushing, and colliding going on beneath Tibet, the ground often moves, bringing death and destruction to humans on the surface. Northeast Kham is especially quake-prone, for much of it rests on the Xianshuihe fault, one of the most active faults in China. Mountain ranges bury the fault at both ends, but for about a hundred kilometers, the strike-slip seam closely follows the Xianshui River (Tib: Zi Chu). The valley of the Zi Chu is fertile and well-populated, which makes the Xianshuihe fault an arc of destruction not unlike California's infamous San Andreas. Since 1786, it had unleashed eighteen quakes of magnitude 6.0 or higher. Of these quakes, four had epicenters in Ta'u or Drango, two counties that sit like bull-riders astride the middle of the fault.

The Xianshuihe fault is one of the most active in western Sichuan but is by no means the only threat. The Longmenshan fault, which lies at the northwest perimeter of the Sichuan Basin, is also a grave threat. In 2008, it would unleash a massive quake affecting millions of people. However, the Gokar Quake came from neither of these two famous faults. Its source was an obscure fault called Zihe. Like so much of Tibet's geology, the Zihe fault was poorly understood because its remote location made research difficult.

Dartsendo's capital, home to about a hundred thousand people, lies near the eastern terminus of the Xianshuihe fault. The city's buildings, most seven stories or higher, are made of reinforced concrete. A Canadian architect who observed construction there told me that Dartsendo's building standards appeared adequate for an earthquake zone, although the strength of structures also depends on the quality of the concrete, which he could not discern.

Dartsendo is an affluent place, accessible to building inspectors, but out in the boondocks, anything goes. Ordinary Tibetans, constrained by poverty, build as cheaply as they can, relying on charms and prayers to keep their families safe.

Timber is essential to a safe, stable traditional Tibetan house, and it is expensive. After commercial logging was banned in 1998, logs often had to be transported long distances. Only in Ta'u County, where timber is cheap and the memory of earthquakes is strong, did I see frames made of giant logs securely interlocked in three dimensions at both ceiling and floor level. Outside Ta'u, people were blasé about earthquakes, and even the rich would usually opt for a big house rather than a strong one.

Out of eighteen counties of Kandze Prefecture, one-third of them—Dartsendo, Nyakchukha, Gyezur, Rongtrak, Dabpa, and Nyarong—traditionally build walls out of random stone mortared with clay.[37] Such a wall is little better than a vertical pile of rocks

---

37 This type of construction is also found in Ngawa Prefecture and many other regions.

pasted together with dirt. These unstable walls must support the heavy clay roof. Beneath the roof, horizontal ties typically run in just one direction, so the building has little sheer strength. During an earthquake, walls crumble, and pillars topple, bringing timber and clay down on the heads of people inside. The Gokar quake victims lived in just this type of home.

Wu's report conveyed the residents' terror, even weeks after the main quake: "I heard the giant noise of the aftershocks," he wrote. "[I] saw many flying rocks." Then he described the barriers that lay in the way of recovery:

> Of the 316 families in Gokar Township, only 66 got tents, though the houses of 53 families collapsed and 43 semi-collapsed, and all of the other houses suffered different damage with cracked, distorted and inclined walls and tilted pillars, and none of these houses are fit for the people to live in. The people without tents only live in the temporary sheds covered with plastic. Families are crowded together in small tents, which adversely affects the health of older people and young children.

> For the immediate future, the main goal of the local people is to earn enough income to recover their normal lives. In these villages, the main agricultural products are maize, wheat, barley, mushrooms. Because of the geographic situation, the products cannot be delivered to the market quickly enough for the farmers to get a good price. Agricultural land is also in shortage. In Gokar Township, the average farming land for each people is only 0.75 *mu* [1/20th of a hectare].

In the affected area, steep mountain limits pasturage for livestock, and this contributes to general poverty. The average family in Gokar has only three animals. The earthquake disaster killed more than 800 animals, which were struck by flying rocks or fell down the steep slopes. At that time, people were concerned about their lives; they could not take care of their livestock. As a result, they will face severe economic hardship in the next few years.

Through my contacts at the American consulate in Chengdu, I learned that the State Department could make modest grants for disaster relief.[38] I assigned Mr. Wu the task of developing a credible proposal that we could take to the embassy in Beijing.

Wu found that people in the disaster zone had endless needs—and endless ideas about how to spend American money. Gokar Township leaders said that they needed a running water system to replace a channel damaged by the quake. This would be fine for Gokar but useless for the other three townships. They said that many families needed help to rebuild their homes, but selecting families to help would be tricky and would likely embroil us in conflict among neighbors.

Mr. Wu reported that the biggest challenge faced by all four townships was economic: they could not easily rebuild their homes or replace their animals because they had no cash income, and they had no cash income because it was difficult to access markets in the world outside. Gokar was so isolated that locals could recall no foreigners visiting

---

38  For a history of U.S. government assistance to China and Tibet, see Thomas Lum, "U.S. Assistance Programs in China," Congressional Research Service 7-5700, May 9, 2013.

since a Japanese man stopped by during World War II. The residents of Benyukrong Township were even more isolated; few had ever seen a bicycle in their lives. If the region was better connected to the outside, the people could make some money and rebuild what they had lost.

As it was to so many development challenges in Kham, transportation was key to disaster recovery. Many roads and footpaths needed repair and improvement, but any roadwork we might try to do would need regular maintenance, or else it would fall apart within a few rainy seasons. Such projects are better suited to the government, which has a long-term presence.

However, there was one transportation need that KhamAid could reasonably fulfill. Wu's report explained:

> There used to be a wooden bridge [over the Gokar River] for tractors to pass through, but the earthquake damaged it. To carry the relief goods for the victims of the earthquake, the county government has set up a temporary wooden bridge, but it will not stand up to summer floods. . . . A [new] bridge there will benefit all 6,638 people in the four severely afflicted townships.

I sent Mr. Wu's report to the American consulate in Chengdu along with a request for a US$40,000 grant. The State Department did not normally fund reconstruction, but the officials agreed with Mr. Wu that a new bridge was essential to support the relief effort. Still, they had questions. If an American grant pays for the bridge, will the government commit to improving nearby roads? Will local people contribute labor?

Mr. Wu relayed these concerns to the county officials and received satisfactory answers, although he did have to explain that Gokar residents could not work for free, not while they were trying to rebuild their devastated homes and lives.

To seal the deal, Mr. Wu met with the new American consul general, who had recently arrived to take up his post in Chengdu. Unfortunately, now a delay seemed certain because of two inescapable forces of nature looming on the calendar: the start of caterpillar fungus season and the summer monsoon.

Caterpillar fungus—*yartsa gunbu* in Tibetan—is a natural product that Tibetans gathered on the highlands from early May to mid-June each year. Across the Chinese-speaking world, *yartsa gunbu* is a famous and much sought-after traditional remedy that fetches a high price. As a result, during the digging season, all able-bodied Tibetans who lived near fungus habitat vanish to the highlands to join the money-making jamboree occurring in thousands of localities. The income derived from *yartsa gunbu* is the lifeblood of rural families and finances a substantial fraction of economic growth in Kham.

There would be no laborers during the month and a half that *yartsa gunbu* held sway. After that would come another showstopper: the summer rains, which would worsen the existing landslide peril. Construction would have to wait until autumn.

Mr. Wu hired an engineer to manage the project, and together they reached an agreement with the Number Twenty Engineering Company of Southwest Engineering Team, whose people were versed in the ancient Chinese art of stone arch bridges. The State Department agreed with our plan and sent the first installment of funds.

Even though our attention was on the victims of the Gokar earthquake, I remained determined to do more about health care. Our partners at the Kandze Prefecture Women's Federation had asked us to address the paucity of care for expectant mothers in rural areas. This was a new direction for KhamAid and would be our next big push.

# Maternal Health

*If you want to save a culture, save a mother.*

— Lee Weingrad, founder of Surmang Foundation

Before the Communist takeover of Tibet, no one collected data on life expectancy and causes of mortality. Even afterward, the registration of deaths did not become a regular practice until the 1970s.[39] Nevertheless, the China Tibet Information Center, a propaganda outlet, stated that in 1951 the infant mortality rate in Tibet Autonomous Region had been 43%, falling to an incredible 0.974% by 1990. The same report stated that maternal mortality had plummeted eightfold during that time.

A more reliable source told us that in 2000, the infant mortality rate for Kandze Prefecture was 3.64% and the maternal mortality rate was 0.208%, comparable to those of TAR, but about ten times higher than Beijing. In 2001, more than three-quarters of deliveries to rural women in Kandze Prefecture occurred without a trained birth attendant present.[40]

While the figures are perhaps uncertain, I do not doubt that, since 1980, the situation has markedly improved. Nevertheless, even at the dawn of the twenty-first century, the risk of babies and mothers dying remained unaccept-

---

39 "Mortality Rate and Average Life Expectancy," retrieved from http://zt.tibet.cn/english/zt/society/ in 2014, later removed.

40 The figure was 76.5% for agricultural townships and 83.3% for pastoral townships. Winrock International, "Sustainable Development," p. 9.

ably high. The reasons were both economic and cultural. Health care was expensive and hard to reach, often requiring many hours of travel. In the countryside, hygiene and health knowledge were poor. Women were not highly valued in traditional Tibetan society, an attitude that was also reflected in the low school enrollment rates for girls.[41] Also, most rural people regarded pregnancy as normal, not an illness calling for a doctor's care.[42]

Home deliveries were the norm, a dangerous custom made even more so because traditional people in Tibet regarded childbirth as unclean and did not want bloody afterbirth polluting their dwellings. Customarily, a woman in labor left the living area of the house and went to the stables to deliver her child upon the piles of manure and hay. Nomad women left the family tent and went outside to the grass and sky. Either way, the mother delivered her baby on an earthen floor or on dried animal dung placed there to absorb the blood. Typically, an untrained family member assisted a woman in labor, but it was not uncommon for women to deliver totally on their own.

---

41  For example, in 2001, Derong County schools had a combined enrollment of 1731 boys and 1001 girls. In Kandze County, Gyalten Rinpoche's charity school in 1998 had 87 boys and 51 girls.

42  Michael A. Lev, "9 Days in Labor: In Tibet, harrowing childbirth a fact of life," *Chicago Tribune,* Oct 13, 2004.

## Midwife Training

After I landed in Chengdu for the start of the spring field season, my first act on behalf of mothers and babies was to tell the Books for Schools team that I wanted to put out a book about women's sexual health. Most women in Kham had no idea how their bodies worked and were too embarrassed to speak of such matters. Tsering and Yeshi agreed to find such a book and publish a Tibetan translation along with the eight-volume set of biographies that was their next project.

Riding a bus to Dartsendo, I found that the new tunnel was now fully operational, and the trip took less than eight hours. My first meeting was with the Kandze Prefecture Women's Federation and concerned a training program for village midwives, a major joint project.

Mr. Wu and the Women's Federation had been working hard, and plans were taking shape. Doctors at the Kandze Prefecture Maternity and Pediatric Hospital had agreed to teach the midwives. There would be three weeks of classroom instruction followed by three weeks in the wards helping with actual deliveries. The trainees would learn about the physical processes of pregnancy, labor, and delivery, how to use sterilized birthing equipment, how to provide postpartum care, and, most importantly, how to recognize high-risk pregnancies that required a doctor's help.

Our vision was for the trainees to work in communities with poor access to doctors, similar to China's "barefoot doctors" of the 1960s and 70s. Because the women would likely be asked to treat other medical problems besides pregnancy, the curriculum also included general health care and first aid, especially for children.

The Women's Federation was tapping their network in two counties, Nyakchukha and Litang, to identity ten suitable women from each. The twenty trainees would come to Dartsendo in a few months. Mr. Wu was arranging transportation and lodging for them as well as managing program funds, which were coming from a family in

California whom I had known since my traveling days and who had a longstanding interest in China.

Around this time, an expatriate New Zealander living in Beijing contacted me, wanting to bring a group of friends to Kham for some long-distance bicycling to raise money for Tibet. I seized on the opportunity to turn the trip into a benefit for KhamAid's nascent health care program.

I often got messages in my inbox proposing outlandish, pie-in-the-sky schemes, but this bike ride was looking like it might really happen. The notion brought back misty memories of the long-distance cycling I had done during my free-wheeling traveling days: the Zen of pedaling over ever-changing topography as water-color vistas washed past in slow motion. Heck, if the timing was right, I told them I would get a bike and ride along.

## News and Progress in Degé

Sögyal's tragic death hadn't stopped my quest to find a role for KhamAid in the conservation of the Degé Parkhang. Mr. Wu and I stayed in frequent touch with the county government. The leaders told us that, although they very much wanted our help with funding, they didn't want us to bring wall paintings conservators there. Before any work could start on the paintings, county leaders first needed a condition assessment report that laid out, in detail, the state of preservation of the building and its contents, and the threats they faced.

Degé County did not have the money to do such a condition assessment, especially since the 1998 logging ban, which had slashed the county's income from logging permits.[43] The national government

---

43  During the 1990s, the timber industry contributed from 15% to 22.3% of Kandze Prefecture's GDP and was responsible for up to 80% of the revenue of individual counties. Winrock International, "Sustainable Development," p. 15.

would not give them money unless the condition assessment showed that investment was needed and how it would be spent. To break the logjam, county leaders needed outside help.

So, I had pressed forward with fundraising, hoping that the goodwill earned would later allow us to work on the conservation itself. My funding proposals were enhanced by a technical evaluation of the wall paintings' conservation state, which had been prepared for us by an Italian conservator who had visited the Parkhang as a tourist the previous year.

Earlier in 2001, we had learned that KhamAid won a US$40,000 grant from the Ambassador's Fund for Cultural Preservation, a program administered by the U.S. State Department. The money would pay for the Parkhang's condition assessment, with the work to take place during summer.[44] A delegation of Degé officials came to our office to discuss project planning.

The county had contracted for the assessment to be performed by a team of Chinese specialists from the Sichuan Archeological Institute. This group had previously worked on conservation projects at several Chinese Buddhist monasteries in Sichuan and Yunnan that included wall paintings. In June, the team would travel to Degé to perform a comprehensive assessment of the Parkhang's conservation needs.

Although I preferred to use foreign consultants, I agreed to the county's proposal to use Chinese, for they would be far quicker and more cost effective. After all, the main thing was to get the work started so that the building could be safe.

Liberated by recent highway improvements, I set out on a long looping field trip around Kandze Prefecture, accompanied by Mr. Wu

---

44   This grant was supplemented by $5,000 from the Rubin Foundation.

and several others. We visited sponsored students, met with midwife trainees, and spent an enjoyable time at a festival in Litang. By the time we reached Degé, the assessment was already complete. The County leaders showed me a copy of their report: a thick book of beautiful architectural renderings and pages dense with Chinese characters. We leafed through it, amazed at the sheer volume of work accomplished. The assessment team had been very thorough. They had compiled a full set of architectural drawings, topographical maps that highlighted drainage issues on the north and east sides of the building, and page after page of detailed recommendations for the work to be done.

KhamAid's own expert, an American conservator trained at Columbia University, looked over the report and its recommendations and asked many questions. The Sichuan Archeological Institute had ideas on how to remedy the moisture issue, but our expert expressed concerns about their proposal to use tar and cement to waterproof some parts. He diplomatically urged the county officials to proceed with caution. He also politely suggested that the county set up a main-tenance plan and a program for managing visitors, for the numbers were growing rapidly.

I wanted to make photocopies of the report, or at least take pho-tos of it, but the Degé officials said that was not allowed. I was mildly outraged by this, but still proud of what we had accomplished. Now Degé county could apply to Beijing for the money needed to carry out conservation.

At this time, China's capacity for protecting its historic sites was growing and maturing rapidly. Collaborating with the Getty Conservation Institute, China's State Administration for Cultural Heritage had recently issued national guidelines for cultural heritage conservation and management. They were applying these principles at sites of international significance such as the Mogao Grottoes at Dunhuang, and they were training a cadre of Chinese experts. Although KhamAid would not likely participate in future Parkhang conservation, I was glad to have helped initiate protection of the historic site.

After a few more stops, I headed back to Chengdu for a respite. I needed a break because the long-distance cycling team would soon arrive, and I would be biking with them while we looked at hospitals and clinics along the northern highway across Kham.

## Assessing Health Care Needs

To kick off the bike trip, I organized a welcome party and press conference at a Chengdu dive popular with foreign backpackers. The other cyclists had landed only hours earlier on a flight from Beijing and were on their way over. I had just commandeered several tables and set out stacks of literature when in walked the ringleader, David Oliver.

Oliver was a strapping bloke from Kiwi sheep country who vibrated with animal energy and looked like he could buck hay and pull trucks with ease. He introduced me to his three friends. One was a former rugby player, Irish, broad of shoulder and exuding vigor. Another fellow was young, lanky, and supple; he was also from New Zealand, and he had brought a very fast bike with him. The fourth was our medical expert, Dr. Bruce Beattie, from Australia. He worked for a company that provided health care to expatriates stationed in China, and his job was provisioning clinics in remote areas. Dr. Beattie was the tallest of the four at about six foot four (1.93 m); he looked lean and steely-eyed, like a marathon runner.

The four men towered over me. Suddenly, I was clobbered by the reality of what I was about to attempt. I was on the north side of forty, hardly in peak condition, and female. What had possessed me to sign up for this ride, and how was I going to keep up?

A crowd of well-wishers had gathered to celebrate our upcoming adventure. A few Chinese journalists were also present, with their lights, cameras, and notebooks. The restaurant's customers—stringy-haired travelers, foreign teachers, and a few locals in addition to our invited guests—were made to listen to speeches from Oliver and me about the great cause of bringing better health care to Tibetans in Sichuan. In the course of the evening, our donation box picked up 1,788 yuan (US$220). Not a bad way to start.

We would start riding our bicycles at the top of Gyu La, the first big pass west of Dartsendo, from which we'd do an easy downhill run to get acclimated. Cycling to Lhasa was out of the question due to the time and special permits required, so Degé was our goal: nine days, 563 kilometers (352 miles), and five passes with a total elevation gain of 4,300 meters (14,000 feet).

Mr. Wu had phoned the Dartsendo bus station and hired a minibus: one of the peppy little Ivekos that were supplanting the creaky Leshans and making road travel more bearable. The deal was that we would have the entire vehicle, the driver would go very slowly, and his wife would come along to help cook for us on a portable propane stove when we stopped between towns.

Along the way, we would visit clinics and hospitals, where Dr. Beattie would assess medical needs. Money raised by the ride would go toward meeting the needs we identified.

Doctors Without Borders does not operate this way, but KhamAid had far fewer resources, so we had to be creative.

Around noon on the second riding day, the bike team reached the seat of Lhagang Township, an area inhabited by Tibetan herders.

The township's elevation ranged from 2,700 to 4,300 meters (8,860 to 14,100 ft), and its population of 7,155 was spread over 849 square kilometers (328 square miles), none of which was cultivable but included excellent pasture.[45] Excepting a few officials, doctors, teachers, and entrepreneurs in the township seat, Lhagang's permanent residents were virtually all Tibetan. Many were illiterate and lived at the fringes of the cash economy.

(We didn't know it yet, but later, KhamAid would do great deeds for herders in Lhagang. We would also commit some stupendous blunders.)

On a pasture outside of town, a *lingka* (festival) was taking place. The fairgrounds thronged with a phantasmagoria of people in sumptuous garments. Damsels wore long woolen women's chubas, their rivers of glistening braids strung up with headdresses of magenta yarn, silver amulets, and giant beads. Men sashayed in their shorter chubas, their Stetson knockoffs cocked at a jaunty angle and knives swinging from their belts.

I sent word to the local clinic that we wanted to visit, then joined the crowds. A group of male dancers were leaping and twisting in synchrony, their ultra-long sleeves tracing giant cursives in the air. I was busy snapping photos when word came back that the clinic director was waiting for us. Reluctantly, I rounded up the others, and we headed over.

Dr. Zhang Lin, the director, was waiting for us at the compound gate, a bundle of keys in her hand. Unlocking the gate, the doctor led us over a patchwork of mud puddles and broken cement. The clinic buildings were squat, concrete bunkers with bars on the windows. She

---

45  The population figure is for 2004.

unlocked the biggest building, which contained an examining room, pharmacy, and office.

Inside, the place reminded me of the Degé County Hospital, where Sögyal had died: unheated rooms, peeling paint, cold cement floors, and battered steel furniture. There was no running water, either hot or cold, and no indoor latrine. The clinic had electricity, but it was unreliable, and there was no backup. The staff lived in rustic longhouses that looked more suitable for lumberjacks than physicians.

The director, an earnest woman in her late 30s, told us that when the local people got sick, they were likely to try traditional Tibetan medicine first. If that didn't work, they'd come to her clinic, and if they were seriously ill, they'd go to one of the hospitals in Dartsendo, a journey of many hours.

She took us on a tour of the clinic's electronic gadgets, starting with an ultrasound unit resting on a desk. Dr. Beattie switched it on—luckily, the electricity was working—and tried it on his stomach. Squinting at the display and frowning, he fiddled with the knobs for a minute, then shook his head. "That's a poor-quality image. What training does the technician have?" I translated the question into Chinese.

"He trained for a month," said Dr. Zhang. "He can only do simple procedures."

I asked her about the other clinic workers. She replied that, of the six professional staff who were called *yisheng* ("doctors"), none had more than three years of medical training. I wondered if Dr. Zhang realized that none of her staff could even qualify as nurses in America.

We moved on to another building, a ward. The bedframes were rusty, and years of reuse had blotted the sheets with faded red-brown glyphs. One room had an oxygen concentrator, a useful machine at this elevation. Another had an incubator for premature infants, covered with a cloth. Dr. Zhang didn't seem overly proud of it, and I guessed that they didn't use it, probably because no one knew how.[46]

We returned to the main building where Dr. Beattie began rummaging through drawers and storage cabinets. He found a box of reusable hypodermic needles piled in a jumble.

"We use disposable needles when we do vaccinations in the countryside," said Dr. Zhang, responding to his question. "We use the reusable needles here in the clinic." She indicated an autoclave sterilizer sitting on a desk.

Dr. Beattie looked it over. "This is antiquated technology, not up to international standards at all," he said, "but it looks like it would work if they use it properly. Can we see their vaccines?"

Dr. Zhang opened up a cabinet to display neatly stacked boxes labeled in Chinese. Dr. Beattie took one out and checked the date. "No refrigeration?"

She shrugged. "We haven't got the conditions for that."

The bulk of care offered by the Lhagang clinic seemed to be handing out pills, giving injections and immunizations, stitching up wounds, putting people on intravenous drips, and delivering the occasional baby. Dr. Beattie concluded, "There's a lot that can be done for this place in terms of training and equipment, but there's a limit to what you can accomplish because of the background of the doctors. You could drop a lot of money here, and it will just disappear."

He recommended that KhamAid buy them a refrigerator, a set of scales, disposable syringes, a stretcher, and a delivery bed. Dr. Zhang

---

46  In my experience, many officials in China didn't appreciate the importance of
    training. Later, I visited a clinic in Nyarong that had an ultrasound machine,
    gastric lavage machine, oxygen concentrator, and an abortion machine—all
    untouched and still in their original packaging because no one knew how to use
    them.

also asked for training and several high-tech machines, but I thought it unlikely that we could raise that much money. We did have something to give immediately: a fancy expedition medical kit in a big red backpack crammed with supplies, one of eight donated to our project. Ceremoniously, we handed it over to Dr. Zhang. About her wish list, I told her we couldn't promise, but we'd try.

Lhagang was the first of eight facilities that we would assess on this trip.

Later, an informal survey of Lhagang people found that they commonly suffered from complaints of the heart, lung, liver, and skin, as well as gynecological ailments and arthritis. They reported incidents of "encephalopathy" characterized by convulsions and sudden death, which may have been caused by a parasite.[47] Because of the primitive medical system, precise diagnoses and rates of incidence were unknown. Many encampments were four or more hours' travel from the clinic, so people came only if the need was dire. The improved health care system that China had built in Kandze Prefecture still gave poor service to Lhagang herders.

The quality of life in towns like Lhagang was too low to attract skilled professionals. Rural people knew that their clinics got the dregs and therefore had low confidence in the care they received.

A further challenge was patients' lack of education, which was a handicap both in preventing disease and making sensible use of health care when they did get sick. In rural Tibet, folk beliefs prevailed. For example, I've heard of patients giving pills prescribed for one malady to a family member who had a completely different illness. I've heard of people who believed tooth brushing is purely a vanity unrelated to

---

47  Winrock International Project Baseline Research Team, "Tagong County Research Report," Sustainable Tibetan Communities Project, (2005), p. 54.

health. I've heard of people who thought the way to treat diarrhea is not to administer fluids but to *withhold* them.[48] Patients often stopped taking their medications too soon and were at high risk of relapse.

In many parts of China, especially rural areas, even doctors had weak medical knowledge. One result was that doctors improperly used antibiotics to treat viral diseases like colds and flu, making China's per capita consumption of antibiotics ten times the world average. The country's health care system had so many problems, it was hard to know where to start.

## Biking the Road to Degé

Having finished at Lhagang, it was time to mount our bikes and move on. Heading northwest, we vaulted easily over a low pass to reach a pleasant town called Bamé, where there was a monastery that had once been home to the Seventh Dalai Lama. I was all for overnighting there, but the men wanted to continue, so we set our sights on Ta'u, 69 kilometers (43 miles) farther west.

Now we were starting our first serious climb, and it seemed to go on forever. My bike was a Chinese knockoff: sixteen kilos of low-grade steel and knobby rubber. When I finally caught sight of the stupa marking the pass, I felt like crying with relief. The stupa was strung with red-white-green-yellow-blue *lungta* (prayer flags) snapping in the wind. The fluttering of their sacred words was a prayer that bestowed grace on all sentient beings.

When all five of us had gathered, I got out packets of paper

---

48  Ciren Zhuoga (Tsering Dolkar), University of Calgary, "A Critical Analysis of Health Program Design, Implementation and Changes in Nagchu and Dranang Counties of the Tibet Autonomous Region: Findings from an Embedded Case Study Research." (Paper delivered at the 12th Seminar of the International Association for Tibet Studies, August 18, 2010).

lungta, and we flung them to the sky, shouting *Oh lha-so, lha solooooo!* as Tibetans do when crossing the high passes. Far and wide, lungta littered the ground like confetti. We rested a while, but it was too cold to wait long. There was no sign of our Iveko bus, so we started again, the five of us rolling downhill toward the west.

Reaching Ta'u in the late afternoon, we checked into a guest house and made a beeline for the showers, mindful that hot water would be scarce in the days to come.

In the morning, when I stretched my legs under the comforter, I was rewarded with electric agony as lactic acid erupted from every cell. Glumly, I lay in bed and contemplated what lay ahead. Three more passes, each higher than the last. Three hundred and sixty-nine kilometers. Unreal.

Today's itinerary included stops at one hospital and two clinics. The team would need me to translate. There was no staying in bed.

I pulled on my clothes and made my way to the hotel dining room, where the others were sitting down to a Chinese breakfast of watery rice gruel, hardboiled eggs, soggy steamed buns, and pickled turnips.

After eating, we pedaled a few blocks to the Ta'u County Hospital. Compared to the Lhagang clinic, it was a model of cleanliness and efficiency. Hallways reverberated with the clamor of workmen painting and laying tiles. We learned that the hospital had recently received one million yuan from the government, which they were using to upgrade the building, buy equipment, and train staff.

The deputy director who took us around seemed rather proud of the place. The hospital had two buildings, both three or four stories high, and fifty beds. Their electronic equipment included machines for analysis of blood and urine, an ultrasound, and an electrocardiograph. We did not discover if their technicians knew how to use the equipment or if it was there just for show.

The population of Ta'u County was about 46,900, and this hospital sat at the pinnacle of its health care system. Its sixty medical personnel included doctors, nurses, dentists, technicians, and specialists in Tibetan and Chinese medicine. Despite the sheen of the facilities, none of their people had attended medical school for more than four years.

The hospital had a delivery room with two beds and an incubator like the one we had seen at Lhagang. They told us they delivered about ten babies a month. Their operating room was used once or twice a week for simple procedures such as appendectomy and gall bladder surgery. They could also perform Caesarian births. I couldn't imagine how doctors with so little training managed to cut people open and sew them up again. I thought of Sögyal's death on the operating table in Degé.

Despite its flaws, the Ta'u hospital was much better than average. Dr. Beattie concluded that our resources would be better spent on small, struggling clinics like the one in Lhagang.

We set off biking through the fertile valley of the Zi Chu. After nine kilometers, we stopped at a clinic in Mazur Township. It was in good shape due to its nearness to the county hospital and easy highway access. Nothing for KhamAid to do here.

Sixty-two more kilometers (39 miles) to Drango. No passes to cross, but scores of pitiless little climbs. Sometimes a gale shrieked in my ears. At other times, in the lee of the mountains, the air was eerily still. Clouds covered the sky, flattening the land gray. I often thought of getting on the Iveko, but each time I decided to bike just a little further. The wind abated, and I was still going. After seven hours, to my astonishment, Drango sprang up in front of me. I had made it.

The next morning, my legs were pulsing a steady complaint, but the clouds had flown away, and the land was green and shiny, so after breakfast, I got on my bike again. Leaving Drango town, we climbed above the tree line onto a heaving pile of dense, juicy pasture. Chugging past yak-hair tents, I found a cadence that was slow but steady.

Suddenly my fugue was broken by pandemonium ahead. I looked up and saw two foul-looking mastiffs chasing Dr. Beattie. My heart leaped into my throat: I had been mauled once by feral monastery dogs, and I still had the scars to remind me what damage those animals could do.

As I watched, the doctor's mighty legs bore down, mud spat from his tires, and he jetted forward. The dogs gave up chasing him and looked around for easier prey. That was me, wobbling up the road a hundred paces back.

Heart pounding, every hair on end, I carefully dismounted, placed my bike between the dogs and me, and proceeded on foot. The dogs stayed back and away. Fifteen minutes of walking put me at a safe distance. Seeing no more encampments or dogs, I remounted and pushed off, impatient for the pass where the hard work would be over.

When I saw paper lungta on the road, wetly luminous like stained glass, I felt a surge of relief, for the pass must be near. But no, the printed squares had fluttered down from an unseen summit that lay higher still. I climbed some more, all alone, for the five of us were scattered now. The valleys shrank, and the mountains curled around the horizon like God's stone hand. Then came the pass at 4,140 meters (13,600 ft) where the other riders stood waiting.

The descent was long and thrilling, and my tiredness flew away as the summer breeze stroked my hair and laid a thousand kisses on my face. We dropped out of the scintillating heights onto the breast of farmland and homes.

In the Kandze County seat, after eating, washing, and resting, we resumed our health care survey. Here we skipped the county hospital and headed to a charity operation run by a soft-spoken man named Lobsang Nima Soghatsang. Nima had left Tibet in 1959, lived in India for some years, then found his way to Switzerland, where he worked as an x-ray assistant. Realizing that Tibet needed help, he and his wife set up a nonprofit and, in 1999, returned to their homeland. The Chinese government permitted them to establish a home for the elderly and a tuberculosis treatment center, both within a tidy, Tibetan-style compound. A Swiss doctor was helping them, at least until her visa would expire after a few more weeks.[49]

At that time, China had the world's second-largest tuberculosis epidemic (after India), and the disease was especially problematic in the country's far west. Later, a Pelyül County official would tell me that, in 2001, more than half of all families in that county included at least one member with TB.

Nima took us around his facility, which he had built from the ground up with the help of Swiss supporters. The ward was Dickensian: dark, bleak, and empty but for a single iron bed covered with a blanket of gray wool. It took me a moment to realize that the slight bump in the blanket was a human being. The coverlet stirred, and an elbow appeared, then a wan face and a tangle of black hair.

"This is Dolkar," said Nima. "She's only twenty-eight, but when she came here, she was close to death. We've been nursing her and giving her medication, and now she's doing better, but she's still very sick."

"Tuberculosis is caused by a bacterium," Dr. Beattie explained for us non-experts. "It spreads when infected people cough or sneeze. It's very nasty. Twenty-four hours after a TB patient coughs, you can

---

49   Later, the government withdrew approval for their healthcare activities, although the organization continued to house elderly Tibetans; they also established an orphanage.

still find the active virus in the air. It often gets passed around between family members."

At this time, China had a national program to combat tuberculosis, but it wasn't making much headway in Tibet. One difficulty was people's reluctance to go in for testing because they lived too far away or were too poor or stoic. Many community-level health care providers lack the skills needed to diagnose and refer TB patients. Despite the government's promise of free treatment, patients were still paying too much for care.[50] Also, even when people got treated, the medicines prescribed for them sometimes didn't work because of pharmaceutical fraud.

We were impressed with the work that Nima was doing, but because he already had Swiss support, we decided that his facility did not need KhamAid help as much as others.

Our next stop was Rongpatsa, the home of my old friend Gyalten Rinpoche. The tulku was away, but housekeeping staff opened up the attic of his small temple for us to camp in. We dumped our gear and then raced off to nearby hot springs to scrub away the miles. The sun flitted around breaking rainclouds, and village boys, naked as jaybirds, splashed and carried on around us.

Back at the temple, our driver and his wife had prepared a feast. After dinner, we played cards for two hours, knocking back bottles of beers and getting quite silly in the process. Silently, I willed my tired sinews to mend and my strength to return.

After a night's sleep in the sweet silence of the countryside, we rose to face a full day's ride to the herder outpost of Manigango. There

---

50  Xiaoyun Liu, *et al.,* "How affordable are tuberculosis diagnosis and treatment in rural China? An analysis from community and tuberculosis patient perspectives," *Tropical Medicine and International Health,* 12:12 (Dec., 2007), pp. 1464–1471.

we visited a township clinic that was the grimmest we'd yet seen. The director was away. A young doctor took us around but couldn't show us several rooms because none of his keys fit. They had some impressive equipment: x-ray machine, ultrasound, electrocardiograph, incubator, but none of it worked because their generator was broken. The place was dirty and cold.

An hour's ride west, we reached our overnighting place, a valley that at first seemed uninhabited but for tire tracks in the mud. We pushed our bikes up a grassy ridge, then laid them on the dirt and continued climbing on foot. Summiting the brow, we found ourselves standing before a mirror-smooth lake called Yilhung Lhatso, stretched like glass to a distant rounded shore. The edge was dotted with dome-shaped boulders carved and painted with the mantra *om mani padme hum*. Conifers blanketed the slopes spooned around the water; above them, glacial melt tumbled from a mighty mountain backdrop.

A barefoot Tibetan approached us wearing scruffy monk's robes and a garland of tattered protection yarns. The man's hair was in long dreadlocks, and he had a wild-eyed, disengaged-with-reality affect.

The man introduced himself as Dorje, although the Rastafarian fellow wouldn't speak to me or even look at me; he would only converse with our Han driver and his wife. "She understands Chinese!" they kept repeating, but the man didn't want to hear it. Trying not to smile, they "translated" his Chinese verbatim into the same Chinese for me. He said he was in charge of a nearby stupa that was taking shape under a layer of scaffolding, and showed us a guest book in which donors had inscribed notes in various languages.

With the dreadlocked lama's permission, and upon payment of a fee, we took a rest day at this holy place, camping in huts on the lakeshore. I lay down on the grass and slept solidly until sunshine turned to rain, forcing me to rise and seek shelter. At dusk, our driver and his wife, under my direction, made a sort of fake spaghetti with a can of tomato paste, chopped vegetables, and instant noodles. The green peppers seared my sunburned lips.

The last and hardest day of riding unfolded to intermittent drizzle and a dank cold that sucked like an octopus on my skin. Soon after leaving the lake, we passed a cluster of nomad tents, the last habitations we would see for a while. The occupants ran after us, waving their trinkets in our faces and shouting *nyo!* (buy!) as we pushed slowly uphill.

Now the road tilted skyward, and our home planet slipped away: no trees, no dirt, no sign of earthly life apart from jade- and fire-colored lichen flecked on stones. We bumped over boulders, splashed across puddles, and tunneled through banks of roiling mist. I squinted through the fog and tried to remember the shape of this mountain. How many switchbacks? How much higher? David Oliver had pulled out of sight, but I could see Dr. Beattie's red jersey in the far distance. The Iveko minibus, my golden chariot and fount of salvation, was an impossibly tiny dot.

Six hours into the climb, my brain had shrunk to a dozen neurons with the sole function of pressing weight onto pedals, when suddenly I came upon two other bikers waiting in the mist. They pointed up the road, and it took me a moment to register the familiar sight: the small pagoda and strings of prayer flags that marked Tro La.

Together now, we all pedaled the last hundred yards.

On the summit, I could only think of how tired I was. I tossed lungta to the sky and faked a victory smile for the necessary photos. Then the firmaments broke open, and fat raindrops began slapping down. I ran to the Iveko to take shelter and retrieve my warmest mittens for the descent.

As I was rooting through my bag, sudden comprehension hit: WE DID IT! We had climbed the highest, hardest pass of the journey. From here, it was a long downhill run to the Degé County seat. Despite Sögyal's tragic death in that town, Degé was still the diamond paradise of my deepest yearning, a euphoric dreamtime of sunshine, contentment, and rest.

My face was wind-flayed and sunburned. My lips were cracked and bleeding, and a trapezius screamed whenever I turned my head. Clean, dry clothes belonged to a faraway galaxy that I could barely recall. Several of our mighty team had, for various reasons, taken brief rides on the sag wagon. But I had defied my own expectations by cycling the entire way.

During the trip, we saw several poor and dreadful clinics and a few clean, sharp ones. We met doctors with energy and vision, and we met doctors with neither. My fellow cyclists raised the proud sum of US$10,195, which we would now use to buy things for the neediest clinics at Lhagang, Hrehor, Rongpatsa, Manigango, and Khorlondo.

Another KhamAid health program had been launched.

## The Bridge is Finished

All this while, at quake-savaged Gokar Township, our contractor was building our bridge. In autumn, as it neared completion, we learned that the US consul general in Chengdu, a man named David Bleyle, wanted to attend the ribbon-cutting. This was a publicity coup for KhamAid, although it no doubt set off an anxious frenzy for our old friend Zhu Changcheng at Foreign Affairs.

The Gokar bridge grand opening was set for a date in early December, but then Consul General Bleyle was held up for a few days. The people of Gokar wanted to start using their new bridge without delay, so the local government adroitly changed the ribbon-cutting ceremony into a sign-unveiling ceremony.

When the American diplomatic delegation, duly shepherded by Chinese minders, turned off the main highway toward Gokar, the road was still too narrow for cars, so they rode in tractor-pulled carts, just as Mr. Wu had done eight months earlier. Their driver sounded like the same guy, too: a cheerful farmer who zoomed along without a care in the world. According to Bleyle, the Consulate gang was loving the adventure, although the county official accompanying them was growing paler and greener every time they careened around a corner or veered close to the precipice.

Noise from the *tuolaji* motor made conversation difficult, but at last, the county official was able to get the driver's attention. "You know," he said through clenched teeth, "if we come to any dangerous spots, we *could* get out and walk."

The driver glanced back and grinned. "There *are* no dangerous spots!" he said and kept going as fast as before.

When they arrived at Gokar, the headman Geram Tseren draped the travelers in ceremonial white khata and brought them down to the river where the entire community was gathered beside their lovely new bridge. It had a fifteen-meter (35 ft) span, was six meters (18 ft) wide, rose several meters above the water to avoid summer torrents, and was strong enough to carry cargo-laden trucks.

At one landing stood a concrete stele covered by a red cloth. With great pomp, Bleyle and the official together pulled off the fabric, exposing a sign lettered in three languages. The stele named the bridge sponsor as the United States Office of Disaster Assistance; it also said the project was "supervised by Kham Aid Foundation."

That evening, the community sang and danced to entertain the

Americans while they ate a big feast. Lodging was in a Gokar home. "I slept on the headman's bed," Bleyle later recalled. "They told me it was the only bed in the village. The others slept on matting on the floor."

A few days later, a regional newspaper, *Ganzi Bao,* ran a story about the Consul General's visit, naming the American government as the project sponsor.

With the hindsight afforded by subsequent earthquakes, I am now amazed that the Chinese government not only accepted direct American assistance to a Tibetan area, they allowed diplomatic personnel to travel there and the local newspaper to write about it. But at the time, I thought nothing of it. Instead, I thought about how vulnerable Tibetans are riding in their death-trap houses on top of a tectonic combat zone. This problem, like several others, would jangle around in my brain until the time was right to tackle it.

# Part III

# Income Generation

*A horse is judged by its saddle;*
*a man is judged by his work.*
— Tibetan proverb

One gate of the development mandala has the power to open all others: jobs. Income is the holy grail of development, for it empowers people to meet their own needs. Yet, ever since the founding of the People's Republic, the word "job" in Tibet has nearly always meant working for the government. There were few other employers and none that could match the stability, benefits, and opportunity for advancement that the government offered.

Tibetans did operate small businesses, but Han migrants from outside operated many more. Capital was not the biggest problem: although Tibetans had poor access to credit, they could still raise cash from gathering caterpillar fungus or by borrowing from family members who did so. The biggest problem was knowledge: they had little exposure to the new types of businesses that were popping up in towns and cities across China: internet cafes, print shops, salons, karaoke bars, mobile phone stores, automotive shops, photography studios, pharmacies, clothing boutiques, and more.

In Kham, Tibetan entrepreneurs mainly ran restaurants and drove taxis, but even in these industries, they struggled to compete with Chinese migrants, who were quick to spot opportunities and toiled ceaselessly to capture market share. Migrants outcompeted indigenous Tibetans even in many traditional Tibetan trades such as tailoring, silversmithing, and home construction. Competition from migrants was a big reason why the microcredit model, so successful in South Asia, faced stiff headwinds in Tibet. Tibetans also lacked role models and networks to help them source the manufactured goods needed in the new economy.

Tourism was the only sector where the playing field tilted toward Tibetans, but tourism in Kham was still tiny and seasonal. Were there any other business models they could use? That was the riddle I yearned to solve.

## Modernizing Agriculture

Early in the year of the male Water-Horse (2002), my own mother solved the jobs problem by proposing that KhamAid should help Tibetans grow vegetables. The traditional Tibetan diet—tsampa, yak-butter, and tea—fell light-years short of her nutritional standards. She wanted me to fix it.

Apart from a few hardy varieties of cabbage, potatoes, and turnips, most vegetables will not grow in the Tibetan climate unless they are protected from the weather. My mother agreed to donate five thousand US dollars if KhamAid would start a program to construct greenhouses. Families would grow vegetables for home consumption and for sale. As development ideas go, this one was pretty groovy: it would solve two problems—poverty and malnutrition—at once.

My staff and I explained the concept to the Women's Federation, our partner on other successful programs, and they steered us to Nyarong County. The county Agriculture Bureau was keen to see a model greenhouse project, and the county Women's Federation knew some farmers who wanted to grow produce instead of barley. Nyarong County was isolated and poor and needed to boost its economy. No vegetables were grown locally; instead, they were being trucked from the Sichuan basin and were fiendishly expensive.

I put Linda Griffin in charge of the program. She was a new recruit, a British traveler and spiritual seeker who lived in China and spoke fluent Mandarin. Petite, soft-spoken, young, and pretty, she inspired trust and worked well with Chinese officials. She worked for us part-time, filling the rest of her time with freelance writing.

The Agriculture Bureau sharpened their pencils and designed a program that would build five greenhouses and train five families how to grow, but the cost was nearly $4,000 per family. I couldn't countenance spending that much money on one family, not when other forms of assistance, such as scholarships, were so much cheaper. Linda Griffin and I dissected their plan, looking for expenses to shave.

The county seat was at a relatively balmy 3,080 meters (10,160 feet) above sea level. As in many other developing countries, subsistence agriculture in Kham was very effective in keeping people on their land and soaking up excess labor, but it provided an inadequate diet and put farmers at grave risk if their crops failed. Yet cash crops were not readily accepted by people who cherished their fields of barley as insurance against hunger.[51]

It was therefore remarkable that some farmer women in Nyarong had shown unusual initiative: they had hired workers from eastern Sichuan to grow lotus root, asparagus, spinach, and other vegetables

---

51  Chinese law kept families on their land by making it difficult to transfer the right to use a given plot except to descendants.

on their land, without a greenhouse. The experiment wasn't going well: the tomatoes were hardly out of the ground before frost killed them, and other crops were barely hanging on. Still, the women had entrepreneurial spirit and the courage to take risks.

One of the women slated to benefit from the program was Ajeh, forty-six years old. She had been to primary school but was functionally illiterate. When I went to her home to meet her, she had just come in from the fields, and her chuba was dusted with soil. Decades of outdoor toil had darkened and lined her face. In addition to their cropland, the family owned a tractor that her husband drove. His earnings of twenty yuan per day (less than US$3) was enough to make them middle-income by local standards.

While walking around the hamlet, I met a girl who was just skin and bones and looked far younger than her stated age of ten. Food was evidently a problem for some Nyarong families.

At that time, *Tuigeng Huanlin* ("Grain for Green") was transforming the Nyarong countryside. The program's objective was to restore ecological balance, halt soil erosion, and reduce siltation of rivers. It gave technical assistance and financial incentives to farmers so that they would take slopes exceeding 25% out of production, shifting the burden of agriculture to less fragile areas elsewhere in China. Former agricultural lands were to be treated in two ways: those deemed as "economic areas" would be planted with trees to produce timber, fruits, or nuts. Those deemed to be "ecological areas" would be left alone to regenerate natural grasses and trees. Nyarong was an "economic area" where the owners of the freed-up land would get cash to buy seedlings. They would also receive subsidies in the form of grain, which would continue for five years or until the new orchards were mature enough to produce an income. In some areas, participation was voluntary; in other areas, farmers were obliged to take part, whether they wanted to or not.[52]

The land under our future greenhouses was not sloped; it was flat, fertile, and easily irrigated: really, too good for barley. It would inevitably be converted to other uses. We hoped to make the owners agents and beneficiaries—not victims—of that process.

Working with the Agriculture Bureau and the Women's Federation, Linda Griffin and I redesigned the program. Ten women would participate. The greenhouses would be simple in design and easy to maintain and repair. There would be one hired hand: a trainer to teach the women how to grow. The Agriculture Bureau would manage the construction and provide tools and seeds, all as an interest-free loan, which the women would repay over five years. Repaid funds would be rolled back into the program, allowing more greenhouses to be built and additional families to take part.

I soon found a second sponsor: Trace Foundation, a medium-sized NGO in New York City that ran several assistance programs in Tibet. Together with my mother's donation, we now had enough money to fund the program. We had a product with high margins and proven demand, firm support from the local government, and motivated participants. Everything looked set for success.

---

52  The program was halted in 2007 except for forestation of barren land. Liu Can and Wu Bin, "Grain for Green Programme' in China: Policy Making and Implementation?" China Policy Institute, University of Nottingham, April 2010, http://www.nottingham.ac.uk/cpi/documents/briefings/briefing-60-reforestation.pdf, accessed 11/11/14.

## Tourism Takes Off

Meanwhile, in the outback of Degé County, the guest house that I had jump-started at Palpung Monastery was gaining momentum. Thanks to KhamAid's website and the *New York Times* article, a steady trickle of backpackers was finding their way there. A writer for Lonely Planet guidebooks—a publication carried by virtually all backpackers—made the trek and loved it, so updated editions included instructions on how to reach Palpung. Traffic began to grow.

Outfitters caught on, and before long, half a dozen agencies had slotted Palpung into their itineraries. As China developed, increasing numbers of urban Chinese developed a desire to be in the wilderness or wanted to learn about their country's ethnic minorities. Organized groups, both foreign and domestic, began showing up at Palpung.

The year 2002 brought a communication revolution thanks to new fiber optic cables striping western Sichuan. No more reliance on flimsy wires strung from poles; the new cable was safely underground. No more dialing and dialing and dialing to connect to far-flung towns; now anyone in China or overseas could connect on the first try. You could also walk up to a public phone in, say, the Ta'u County seat, and direct-dial California. Later, the government would shut down international direct-dialing, but in the early years, the services were gloriously unfettered.

Even better: the system's bandwidth was sufficient to carry thousands of simultaneous internet users, spurring internet cafes to open in every town. I bought a gadget that plugged into my laptop and allowed me to dial up a local internet service provider anywhere there was a mobile phone signal—a rapidly expanding list of places. The "Great Firewall" (as it later came to be known) was still embryonic, so you could surf almost anywhere you wanted.

The improved communications were a boon to residents, business people, and travelers. No longer did traveling in Kham mean being incommunicado for weeks. The Chinese government blocked websites for international Tibet advocacy groups, but they didn't block khamaid.org. Backpackers could gather information, make a spur-of-the-moment decision to go to Palpung or other places, and later share their experiences with friends—all from internet cafés, without leaving the high plateau.

Rural areas would have poor access to the internet for a long time to come, but in towns and cities, the internet was making Tibet's isolation a thing of the past.

## Clinic Aid Delivered

In midsummer, following Dr. Beattie's recommendations, Mr. Wu and Linda Griffin placed a large order with a medical supply house, and then accompanied the delivery truck to the five clinics we had selected the previous year for assistance. They received a warm welcome. "It's a great encouragement to us doctors," one medic told them, "when you bring support from such a faraway place."

Encouragement mattered because the doctors were miserable. Primitive conditions and loneliness were two big reasons for dissatisfaction. Linda Griffin observed that the doctors at Manigango, a remote, high-altitude outpost, seemed entirely dependent on each other for a social life. Although nearly all were ethnic Tibetans, they had difficulty communicating with local herders whose dialect they didn't understand and who had a very different outlook on life.

The doctors had few advanced diagnostic tools, so they relied on stethoscopes, otoscopes, thermometers, and blood pressure cuffs. This equipment, however, was old and worn, with several doctors sharing a single set. KhamAid gave each clinic multiple new sets.

The doctors frequently gave injections, but Dr. Beattie had observed that the clinics lacked adequate supplies of disposable needles, and their sterilization equipment was not up to modern standards. KhamAid gave ten thousand disposable needles and syringes to each clinic and electric autoclaves to four of the five. To keep vaccines from losing effectiveness, KhamAid gave each clinic a refrigerator and cold boxes to use for transportation.

The clinics often received accident victims and people needing emergency surgery. The director at Manigango had learned surgical techniques in a year-long training program but could not use his skills because the clinic's operating theater was not sterile enough to perform operations safely; in addition, the patients could not afford the fees. We couldn't fix these problems, but we did give the clinics equipment to stabilize trauma patients for transportation to a hospital: stretchers, suture kits, bowls for dressings, and a range of scissors. To help the doctors deliver babies safely, we provided delivery bundles with all the necessary equipment, as well as baby scales and charts to monitor the growth of infants in the critical early months.

Wu and Griffin also gave them books: a comprehensive doctor's manual and a rural health care guide. So intense was the doctors' thirst for information that many of them immediately grabbed the books and started reading. In Manigango, where KhamAid staff stayed the night, Griffin rose the next morning to find one doctor with his nose still buried.

Griffin and Wu also noted that the ward beds in Manigango were so decrepit that one patient declined to use them, preferring to pitch a tent in the yard. Later, they arranged for delivery of a dozen mattresses, quilts, covers, and sheets to that place.

Everywhere they went, Griffin and Wu heard that many patients could not afford to pay for treatment. A doctor told them that, in cases of genuine poverty, the government was supposed to subsidize care, but for reasons that weren't clear to Griffin and Wu, this rarely happened in practice.

To meet the need for affordable health care, several tulkus had opened charity clinics at various locations around Kham. Gyalten Rinpoche was building one near his school that would be staffed by graduates of TAR Tibetan Medical College. I learned that many if not most doctors of traditional Tibetan medicine who had graduated from government medical schools also learned the basics of Western medicine. This gave me more confidence in the care provided by the Tibetan medicine doctors at charity clinics.[53] The next year, we would raise nearly three times as much money and spend it at Gyalten Rinpoche's clinic as well as ones operated by Shangye Rinpoche, Palgya Rinpoche, and Shechen Monastery.

Another effort that supported health came from Gyalten Rinpoche's school. We had raised a sum of $14,600 for them, allocated to teacher wages, a tractor for general transportation, and last but not least, a toilet, the school's first.

That's right. Throughout the school's eight-year existence, it had had no lavatory whatsoever, nor were there any trees or bushes in the vicinity. Children and staff took long walks outside the walls to relieve themselves in the open. I had done it a few times, and you bet I stepped carefully to find a fallow patch of ground. KhamAid's toilet grant would provide a handsome concrete outhouse painted white. It would have no running water, but compared to what they had before,

---

53 Shangye Rinpoche's hospital staff was led by a highly regarded Han physician from the city of Xi'an.

the new latrine with four solid walls, separate sides for boys and girls, and a roof overhead, would be a palace.

Meanwhile, back in Dartsendo, we had just completed the training of our third class of ten midwives. Each of the women had returned to their rural homes carrying with them delivery bundles that included stethoscopes, blood pressure cuffs, baby balances, tweezers, scissors, needles, and autoclaves that could be used on a wood stove to sterilize tools. Each got a package of medicines, and the Women's Federation set up a circulating fund so that they could replenish the drugs as needed. It was too early to tell whether our midwives would be effective, but our hopes were high.

## Scholarship Challenges

KhamAid's scholarship program was growing rapidly, and we were now operating in six counties. Program director Dana Isherwood embraced it with passion, spending personal funds to fly between California and Kham. In 2002 alone, she found sponsors for 33 more students. Yet the program was not without problems. One mistake was an early attempt to include primary school pupils. Things went well at first: the cost per student was much lower than for older kids, attracting new donors. But keeping track of so many children and sponsors was exhausting. Then we discovered that one school was accepting tuition money from us and another NGO for the very same students. We pulled out of the double-dipping school and began to phase out the primary school program altogether.

We kept going with older children and, in the fall of 2002, we had 86 girls (our one boy had graduated). The kids were universally grateful and happy to be in school, but many had difficulty meeting a key program requirement: to write an annual letter to their sponsor.

They could write well enough in Chinese (usually less well in Tibetan); they just didn't know what to say. After one girl had fashioned a decent letter, her classmates would want to copy her, producing a stack of very similar documents. We had to look over their shoulders and make them personalize the letters. Otherwise, many would have employed identical turns of phrase.

On one occasion, we faced an existential crisis when we found out that a student in our program, a girl who looked, dressed, and spoke Tibetan, officially belonged to another ethnic group, the Naxi. Her village was an anomaly: a pocket of Naxi people surrounded by Tibetans. What *was* she, really? Had we misled her sponsor? Should we cancel her scholarship?

*That* begged even harder questions such as: what does it mean to be "Tibetan"?

And was KhamAid, by design, a racist organization?

In the end, we took the easy way out: we kept the girl on our rolls and said nothing to her sponsor.

A smaller but persistent headache was children's names. Most Tibetans do not use surnames; instead, each individual is given two names by their parents or by a lama.[54] The two are chosen from roughly a hundred common names, but some, like *Tsering*, which means "long life," and *Lhamo*, which means "goddess," are especially popular. At one time, we had six Tsering Lhamos on our roster.

Although we liked to use Tibetan names, school records were in Chinese. We struggled daily with name bewilderment and lived in constant terror of sending a child's letter to the wrong sponsor.

Yet despite the huge distance and infrequency of contact, I was

---

54 Surnames exist but are not common among Tibetans in China.

touched—and sometimes astounded—by how much sponsors cared about their students. Sponsors sent us cash to give them, sometimes more than was appropriate, so that we eventually had to impose a limit. Sponsors mailed gifts to our California office; I packed them in my bags for the long trip to Kham, handing them off to staff who carried them on marathon bus journeys, through all sorts of weather, to the faraway towns where our students lived.

One unwitting sponsor put a "Free Tibet" sticker on a letter he sent to us for his student. Another person kept inviting his student to travel with him and didn't seem to understand why this was a terrible idea. We began to worry that our program might attract pedophiles looking for vulnerable children to exploit. We ousted the inappropriate sponsor, found the child a new one, and enacted policies to better protect students.

Out in Derong County, the girl Metok Tso was studying in junior middle school. As she grew older, her confidence and vivacious personality bloomed. When the English teacher asked questions of the class, other girls would hang their heads and mumble, but Metok Tso was eager to speak up, to test herself.

Metok Tso's best friend was a girl named Rinchen Dolma, whose sponsor happened to be Dana Isherwood herself. When Dana visited their school, she wanted to spend time alone with her girl, but Metok Tso was already a force to be reckoned with and couldn't be easily dismissed. "Metok Tso was so annoying," Dana recalled, "because when I would ask for information from Rinchen, Metok Tso would volunteer it before Rinchen could open her mouth. Metok Tso loved the limelight. She was always cheerful. She had energy, and that's what made her attractive to so many people."

But I was starting to realize that putting children in school was not enough, for some of the schools were awful, especially in the remote countryside. One reason was brain drain. In the past, under China's centrally controlled economy, teachers were obliged to accept any job assigned to them. Now China was liberalizing its job market, and the best teachers were quitting in droves. To fill vacant posts, schools hired anyone they could find, qualified or not, with the result that only 15.6% of teachers in rural West China had a college diploma or university degree.[55] An exceptional child like Metok Tso could succeed in that environment, but many more children were left behind because teachers failed to engage them.

One action we took was to find US$7,927 of support to help eight untrained individuals who were teaching in Nyarong County attend a two-year training program so they could improve their skills and get certified. Yet that was no help for the brain drain problem, which stemmed in part from horrendous living conditions at rural schools, an issue that afflicted clinics, too. To address this, I decided to launch a whole new effort that would harness the yearning of people in rich countries to travel to Tibet and help Tibetans.

I called the new program, "Better Homes." Not only would it improve teachers' lives, but it would allow the volunteers who worked on it to briefly become a part of rural communities. From that close vantage point, we would witness the struggles of ordinary Tibetans to better their lives.

That first year, I would also learn something else that is fundamental to life on the high plateau: how hard it is to get a decent meal.

---

55  Shiling McQuaide, "Making Education Equitable in Rural China through Distance Learning," *The International Review of Research in Open and Distance Learning,* 10:1 (2009), p. 3.

## School Renovation

During the previous winter, Mr. Wu had approached the Nyarong Education Bureau with my proposal to renovate schools using foreign volunteers. To my astonishment, they agreed, and so did the Foreign Affairs Office. A call issued by email got me a team of five volunteers; Linda Griffin would also go. We purchased a truckload of tools, paint, and construction materials according to the sketchy specifications provided by the Nyarong Education Bureau. By late September, we were ready to try out the program.

Our target was a Lharima Township, in the remote countryside of Nyarong County. Heavy rains had closed the main highway, so we changed to a high-clearance truck and set out on a secondary road across the hinterland. Our way was clogged with livestock, for many herders were migrating to lower pastures where they would spend the winter. Eight hours of stop-and-start driving through rain and mud brought us to the school gate.

Thanks to Mr. Wu's advance work, Lharima was expecting us, and we were greeted by a welcoming group of officials, teachers, and a hundred and forty very excited children. I think I must have shaken every one of their hands.

The next morning, we got to work. The teachers lived in twenty-year-old barracks built of logs, squared around a concrete yard. Thanks to poverty and (probably) corruption, the log buildings were rustic and in poor condition. The rooms were dark and depressing, in part because the walls had been papered over with ancient yellowed newsprint to stop the wind from knifing in through the cracks. Ceilings were black from the smoke of wood-burning stoves used for heat and cooking. The wiring, where it existed at all, was a fright.

Even worse, the place stank of indifference. The headmaster was out of town at a basketball tourney. The teachers lolled around smoking and gossiping in the yard while pupils read their lessons unattended. Few teachers had bothered to improve their living quarters. Their salaries were too low, and anyway, most did not intend to stay in Lharima very long.

Our first task was to haul furniture and belongings out of the teachers' rooms and prep them for paint. I totted up the work in front of us: seven two-room apartments. Added to that were eight more rooms at the township clinic, which I had, perhaps unwisely, decided we would also renovate. These twenty-two rooms were to be cleaned of newspaper and painted.

We got to work wetting glued-on paper and scraping it off, but the adhesive was stubborn, and we had to moisten it repeatedly before it was soft enough to remove. The work quickly got bogged down. The volunteers kept at it, but they looked glum. We were planning to stay for only six days. It was plain that I had severely underestimated the job.

As we worked, schoolchildren came wandering over one by one to see what the foreigners were doing. Half an hour later, a few had started scraping newspaper from walls. "Some of them were turning up first with chopsticks," one volunteer said later when I asked her to talk in front of my video camera. "Then, a little later, a piece of glass, not too sharp, and they were scraping with that."

By midmorning, we had children with cleavers, children with hoes, and children with bare fingers. They piled up furniture and fearlessly scaled the wobbly towers to scrape the highest places. They folded themselves into compact bundles to scrape near the floor. A few hours later, the room was down to bare wood.

I went to the next apartment to size up the job there and saw that it was nearly clean, too. Children were everywhere, and now teachers as well, and they were all working. The place had been sleepy and defeated when we arrived, but now there was a whirlwind of industry, a transformation. It was breathtaking.

The townlet of Lharima lay at a lofty 3,750 meters (12,400 feet) above sea level, a puddle of humanity in a shallow valley rimmed by forested slopes that quickly gave way to pasture. Most townspeople were former tent-dwelling herdsmen who had moved here by choice (the county did not yet have a nomad resettlement program). Besides the school, the town had several dozen Tibetan-style houses, a government compound, some badly beat-up 1980s-era longhouses where officials lived, and a small, tidy monastery. Dogs barked all night, and footpaths were strewn with animal feces. Fights, both human and canine, were frequent.

Hard work made for hungry volunteers. Lharima had no shops or restaurants, apart from one fellow who sold liquor and cigarettes out of his home. We had brought along food supplies, but we needed a cook. The teachers could not do it because we had turned them out of their apartments, so they arranged for us to lunch at the home of a retired colleague who lived in the town. We offered to bring our supplies, but they insisted there was no need.

When we arrived, a friendly, middle-aged woman invited us in. Later, I asked her the amount of her pension, and she said 700 yuan ($80) a month. That was a decent sum in Lharima, but there was little to buy, even in autumn when livestock is slaughtered and harvests are in.[56] The closest market town was 43 kilometers (27 miles) away, and there was no bus.

We soon learned that all she had for our lunch was noodles, lard,

---

56  Autumn is the preferred season for slaughter because livestock are fattest and meat keeps all winter long.

and a few spices. After watching the greasy noodles slither into my bowl, it was all I could do to swallow them. Later, I took some food from our larder to give to the family, but it was plain that cooking for our group would be too much of a burden. Besides, their cuisine didn't suit Western palates. I appointed myself expedition cook; it was that or starve.

The teachers' office became my kitchen, and their one-burner electric stove was the focus. I hired a local girl to assist. The first meal would be a simple soup of noodles, meat, and vegetables. We had brought along a pressure-cooker, an essential tool for cooking at high altitude, but I had no experience using it. After forty-five minutes on the stove, at last, the pressure relief valve began rocking and hissing as it was supposed to.

A few minutes later, I took the pot off the stove and opened it. My helper plunged in a spoon and brought up a sample. It was mush. She looked at me balefully. "*Nimen neng chi zheige ma?*" You can eat this?

It was too late to start over. "I'm sorry! I'm sorry! I'm sorry!" I said as my hungry team came in for dinner.

At first, I was a calamity in the kitchen, but slowly I got the hang of it. The stove, an electric coil set into a low table, gave only a feeble heat, especially in the hours before dinner, when the town overstrained its tiny hydroelectric generator. While waiting for the rice-pot to come to a boil, my assistant and I bent over chopping blocks whacking vegetables with heavy cleavers.

Water had to be fetched from a well in the yard in twin buckets slung from the ends of a pole balanced on one's shoulders. This was a trick any twelve-year-old Lharima girl could perform, but I knew my limits. I asked my assistant to fetch the water lest I become the town's laughingstock.

As affluent, fussy foreigners, we had brought fresh produce with us, but it took careful planning to use it before it rotted. Tofu, which came in unsealed plastic bags, was especially perishable. I had planned to buy meat in Lharima, but that proved difficult as people were reluctant to slaughter animals. One afternoon, the township officials procured a sheep that they transformed into a fiery death stew seething with chili peppers and swimming with small bones. It was tough going for palates unused to Sichuan fare; nevertheless, we ate it gratefully. For breakfast, at least, we had local yogurt and tsampa, both very tasty, and plenty of fresh butter.

Hygiene was a constant battle with high stakes for us foreigners unused to local bugs. Enemy Number One: lack of refrigeration, not just at the school but anywhere in town. Residents simply put their leftovers on a shelf, covered with cloth to keep out flies.

Enemy Number Two: the water. Like virtually all tap water in China, Lharima's water couldn't be trusted, and you had to boil it before you could drink it. When I made salads, I had to wash the vegetables in just-boiled water, a commodity known as *kaishui*. Like any Chinese housewife, I had an armada of thermos bottles for storing freshly boiled kaishui until needed. I needed it constantly: kaishui sterilized the cutting board and utensils, removed grease from dishes, made tea, coffee, hot chocolate, and soup, and was diluted to make warm water for personal washing and laundry. Getting enough kaishui was, just by itself, almost a full-time job.

But the greatest enemy was the school loo. It was a putrid shack sitting on stilts that stood by itself in one corner of the yard. To use it, you walked a plank to the boy's or girl's room, which hung over an open cesspool seething with waste and maggots. One's business was done squatting over a hole in the floorboards. More than a decade later, volunteers still had vivid recollections. "[I was always] hoping the morning air would be cold so it would take the bite out of the odor," wrote one, "and being especially mindful to avoid the occasional trail of excrement left near and around the holes by some of the less accurate children."

We installed lights in the lavatory, but that's all we could do for it. So, I always started meal preparations with a good scrub with warm kaishui and soap. Twice each day for seven people, I served up rice or noodles, three stir-fry dishes, one appetizer, and soup. Cooking at Lharima made me understand why Tibetans eat so simply and why diarrheal diseases are commonplace in Tibet.

By the third day, we had settled into our roles. A carpenter from California led the structural repairs. A computer programmer from Pittsburgh installed wires, switches, and lights. Linda Griffin and three other women were masters of scrape, caulk, and paint. I did a little of everything, but my main occupation was keeping the foreigners fed.

After we had cleaned the rooms of newspaper, we moved into the next phase: sealing the gaps between logs to keep out the wind. We had tubes of silicone caulk, but it was nowhere near enough. What to do? The answer was in the gobs of gooey paper coming off the walls. We mixed a test batch in a bucket. It was a sticky, repellant mess—perfect for children. Soon our elfin army was using its tiny fingers to push paper mâché into the walls.

Next was paint. That was a big job, so we brought on twelve local hires to help. Oh my, how they had fun! They sang while they painted; they joked and laughed, gesturing with paint-loaded brushes and sending ribbons of color flying in all directions. Paint dripped, daubed, leaked, spilled, and splattered. It was a good thing we had bought cheap lab coats to use as smocks. Otherwise, a lot of chubas would have been ruined. As it was, we all got polka-dotted on our exposed skin and hair.

The work was hard and dirty, yet our spirits were high. Working side by side with locals, squirting caulk and dripping paint and poking goo, we laughed all day long. Wild characters would occasionally appear in the doorways to watch us work. At night, we sat up late quaffing Snow Flower beer and trading stories about the little incidents of the day and the people we were coming to know.

One person I got to know was a young woman named Yang Ming, one of three Han teachers at the school. She had bobbed hair and was barely five feet tall in heels; at nineteen, she was one of the youngest of the faculty. By day, she was a perky sparkplug with a big smile who got on well with everyone, but once, when she was alone with me, she let down her guard. "Since I came here, I've cried so many times," she said. "I'm so terribly homesick."

Her home was Suining, an impoverished place in eastern Sichuan, the source of legions of migrant workers who did the lowest-paid, most wretched work in China and were treated by many people as disposable. Nyarong County was supposed to be a land of opportunity for Yang Ming. Some years earlier, her father had gotten a job with the county forestry bureau and brought her along with him, transferring her registration to make her a legal resident. They did this because, by attending school in a disadvantaged area, Yang Ming could more easily qualify for vocational training after grade 9. The strategy worked, and she was admitted to Dartsendo Normal College for training as a teacher.

In due course, Yang Ming graduated and was offered a teaching position. She had won the coveted "iron rice bowl," the lifetime of economic security that only a government job conferred, but it was a Pyrrhic victory because her father had meanwhile retired and gone home to Suining. She was sent to Lharima, many days' travel from her home and family. Her job was teaching the Chinese language to first-graders who could not understand even a word and were not much interested in learning. The work was hard and thankless, and she drew little satisfaction from it. She was far too poor to pay the ten thousand-yuan bribe that would buy her a transfer to the county seat. Her prospects for finding a compatible husband in Lharima were dismal. Yet if she quit, she would lose her iron rice bowl. "My mother worries so much about me," she lamented, "alone in this place so very far away." She was not yet 20 years old, and already she had been here for two years.

The painting was moving along nicely. Roof work that KhamAid had paid for was holding up. With the help of teachers and children, we rewired all of the living quarters and the clinic and replaced more than sixty broken window panes. We hired a second carpenter from the county seat who worked for four days fixing broken floors, ceilings, and walls.

By the time we were ready to leave Lharima, we had touched off an epidemic of do-it-yourself fever. People who had been living in steadily deteriorating housing, some of them for years, finally took it upon themselves to paint furniture, hang curtains, and make other upgrades. We left them supplies so that they could continue after we were gone.

The impact of the Better Homes program was not easy to measure, but I still considered it a success. In future years, we would bring it to seven other schools in Kham.

## Education Obstacles and Transitions

At the start of the Water-Ewe year (2003), KhamAid was poised to move forward, but we soon hit a speed bump—a nationwide panic over a flulike disease called Severe Acute Respiratory Syndrome, or SARS. It started in Guangdong province and, because of China's initial coverup, quickly spread, with more than 8,000 reported cases around the world, mostly in China and Hong Kong. By April, normal life had ceased. Counties and municipalities established checkpoints at their borders where officials took travelers' temperatures and sprayed vehicles with disinfectant. Face masks were ubiquitous, and people went to extraordinary lengths to avoid crowds.

While no infections were reported on the Tibetan plateau, the tourism industry suffered.

The SARS epidemic slowed KhamAid's work but didn't stop it. Dana Isherwood went out to visit scholarship students. The Books for Schools team moved ahead with their next translation project. By now, the books program had been going for several years, but we had not, as yet, assessed its effectiveness in promoting school engagement and Tibetan language literacy. I sent Linda Griffin to visit schools to check on the program's impact.

Visiting nine schools in four counties, Griffin found that kids loved our *Children's Fun Science* series thanks to the cute pictures on every page, but the rest of the news was not good. Our second series, titled *Window to Science,* was being read at only two schools. At all the others, the books appeared untouched.[57] When Linda asked why the books weren't useful, teachers seemed embarrassed and insisted that they were using them, even though the books appeared pristine.

Griffin learned that the science books were gathering dust because primary school pupils could not read Tibetan well enough to make heads or tails of them. Professor Palden Nyima, whose brainchild this program was, checked several other schools and found the same thing. He was stunned. Ensconced in his ivory tower in Chengdu, he

---

57  Two Tibetan middle schools that routinely assigned extra reading used the *Window to Science* books.

had not realized how Tibetan language literacy had deteriorated in the countryside.

Teachers explained that the bottom line was jobs. How many jobs used the Tibetan language? Very few. "Education is a big investment for families," Linda wrote. "Both kids and their parents know that Tibetan [language] won't get you a good salary in the future."

Our newest project was a seven-volume set of biographies called *Famous People in China and the World,* plus an eighth volume about women's health. After I read Griffin's report, I asked the professor to pull them from production, but it was too late: 130 sets had already shipped; another 2,700 freshly printed sets were sitting in Chengdu. So, we tore up the list of primary schools that were supposed to receive these books and made up a new list of high schools, colleges, and universities where people could read at a more advanced level. Despite the political sensitivity, we included several monasteries and nunneries. Then we shipped the books out.

In all, our Books for Schools program had purchased or printed close to 60,000 Tibetan language books and distributed them to more than a hundred schools with a combined enrollment of at least fifty thousand students. But other aid organizations were jumping on the book-printing bandwagon, and some schools now had more than they could use. It was time to move on.

Out at the Derong Middle School, Metok Tso and the other girls in her cohort were graduating from grade 9. In China, for students who plan to continue studying, graduation is a time of acute stress. After classes are over, students face grueling exams, then several weeks of tortured waiting. Girls like Metok Tso who lived in far-flung villages could not even find out their exam scores without a long trek to town.

We wanted to know whether our graduating girls intended to

continue their education, and if so, which schools they had qualified to attend. Anyone who knew Metok Tso would not have been surprised that she passed her exams. However, we at KhamAid didn't know her very well yet. We received no news and had no idea what her plans were. Each August, families scattered across Kham were simultaneously making decisions about their newly graduated children. We asked girls to phone us with the news, but they seldom did. Parents were even less help: they had no phones of their own and were too poor or intimidated to use the public phones in the county seats.

We did not find out that Metok Tso was admitted to Kang Nan Senior Middle School until she and her mother showed up at the school, baggage in hand, naively assuming that KhamAid would continue to pay Metok Tso's fees. As it happened, her sponsor had already committed to two other girls and couldn't continue to sponsor Metok Tso. Oops.

We faced this situation at the start of every school year, and it gave us much heartburn because we hated like anything for children to drop out. We scrambled to find her a new sponsor, which is when Richard Harlan entered her life.

Richard Harlan was a tall, gray-haired, mustachioed gentleman, a retired aerospace engineer, an unlikely explorer for he was not young, nor did he speak any Tibetan or Chinese. Nevertheless, starting in 2003, the year of his 70th birthday, he had begun spending his summers roaming far and wide across Kandze Prefecture. Improvising transportation as he went, he traveled solo or with Tibetans he encountered. Harlan had no political or religious agenda; like me, he was simply in love with the place.

Along the way, Richard Harlan discovered KhamAid and began sponsoring Metok Tso and several other students through our scholarship program. Metok Tso was all of fifteen or sixteen years old and hardly started on her life's journey. Now, with Richard's help, she could take on the world.

# Information

*Knowing just one word of wisdom is*
*like knowing a hundred ordinary words.*
— Tibetan proverb

What food is best for health? Why did my concrete crack? Will it rain tomorrow? Where can I sell my meat and yogurt? What does "democracy" mean?

A healthy mind asks a hundred questions a day, and the answers matter. In remote rural areas, lack of information matters, too. If travel to the outside world is a useful thing, then its vital complement, a conduit that brings the outer world in, is also absolutely important. Yet throughout history, Tibet's communication with the outside world has been tenuous, especially for people living off the major trade routes. Now, the roads were lessening isolation, but news and information were still slow to filter in. Electronic communication was key, but KhamAid could do little to open this gate, for it lay beyond our means.

A year after the work in Lharima, I brought another volunteer team to a different township in Nyarong County. Bangmé was a farming community deep within the Nyak Chu gorge. The Education Bureau had arranged for us to lodge with a local family. From this family, I would learn much about the contours of rural poverty and the human hunger to connect.

## A Poor Family

Thubten, the father of our host family, worked as the school cook. He had a wife and three children. A sign over the door to their home said, "Charity House," meaning that it wasn't theirs. All they owned in the world were three skinny cows, some household items, a bit of furniture, a television, and a VCD player.[58]

Thubten told me his hard-luck story. At the height of the timber boom in the 1990s, he borrowed money to purchase a truck that he intended to use to haul logs. Before he could pay back the loan, however, he had an accident, and his truck was wrecked. No insurance, of course. To repay what he owed, he had to sell the family homestead.[59]

Without land, one cannot grow food. The couple and their children would have wound up as beggars, but the local government allotted to them an abandoned home that it had somehow come to possess. With a roof over their heads and Thubten's wages of 400 yuan (about US$50) per month, the family muddled along.

The house was mostly empty but plenty big, and we found it a decent base of operations. Not that there were any frills. The walls were bare clay except for plastic tarp and some faded posters. There was no proper stairway: a notched-log ladder led from the ground floor stables to the living quarters on the second floor. Three of us slept in the living room on carpet-covered benches; our displaced hosts slept on blankets spread over the floorboards. Another log ladder led up to the roof, where the rest of the team pitched tents. For cooking, the family had a wood-burning stove and an electric coil heater. For

---

58  VCD is a digital video standard common in China.

59  Under China's laws at that time, private parties could not buy and sell agricultural land. I surmise that Thubten did not sell it outright; either the government purchased the property or Thubten entered into a long-term lease arrangement.

water, there was a spring-fed stream running past the house. There was no toilet; you had to climb downstairs, head outside, and improvise. It was basic, but it was enough. The place soon became home.

Thubten was 38, his wife, 39. Her health was not good. Thubten said she had been coughing up green sputum for some months. One of the volunteers was a doctor; he examined her and declared that she was malnourished, albeit not severely, but could not diagnose her cough. Thubten and his wife were both extremely thin. But then, everyone was thin in that place.

Thubten's oldest boy, a monk, was fifteen years old but small for his age. Before donning monk's robes, he had completed sixth grade, which made him the family's most educated member. He was on home leave during our visit, and so we hired him to work for our project, paying him twenty yuan (US$2.50) a day, the going rate for unskilled labor in that area.

Thubten and his wife told us they had sent their son to a monastery because they feared he was too poor to marry. With no land and no steady job, he would either be a lifelong bachelor or share a wife with his younger brother. Such was the lot of very poor men in the Tibetan countryside.

Polyandry was not rare in Kham. Two brothers sharing one wife was a smart economic strategy: it prevented property from being divided, and an extra breadwinner is a tremendous help to a family on the margins of survival. Someone once told me that the wife benefits from the arrangement because she is "less likely to be beaten" when there's a second husband around. A man once explained that, in his household, the husband who desired to sleep with the shared wife would place his shoes outside her bedroom door, signaling to his brother to slumber elsewhere. Both dads raised children, and no one cared whose genes they carried. In Nyarong, polyandry was not uncommon; indeed, across the road from Thubten's house was just such a family.

Thubten's second child was a ten-year-old daughter. She had recently undergone an appendectomy and was recuperating at her grandparents', so we never saw her. I couldn't imagine how Thubten managed to pay for the operation. She was reportedly an excellent student.

The youngest child was a boy of about eight. We dubbed him "Brat Boy" because he was an unkempt, ill-mannered child. His father admitted that he was a poor student and often fought with other children. Because their eldest son was a monk and their daughter would most likely marry into another family, the couple would have to depend on Brat Boy to care for them in old age. This was not a hopeful prospect, and I worried for their future.

There wasn't much to do in Bangmé Township, especially after dark. Oh, how the family loved their television. Whenever there was electricity (about half the time), the TV was blaring. Like children everywhere, Thubten's were mesmerized by the flickering screen. Adults watched, too. Families visited, and everyone watched together.

No signal could reach Bangmé deep within the gorge, and the family didn't have a satellite dish as did many of their neighbors, so they got programming from their family library of VCD disks.[60] Their collection included several Tibetan music videos, a ponderous Indian-made epic about the life of Padmasambhava that had lots of psychedelic visual effects, three or four chop-socky Hong Kong action flicks (highly favored by the boys), and a disk of American animated shorts. All of these recordings they watched over and over.

---

60  At this time, residents of towns in Kandze TAP could usually access cable and broadcast television, including a local station offering Tibetan language programming, as well as provincial and national television stations.

Nyarong County was one of the Sichuan's poorest; in 2002, the per capita income was only 798 yuan (US$90) per year. Each Nyarong resident had, on average, only 0.13 hectares (0.32 acres) of arable land, for most of the county was too steep or too high for farming. Isolation was another reason: Kandze Prefecture's two main arteries, national highways 317 and 318, both gave Nyarong a wide berth, and the road through the gorge was often closed by summer mudslides or winter ice. Public services were poor because skilled people did not want to live in such an out-of-the-way place.

Through our scholarship program, Dana Isherwood found out that, unlike schools in other counties, girls dominated Nyarong's middle school because many boys were dropping out to work on road crews. Wages were depressed, and the region's poor services were perpetuating the cycle of poverty.

We told Thubten's sickly wife that she should get more sun and consume more fruits and vegetables, and we gave them fresh produce, but she kept on eating the noodles, tsampa, and butter that were her family's staples. Instead of seeking foodstuffs to improve their diet, they spent their spare time staring into their electronic porthole, gazing at the glowing, inaccessible landscape beyond. Even so, they felt their video library was inadequate; they wanted more and better programming. So Thubten politely inquired, would I please buy his family a satellite dish?

I said no, for I thought TV was mental pollution that I should not invite into their lives. But later, I wondered if I had been wrong. Who was I to tell Thubten what should be important to him and his family? Perhaps television, more than vegetables, was what they needed.[61]

At least we did give them ten days of wages plus rent for staying

---

61  In 2010, I heard that the township of Bangmé had gotten connected to the internet.

in their house, our leftover food, cooking utensils, and many miscellaneous gifts (including vitamins) from the volunteers. Yet I doubt that our gifts and cash had much long-term impact.

Income generation was surely the way to maximize impact and open other gates of the mandala. About 25 kilometers north of Bangmé, our ten families were laboring in their greenhouses to grow vegetables for the market. Already, their enterprise was struggling.

## Greenhouse Setbacks

The greenhouses had been built the previous spring and covered about half an acre of land. They were operated jointly by the ten women. The Nyarong Agriculture Bureau put in extra money on top of KhamAid's funds so that the greenhouses would have steel frames instead of wood. By October, the women had brought in three harvests.

The crops were selling well but didn't bring in as much as we'd hoped. Still, the women were able to pay back a little more than half of the scheduled amount, which was already low because this was the first year. The county government made up the difference and added a bit more to enable two more families to join our original ten.

All seemed well, but problems were starting to surface. The repayment schedule was based on Agriculture Bureau projections, which were now proving inflated. The families worried that they wouldn't earn enough to pay what they owed. The bureau had also failed to foresee two major technical problems. First, the plastic sheeting on the greenhouses was too thin to retain heat during the winter. Without special heat-retaining covers, it would be impossible to grow crops during the coldest months. To buy covers for all the greenhouses would cost 70,000 yuan (US$1,200).

There was no way we could add the cost of buying covers to the loans; margins were already too thin. After some discussion, Linda Griffin and I decided to buy covers for half the greenhouses and have the families share them for the first winter to see how things went. The families would pay only a nominal 'rent' of 100 yuan per cover.

The second technical problem also concerned temperature: during the summer, the greenhouses got too hot. To allow air to flow, each morning, the women were unfastening the plastic from the frames and hitching it up. If we installed roll-up windows, then it would be a lot easier, but that would cost more money. We decided to leave it up to the families whether to make this investment.

It was also becoming apparent that the Agriculture Bureau was supervising the program so closely that the women had little sense of ownership over the business. The women liked and respected the trainer, a man from Miyi in eastern Sichuan, but were so dependent on him to tell them what to do that they seemed more like employees than owners. Meanwhile, the market price of vegetables was falling as new greenhouses, most owned by outsiders, were popping up around the region. Also, roads were improving, making produce easier to import.

Linda Griffin was pessimistic: "Given the difficulties that have cropped up so far," she wrote in a report, "I would be surprised if the five-year repayment schedule can go ahead as planned."

Nevertheless, the county government was determined to make it work. They wanted a shining example that would bring acclaim to Nyarong and encourage more people to give up subsistence agriculture and grow cash crops. In addition to what they had already put in, the county invested funds to build a perimeter wall around the greenhouses to keep out livestock and thieves. They dug a reservoir and irrigation channels to bring water to the site, and they also put the trainer on contract and paid him for two years.

During the winter, Linda Griffin decided to leave China and start a new life elsewhere, so Mr. Wu stepped in to replace her as director of the greenhouse program. In early April, he emailed me with bad news. "On March 31st," he wrote, "there occurred continuous gale… All of the plastic covers are completely destroyed, and some steel frames are [bent] out of shape. The different kinds of well-growing vegetables suffered from damages to a certain degree. It is still frost season, so the losses might increase."

County officials calculated the losses at around 120,000 yuan (US$14,600)—a terrible setback. From the wreckage of their greenhouses, the discouraged women gathered up bruised and frost-nipped vegetables that had been almost ready for harvest. Mr. Wu and I waited helplessly to hear what the women and the county government would decide to do.

## Mother to a Whole Village

By the start of the male Wood-Monkey year (2004), we had trained forty women as midwives and sent them back to their villages, but no one had checked to see how they were doing. We decided to assess our program.

The gold standard for program impact assessment would have been to measure changes in mortality rates in the townships where our midwives were practicing, but the government would not give us the data. Even statistics for much larger areas, prefectures and provinces, were hard to find.

As I have said, women in Tibet at that time commonly delivered babies in the stables or outdoors, a dangerous practice, so the doctors who trained our midwives taught them what they called the "new method" of delivery. This "new method" was giving birth indoors on a clean bed and tending the mother carefully rather than sending her downstairs or outside. This "new method" might be old news in the developed world, but in rural Kham, it was a departure from custom.

Lacking data on mortality, we prepared interview questions to gather information for our assessment. Given our limited resources, we could not go to all forty of the far-flung villages where our women lived, but we aimed to track down as many as we could. Accompanied by Women's Federation representatives, Mr. Wu and I headed out on a road trip to the four counties that had so far sent women to the training.

Our first stop was the Nyakchukha County seat, where the Women's Federation delivered up a nervous, reedy woman who had traveled into town to see us. She quickly confessed that, in the three years since the training, she had attended only *one* delivery—watching the entire birth without mustering up the courage even to touch the mother. This was very discouraging, but we had many more midwives to see.

The next morning, we set off on foot, crossing a bridge over the Nyak Chu and then turning onto a dirt track heading up the mountain. As we climbed, the local official accompanying us told us about the odd features of the place we were going to. She said that the residents of Shanbeihou Village spoke Chinese rather than Tibetan, but not a standard Chinese dialect; instead, an ancient tongue with a peculiar upside-down grammar that was unique in China. Although the people were ethnic Tibetan, dressed in Tibetan clothes, and worshipped as Tibetan Buddhists, no one could recall a time when the village spoke Tibetan.

After about an hour of walking, the village midwife appeared, having come down to meet us. Sonam Drolma was a plain-spoken and unpretentious woman, about 40 years old, with a big smile, ruddy cheeks, oversized silver earrings, and red yarn woven into her jet-black hair. Her strong, capable hands took mine warmly in hers to greet me like a long-lost sister.

The people of Shanbeihou were lucky: their village was only three hours' hike from the county hospital, yet most expecting mothers did not bother going to town for checkups and also chose to give birth at home. Sonam Drolma said that, among the fifty-eight families living in Shanbeihou, five or six new babies were born each year. Although she'd never had any formal instruction, she was already known as a healer when she entered our program. Now she delivered most of the babies and was like a mother to the entire village.

When we got there, I saw that Shanbeihou was a pretty quilt of stone houses set among wheat and corn fields tilted over a steep fall overlooking the Nyak Chu. We went first to Sonam Drolma's house and had tea. She showed us where she wanted to add a room to the home to use as a clinic, and we discussed a KhamAid grant for this purpose.

Following tea, Sonam Drolma took us to another home in the village, where we met a young wife named Chokyi Yangchen, born and raised in Shanbeihou. Small and pixielike, wearing trousers and a baseball cap turned backward, she looked like a hard worker. She was shy like most girls her age, so Sonam Drolma told us the story of her pregnancy while the girl and her family sat nodding.

As the eldest of three sisters, Chokyi Yangchen had been the first to marry, and in due course, became pregnant. That was the spring of 2003 when she was nineteen. As the seasons turned, her pregnancy had appeared healthy, with no symptoms that might have prompted Sonam Drolma to recommend a hospital delivery. On the night of December 29th, in the wee hours, the pains had come.

Someone had run to fetch Sonam Drolma. The midwife knew what to watch for, and, as the hours went by, she saw two things in

Chokyi Yangchen's labor that worried her. First, the baby was exceptionally large, and second, the labor was lasting much longer than was typical for women in Shanbeihou. Time passed, and the pains came on harder and stronger, until four o'clock the next afternoon, when the infant boy finally presented himself to the midwife and the world.

But something was wrong. The little body was limp and motionless, and he would not take a breath. To his shocked family, he appeared dead.

The county hospital was just three hours away, but it might as well have been on the moon. The horror-stricken family implored Sonam Drolma to do something to save their child.

Before this, Sonam Drolma had already saved the day in two other difficult deliveries. One mother in labor had been making her way to the hospital with Sonam Drolma by her side when suddenly her time came; Sonam Drolma had delivered the baby right on the trail and afterward got them both home safely. Another Shanbeihou woman had had severe bleeding after delivering her child, so bad that the woman passed out and was unconscious for half an hour. Sonam Drolma had been able to manage the bleeding and revive her.

But Chokyi Yangchen's lifeless baby was the toughest case the midwife had yet faced. At first, she had thought the boy was lost. Then she had remembered a lesson from KhamAid's training: cardiopulmonary resuscitation. She had never used it before, but she decided to try.

Sonam Drolma put her mouth over the mouth and nose of the infant boy and exhaled gently. The child's tiny lungs expanded. Minutes later, he was alive and breathing. Now, seven months later, I watched him career about the kitchen in a walker, an active, healthy baby.

Sonam Drolma was undoubtedly a successful midwife, but as we interviewed more women, we realized that she was an outlier. Naively, we had expected that our midwives would deliver babies for humanitarian reasons and not for money. We had underestimated the power of economics to influence women's choices. Lesson learned: many women could not afford to work for free. Our most educated trainees, women who had graduated from grade 12, had quit doing midwifery because they got job offers from the government, most unrelated to health care. Some women had married and relocated to communities where people didn't need or want their services. One woman had moved to town and opened a shop.

About half of our trainees had stopped providing midwife services within a few years, either because they had other opportunities, or because their communities didn't have confidence in them. In three of the four counties, the Health Bureau had little or no involvement with our program, but the fourth, Serthar, was different. In Serthar, the Health Bureau had assigned our program graduates to work at government clinics. I couldn't go to Serthar due to its political sensitivity, but Mr. Wu went there and interviewed several of them.[62] He found that the Serthar women, unlike the others, weren't waiting for women to come to them; they were constantly out making house calls. During these visits, they gave expectant mothers advice on nutrition and other forms of self-care, and encouraged them to come to the clinic for a full checkup.

The Serthar midwives received modest government stipends for their work, which enhanced their standing in their communities. Doctors mentored them so they could continue learning. As government employees, they received additional training on top of what they

---

62  Larung Gar, an enormous encampment of monks and nuns, is in Serthar County. The government's repeated razing of homes there has led to intense international criticism.

had gotten from us. As a result, the Serthar midwives were very successful in meeting our program's goals. We resolved to model our future program on Serthar's success.

## Among Nomads

When autumn arrived, it was time to renovate another rural school. This time we would be working among *drokpa*, or full-time herders, a people whose language and folkways were different from those of *rongpa*, or farmers.

Our destination, Sershul County, was known for having *wu ge zui*, or five "mosts." It was the farthest, highest, biggest, coldest, and poorest county in Kandze Prefecture. It was, therefore, a place of tremendous need.

We traveled slowly to acclimate to the elevation, taking five days to reach Sershul County at the northwestern reaches of Sichuan. Descending from a pass, we rolled onto a prodigiously large rangeland, a carpet of gray-green grass that extended without a tree or shadow to foamy hills in the far distance. Several hours later, as the sun was plunging toward the horizon, we spotted the hydroelectric station at nJu-nyung Township, the landmark that signaled our turnoff.

A jeep was there waiting; it held our project partner, a tulku called Kilung Jigme Rinpoche, and his driver. They led us onto a faint track heading away from the highway. Already at 4,000 meters (13,200 feet) above sea level, we began to climb into the gathering gloom, leaving behind the concrete buildings of the township headquarters and our last link to the modern world.

The track was boggy and dotted with soft hummocks erupting like mushrooms from the earth. The mush was no problem for Kilung Rinpoche's jeep, but it was quicksand to our bus's tires. After fifteen minutes of wallowing, our driver halted the bus and vowed that he would go no further.

I got out to parlay with Kilung Rinpoche and figure out what to do. When I stepped outside, I was lacerated by a scything wind that sliced off the grasslands with not even a bush to slow it down. Rain spattered from a mud-gray sky, and soon it would be dark. The only shelter in sight was a few earthen huts belonging to herdsmen. I gazed as far as I could over the swamp-infested badlands but could not see our destination. This was not a place to get stuck.

The man in the car, his eminence Dza Kilung Tulku Jigme Rinpoche, was a handsome thirty-something Tibetan. He lived part-time in America and spoke fabulous English. "Don't worry," he said. "It's only eight kilometers from here. Everyone can go in my jeep."

His jeep was a smallish, beat-up Cherokee model with many hard miles on it. Even if the tulku's spiritual powers held the car together, I doubted he could get us and our gear to his school next to Ponru Monastery in fewer than ten trips. Luckily, our work materials, cement, timber, paint, and so forth, had been delivered earlier. However, we still had twelve people, their duffles, sleeping gear, food for five days, dishes and utensils, a medical kit inside a steel-frame suitcase, a frightfully heavy toolbox, gifts for the children at Ponru, and the most essential item on any expedition checklist: toilet paper, two twenty-four-roll packs. I didn't want to think about what might happen if people and gear had to wait in the dark while the jeep shuttled back and forth fording streams and wading bogs. We needed a better plan.

I climbed back into the bus where KhamAid staff and volunteers were studying the void outside their windows and chattering excitedly. I explained our predicament. "No problem!" said the team. "We'll walk!" Two offered to stay and guard the baggage while the jeep shuttled to and fro. The others strapped on their backpacks. It was cold, and everyone wanted to be moving. We set off at a brisk pace.

Two hours, eight kilometers, and three jeep trips later, the last stragglers arrived at the school. It was completely dark by this time, but by the glare of headlights, I could make out a line of children by the gate waving silky white khata. They sang and applauded and cheered their welcome as we paraded past. When I reached the end of the line, two of them slid their tiny hands in mine and led me inside.

The school cook had prepared noodles for us. Kilung Rinpoche did not stay; after a quick hello to the staff, he got back into the Cherokee and disappeared into the night. After we had eaten, our hosts led us next door to Ponru Monastery, set on a rise above the school. We were lodged in a row of newly built monk's quarters. I bunked with two volunteers in a bare cubicle. No beds and no heat. We quickly laid out our camping mattresses and burrowed into our sleeping bags, for the temperature was plummeting.

The next morning after the sun peeped over the horizon, we inspected the remarkable planet we had landed on. Ponru School, where we would be working for the next five days, was a private school funded by Kilung Rinpoche's donors for the benefit of local nomads. It was a walled compound, low and squat, floating like flotsam on a billowing grassland sea.

We gathered in the cook's quarters for breakfast, squeezing onto low benches around her dung-fueled iron stove. I had brought along instant oatmeal and coffee—mainstays of KhamAid field cuisine. The cook steamed some buns, which we Westernized by spreading with peanut butter and jam. There was, as always, tea, tsampa, and butter.

We were joined by Dawa, one of two teachers at the school. She was a lovely young woman, warm, unassuming, and down-to-earth.

In her clean clothes and neatly plaited hair, Dawa stood out like a diamond in this place of mud and dung. She was the only person for miles around who had the education to teach math, science, and Chinese to fourth graders. She must have found it lonely, for she attached herself to us from the moment we arrived, becoming part of the team.

The school was composed of two long, flat-roofed barracks set at right angles to each other. It had one classroom for the thirty-one students, four dormitory rooms, each equipped with a low wooden platform used as a bed by five children, a cave-like kitchen where Mr. Wu would be preparing our meals, and Dawa's two-room apartment. In one corner of the yard stood an outhouse, the plank-and-pit type, unlit and terrifying at night.

The structures had been built very cheaply out of clay and were riven with cracks, including one that ran right through the school's only chalkboard, dividing it in two. Whitewash was blistering from the walls, exposing the mud underneath. Half a dozen panes of glass were broken. In the entire place, there was not one door or window that sealed adequately against the wind. There was a mountain of work to do.

After breakfast, we began clearing rooms of furniture. The sky was overcast, and the temperature stayed below freezing. Classes had been suspended for the one-week National Day holiday. The second teacher, a monk who taught Tibetan language, history, and culture, stayed at Ponru Monastery, and we seldom saw him. Still, many children were around: sturdy little ragamuffins in an assortment of sizes. Most had only light jackets, yet they seemed impervious to the cold. Not so the KhamAid team. After we finished moving furniture, I called a break, and we headed back to the cook's quarters to warm up.

As we sipped our hot drinks from enamel mugs, one volunteer remarked that she saw a lot of boy students, but where were the girls?

Someone translated the question for Dawa, who explained that parents were less willing to send daughters than sons. The school had twenty-one boys but only ten girls. "Parents think the purpose of education is to serve religion," she said. "They want their sons to read and write Tibetan so they can enter a monastic institute."[63]

I couldn't blame parents for wanting their sons to be monks, for having a monk in the family is an honor. From the child's perspective, the anguish of leaving one's parents was assuaged by joining a big monastic family that included plenty of other *traba,* or novices. Compared to a tent, a monastery was a palace. Chanting sutras is easier than going out every day, in all kinds of weather, to care for livestock. And a life of celibacy is not a dire prospect when you're eight years old.

Another volunteer asked whether any kids had dropped out. Dawa said that, in the three years since the school started, one-third of the children had left. "If it wasn't for Kilung Rinpoche," she added, "many more would be gone." She explained that Kilung Rinpoche not only endorsed secular education to the surrounding community but also paid parents a monthly allowance to encourage attendance.

I had recently visited an encampment in another county where the government fined parents if their kids were absent.[64] Without such carrots and sticks, grassland schools would be empty.

I would soon come to understand that, compared to Tibetan farmers, drokpa were deeply conservative and profoundly religious. They resisted change, yet during the previous half-century, they had

---

63 Monastic institutes, or *shedra*, are schools where Buddhism is taught, usually situated near large monasteries but administratively separate from them. Notable shedra in Kandze Prefecture are at Dzokchen, Palpung, Lhagang, Sershul, Dzongsar, and Shechen Monasteries.

64 This was in Pelyül County. I do not know how widespread the practice was.

suffered far too much of it. After the Chinese Communists annexed Tibet, they had set out to weaken, then eradicate Buddhism, the bedrock and fountainhead of the herder's world. The government had collectivized herds and formed families into communes to care for them. The Communist management system reduced a once proud and independent people to tallying up work points earned through tasks such as herding, milking, and shearing wool, and then exchanging the points for food and other necessities. The government levied heavy taxes and compelled the sale of a large portion of the animal products at artificially low prices, leaving the herders only enough for bare subsistence.

After many years of suffering under this degrading and inefficient system, relief had arrived when Deng Xiaoping rose to power. In 1982, the communal herds were divided among families, who were now allowed to keep most of what they produced, and the economy was unfettered so that supply and demand determined production instead of Party planners. At the same time, Buddhism had reemerged, and Tibetans began to rebuild and reboot their monasteries.[65]

Throughout the decades of turmoil, one thing on the grasslands remained eternal: the yak, a shaggy relation to the cow, was the economic bedrock. Nomads were nourished by the yak's milk and meat or traded them for other foodstuffs. They sheltered in tents made from the yak's spun and woven hair. They circulated among seasonal pastures to give their yaks the best possible forage. When it came time to move, yaks carried nomads' belongings to the next camp.

A drokpa who lost his yaks lost everything. A herd could never be too large, for you always needed insurance against snow disasters,

---

65  Melvyn Goldstein and Cynthia Beall, *Nomads of Western Tibet: The Survival of a Way of Life*, (University of California Press, 1990), pp. 134–155.

epidemics, and thieves. Some Ponru families had more than three hundred head.[66]

Now, in 2004, caterpillar fungus was transforming the economy, earning a typical Ponru family 7,000 to 8,000 yuan (about US$1,000) per year. The cash brought disruptive technologies like motorcycles and cell phones to the grasslands, eroding herders' isolation. A brave new world was on Ponru's doorstep. It was Dawa's job to make the children ready for it.

"Three years ago, when I started teaching these kids," Dawa said, "I asked them what they wanted to do when they grew up. The boys all said, 'to be a monk.' Now, when I ask them, they say teacher, driver, doctor, or businessman."

"That's wonderful!" said one of the volunteers. I thought so, too. Now I understood why Dawa stayed in this lonely and difficult place. She and I were both hooked on the same narcotic: the feeling you get from making a difference in someone's life. Thanks to her, thirty-one children had a chance to thrive.

Thinking back to the herders I had met while trekking, the young woman Dolma Tso and her uncle, Nyima, I realized that Ponru was a much harder place to live, for the nearest farms were not just a few hours' hike away, they were at least 175 kilometers (110 miles) distant. Ponru's herders could not easily get tsampa, let alone fruit or vegetables. They could not easily replace a broken tent pole in this treeless place. They had no houses to shelter in when they were old or sick or burdened with small children. From cradle to grave, they lived their lives in tents.

---

66  In Lhagang, a family having more than 100 yaks was reckoned as rich, 60-70 was middle class, and 30 or fewer was poor. Winrock International Project Baseline Research Team, p. 29.

I didn't know it then, but big changes were coming for Tibetan herders. Full-time tent dwellers like the people of Ponru would fade into history, for the Chinese government was starting to roll out a massive and controversial effort to settle the nomads into permanent housing, ostensibly to provide better services to them and to protect the rangeland environment. Program details varied from county to county. In most areas, herders had the choice of accepting a subsidized house either on their traditional winter grazing grounds or in a new, planned community, often on the outskirts of town. Some herdsmen sold off their animals; others kept at least a few.

None of this was yet happening in Ponru. But even without a government settlement program, drokpa could not forever resist the modern world. All of those I knew who had left the grasslands and gotten an education had no plans to "follow the yak's tail" again. Personally, I thought a herder's tent was too darn uncomfortable, and their food was unhygienic and unhealthy. A nomad's life was especially hard on women, for they worked constantly and suffered the risks of pregnancy and childbirth.

Yes, change was coming, and sooner or later, the nomads here were going to be part of it. Kilung Rinpoche knew this, which is why he started Ponru School.

The school was doing a great job academically, but the building had been going downhill practically from the moment it opened. I had sent money ahead to repair the roof, work that was already complete. There was, however, much more to do.

We got busy whitewashing the walls, replacing wiring, and installing lights. The weather was endlessly changing, one minute throwing down rain, hail, or snow, the next moment searing us with blinding sun. Despite our slow ascent, we all suffered from headaches and insomnia. Two volunteers also endured a day of nausea and vomiting, although no one was sick enough to evacuate. The team forged ahead undaunted, weather-stripping doors and windows, and pouring a concrete walkway to the toilet so that teachers and pupils wouldn't have to trudge through mud.

On the third day, an early morning snowstorm frosted the valley white. When the sun came out, a surprise arrived: my old friend Tsering Perlo, roaring into the schoolyard on a motorcycle. I had known him since 1998 when he was one of our art conservation trainees; later, he helped KhamAid with several field projects. Now he was working in Sershul County for another NGO, the Bridge Fund. He had once been a herder himself, and he understood very well the problems faced by the people of Ponru.

"I helped do a survey of nomads in twenty-four townships in Sershul County," he told me as we sat in the schoolyard basking in the sunshine while the snow melted into mud. "We were investigating the rate of infant deaths. We found out there was nearly one death per family."

I told Tsering Perlo that, at that very moment, ten Sershul women were getting trained under KhamAid's midwife program. He liked that news.

We chatted about the projects being done by various NGOs in Sershul and other parts of Kham. After Tsering Perlo left, I asked Dawa how people in Ponru got access to health care. Her answer surprised me. "Some people around here are so conservative," she said, "that they refuse to take medicine."

"Even traditional Tibetan medicine?"

"They might take a little Tibetan medicine, but they believe that Western medicine is bad for your health. And they won't use birth control. I've seen families with five or six children born very close together. When I suggest that they should do something about this, they scold me, saying, 'you're a Tibetan girl—don't talk like that!' "

Later, someone from the Sershul County Family Planning Agency would tell me about a survey showing that nine out of ten women questioned complained of gynecological ailments. The government could not provide contraceptive services, wanted or unwanted, to many nomad women because they were simply too hard to reach. Like others living in the world's least developed places, Sershul drokpa were trapped in a perilous cycle of uncontrolled fertility and untimely death.

Yet Kilung Rinpoche's efforts were paying off: Ponru's children had remarkably high test scores considering the remote area in which they lived. They far outshined the nearest government school, which was larger and had better facilities. A lot of credit, I thought, went to Dawa. It was Ponru's great fortune that Dawa was not interested in marrying, or she would have left long ago. She had promised she would stay until the children graduated from grade 6. Then she planned to become a nun.

Five days later, my team's catalog of good deeds included a new chalkboard; new paint; countless holes and cracks plugged; new lights, switches, outlets, and fuse boxes throughout, all with wires neatly and properly hung; a new damper for the kitchen stove to send smoke outside, and add years to the cook's life; a cat door installed in one staff member's home; and a rubbish pit. We also treated several illnesses and gave a toothbrush, with oral hygiene lessons, to every child.

The Ponru School would prepare herder children for life off of the grasslands, but the adults, too, needed new knowledge and skills to be resilient in a world of change. What skills could they learn, and what jobs could they do? This was the great mystery that, a year later, I would set out to crack. Little did I realize what a wild, wild world I was getting into.

# Part IV

# Cultural Heritage

*Although one parts from one's fatherland,*
*one doesn't give up one's language.*
— Tibetan proverb

The mandala is a broken house if people lose the culture into which they were born. Yet in 1966, Mao Zedong launched the Great Proletariat Cultural Revolution, a political movement that aimed to obliterate China's past. During that horrific decade, "Red Guards"—gangs of brainwashed teenage zealots—went on a rampage to obliterate "the four olds": old customs, culture, habits, and ideas. The Red Guards came to Tibet, too, and persuaded naïve youngsters to join them. They plundered temples, burned books and religious artifacts, and attacked monks and anyone else who dared to be openly devout.

During the Cultural Revolution, Tibetans were robbed of their religion, the thing they held most dear. They dared not conduct their sacred rituals, carve prayers into stones, prostrate before shrines, burn incense, or stage festivals. Local committees of the Chinese Communist Party took over the temples and converted them to meeting halls, offices, granaries, canteens, pigsties, and jails. Centuries-old masterpieces of Buddhist art were defaced with graffiti, covered with political posters, or caked in soot from the cooking fires of the temples' new occupants. The rich artistic patrimony of Tibet's Buddhism, accumulated through centuries of toil and exemplifying the finest craftsmanship of the Himalayan world, disappeared virtually overnight.

Tibetans who were of school age during the Cultural Revolution did not learn to read or write their own language; they learned only about making revolution and Marxist-Leninist-Mao Zedong Thought. The ten years of chaos annihilated Tibet's and China's social, educational, and religious institutions, and left the economy in tatters.

The death of Mao Zedong in 1976 brought an end to the devastation, and new leadership under Deng Xiaoping allowed Tibetans to revive their language and traditions. Nevertheless, China continues to wield enormous cultural influence: the hard power of setting school curricula and writing laws, and the soft power exerted by television, popular culture, and millions of migrants flowing to the high plateau. Meanwhile, the many disparate languages and dialects used among Tibetans make it harder for them to coalesce around one cultural identity and resist Chinese influence.

Tibetan culture is therefore evolving, led as usual by the young. Yet Tibetan youth are not all cut from the same cloth: some are staunch traditionalists while others exuberantly embrace trends from across the globe.

## A Grant for Preserving Culture

When I returned from the Sershul grasslands, a blizzard of emails awaited my attention, for I was negotiating an exciting new partnership that would allow KhamAid to return to the cultural preservation arena and build on our previous successes. Earlier in the year, I had been contacted by Winrock International, a large NGO that worked in dozens of countries. They had invited me to collaborate with them on a joint proposal. Together with a third partner, we had won funding for projects in Tibet through the US Agency for International Development (USAID). The work would have three prongs: generating income for Tibetans, preserving their cultural heritage, and protecting the natural environment in which they lived.

The grant was US$2.5 million, the bulk of which would be spent by the lead organization, Winrock International. KhamAid would get $185K, and a similar amount would go to the third partner, Fauna and Flora International, or FFI. Although much smaller than Winrock's share, the amount for KhamAid was substantial, and I was thrilled at the opportunity. We planned to work in Kandze Prefecture, KhamAid's home turf.

The grant was a godsend for KhamAid, given that our income at that time was coming from individual small donors and the occasional one-off grant. Our expenses were rising; in the seven years since we had started, Mr. Wu's salary had tripled, commensurate with rising wages in China and his capacity to take on complicated and sometimes dangerous work with little oversight. We also started giving him health insurance and contributing to a pension for him. I was scraping by on the inheritance left me by my father and part-time consulting work for another nonprofit, so I was looking forward to billing some hours to the USAID grant so that KhamAid could pay me a partial salary.

Sichuan officials were always suspicious of American meddling in Tibetan areas, but the prospect of so much money pumped into their province must have given them pause. Winrock was a well-established, apolitical organization with no links whatsoever to the Dalai Lama, and they were taking great care to be transparent and follow the rules. KhamAid and FFI had both been operating in Tibetan areas for some time without problems. From the Chinese perspective, our three-way team didn't have any obvious show-stoppers. They probably knew that if they refused us, we would take our USAID money to another province—probably Qinghai, which was said to be relatively hospitable to foreign NGOs. I imagine that there were many high-level meetings where officials debated benefits and risks.

In the end, the government agreed that we could work in Kandze Prefecture, but there was a condition: they wanted all of our $2.5 million (less administrative overhead), to be poured into Lhagang Township, to turn the tiny town and surrounding grasslands into a development showcase. Lhagang was the darling of officials because it had a growing tourism industry and was highly visible.

Lhagang was also convenient: it was only five hours' drive from Dartsendo.[67] That was good because road trips in Kham were again becoming unpleasant ordeals. As the Tibetan economy developed, the three-year-old blacktop was already crumbling under the weight of all the cement and rebar and manufactured goods being driven to distant outposts. But it didn't take much traffic to pulverize the roads in many areas, because the pavement had been laid by unscrupulous contractors putting up "tofu-dreg construction," a phrase coined by Premier Zhu Rongji to describe a national headache. The roads in Kandze were now being re-surfaced, and travel would be agony for a few years until the work was complete.

Under the USAID grant, one of KhamAid's assigned tasks would be (in the words of our joint proposal) *preservation of culturally significant sites*. To do this, we first had to figure out what was "culturally significant" in Lhagang—not an easy task, considering that on the big, broad, devout Tibetan plateau, there is a monastery, temple, or

---

67  In 2009, the Kangding Airport opened about an hour's drive from Lhagang, making it even more accessible.

stupa around every corner, and hardly a pile of rocks that isn't sacred to somebody.

To avoid offending Tibetans with subjective judgments about their holy sites, we decided to use age as a proxy for significance: the older, the better. Yet there were very few temples in all of Tibet that were authentically old. Nearly everything still standing had been built or rebuilt since the end of the Cultural Revolution. Ruins were hard to find, and if you did find them, they were invariably too deteriorated to restore.

As winter passed into spring, I was eager to get started; the grant period was only three years, and we had no time to waste. As soon as conditions allowed, I sent a team to survey monasteries in the Lhagang area, but they found no original structures at any of the half-dozen sites they examined. So, we had to refocus our objective. Instead of rebuilding an old, damaged temple, we would instead teach the skills that go into making a new-but-traditional Tibetan building at a culturally significant site. These skills were carpentry, masonry, and roof laying.

Although Lhagang was full of traditional Tibetan-style buildings, most were not very sturdy because the builders took shortcuts—e.g., digging a too-shallow foundation, using poor quality mortar, overloading the roof, or laying roof beams in only one direction, not two. We had seen at Gokar the horrific results of living in an unsound house on top of a major fault. In Lhagang, no large earthquakes had occurred within living memory, and people didn't realize the danger. A prominent tulku attending a workshop on conservation was even heard to say "earthquakes don't happen here."[68] Lhagang houses *looked* solid to the casual observer, but, in reality, they were unstable and unsafe.

The other reason to train people in the building trades was

---

68  At this time, the 2008 Sichuan earthquake and the 2014 Kangding earthquake had not yet occurred.

that too many construction jobs were going to people from outside Lhagang. The jobs went to Tibetans from other parts of Kham and to lowland Chinese, who were quick learners and ruthless competitors. Lhagang people were drokpa; historically, they lived in tents, and what did tent-dwellers know of houses? Thanks to government subsidies, hundreds of new homes were being built for them, but the money flowed out of Lhagang as fast as it arrived. If local people could do construction work, then the money would stay in the community.

I wanted our program to show people that they didn't need to pour concrete and lay Chinese-style tile roofs to have a comfortable home. Many rural people held the mistaken view that concrete was a sign of modern living and economic advancement. In reality, the new materials were not better than the old, especially if the concrete was of poor quality and not reinforced. An old-fashioned Tibetan home, built correctly, was warmer and more durable, too.

But where to offer this training program? USAID rules prohibited us from using grant money to build homes for individuals. We decided to run the training at Senggé Monastery, a Buddhist institution located one day's horseback ride from Lhagang, or about ninety minutes by car. Winrock wanted to promote horse treks to Senggé and other nearby places to create more tourism income. They felt our cultural heritage work should support a master strategy for *integrated* community development: that is, they wanted to simultaneously open several gates of the mandala to achieve synergy so that the whole would be greater than the sum of the parts. That made sense, so I went along with the choice of Senggé as a project site.[69] Lacking any authentically old temples in the township, Senggé was as good as any. Or so I thought.

---

69  Lhagang Gonpa did not receive serious consideration because the monks there were famously difficult to work with.

Senggé Gonpa was tucked in the crenelated western foothills of the immense Minyak Rabgang range that walled off the Tibetan plateau from the Sichuan basin. The monastery was arrayed on a steep slope at about 3,700 meters (12,000 feet) above sea level: too high for farming and too rocky for pasture, but with breathtaking views of the valley below and forests opposite. Above the monastery, footpaths led over a ridge and down to Dorakarmo, a grasslands area inhabited by drokpa.

In front of Senggé, the valley dropped steeply down until it emptied into a larger valley cradling the highway that connected Lhagang with Dartsendo. At the juncture was a farming village called Pasu. Although no Senggé monks hailed from Pasu, it was the starting point of the only motorable road leading to the monastery. It was little more than a rough dirt track, frequently impassable. Many times, I and other KhamAid staff would have to alight at Pasu and climb to Senggé on foot. Later, Pasu Village would have its own role to play as the Senggé saga unfolded.

Senggé's complex of stone buildings was scattered over a south-facing slope. The monastery had one large chanting hall or *dukhang*, where the monks assembled for ceremonies. The Dukhang had been rebuilt from the ground up and looked new, although the workmanship was only average. There was another temple, small and dilapidated, an old cookhouse, and thirty-seven smaller dwellings that belonged to individual monks.

Senggé Monastery belonged to the Nyingma school. The monks told us it had 840 years of history, and they proudly recited the names of famous sages who'd visited at various times. They also claimed it had a hundred monks on its rolls, but we never saw more than a dozen. I surmised that the other monks lived with their families most of the time, and came to the monastery only for special events.

## Changes on the Grasslands

All of Senggé's monks came from the Dorakarmo grasslands and reflected attitudes common to drokpa: conservative and distrustful of outsiders. Dorakarmo people would also comprise most of our trainees. Consequently, the mindset of Dorakarmo's people and the attitude of its leaders were of central importance to our project, a fact that I did not initially understand but would come to appreciate later.

The government at that time was spending vast sums to coax Dorakarmo and other herders into permanent housing. Typically, herders built the houses first; then, if approved, they received a subsidy of 2,000 to 5,000 yuan.[70] The subsidies were transforming Dorakarmo, and new houses were popping up like mushrooms on winter pasture sites. Although widely spaced and built without any central planning, the houses formed the nucleus of a new settlement that was bound to grow.

The people of Dorakarmo were willing to accept the government's free money, but the early homes were little more than huts of piled stones—just barely enough to collect the subsidy. The houses in town were better, but still, about a quarter of the owners did not bother to live in them, using them for storage only, or leaving them vacant. They kept their tents and herds and took them to high pastures during the summer and autumn months, just as they always had. The weakest family members, children and the elderly, were most likely to stay in the houses. Strong, healthy adults lived indoors only during winter, and some not at all.

A major problem in Dorakarmo was that pasture was deteriorating, and there was less good quality grass for livestock. Consequently, yaks were smaller, and fewer calves were surviving. Residents had various opin-

---

70  My sources differ on the exact amount.

ions on why this was happening: greater extremes of heat and cold, more frequent heavy rains and snow disasters, and damage from the mining of gold and tungsten that had taken place from 1981 to 1999. Residents also sometimes dug up sod to use for building walls and animal shelters.

Fencing of pasture was a controversial topic, with the more affluent nomads generally in favor of it, and poorer nomads opposed due to the constraints that fences imposed on movement. Winter pastures, which were clearly demarcated and considered private property, were more likely to be fenced, ensuring adequate fodder during the colder months. Money for fencing came from both government sources and the herders themselves.

The conservative culture of Dorakarmo limited economic opportunities. As devout Buddhists, people disliked killing livestock, and some took vows to refrain from slaughtering animals or selling them for slaughter for a period of years. The Lhagang area was famous for its tasty yogurt, but Dorakarmo people did not sell their yogurt because they lacked an organized system of collection and transport. Also, Dorakarmo folk considered that selling things on the street was low class, and they looked down on street vendors.

When a herdsman got a hold of some disposable income, usually by collecting caterpillar fungus, his first purchase was likely to be a motorcycle, which was rapidly replacing the horse for everyday transportation. Alternatively, a family might go on pilgrimage, invest in women's jewelry, or buy a fancy fur-trimmed chuba, which conferred prestige.[71] Nowadays, they were also building houses and fencing off

---

71  Later, the Dalai Lama spoke out against wearing pelts, at which point the Chinese authorities took the contrarian stand that wearing fur-trimmed robes signified loyalty to the state. The events described here occurred before furs became politicized.

plots to grow winter fodder. They rarely thought of investing cash in a business to create additional wealth. Herding was the only business they knew, yet an epidemic or snow disaster could wipe out their herds and leave families hungry.

The traditional economy of Dorakarmo was about the ceaseless quest to nurture ever-larger herds and to keep them healthy. Many yaks meant greater security, but the grasslands could support only so many animals. On top of this were the government's efforts to regulate rangeland usage and push herders toward a market-based approach to managing their livestock. This ran directly counter to herders' Buddhist beliefs and their traditional strategy for survival.

For Senggé Monastery, the subsistence herding economy meant plenty of butter offerings but not many cash donations that might have been used to build, decorate, and maintain their temples. The monastery had very few trappings of wealth, such as fancy statues, elaborate wall paintings, and gold leaf. Yet people told us that Senggé had been wealthy once. No doubt much was stolen or destroyed during the decades of turmoil that began with Communist rule.

Senggé's abbot, Khenpo Yonden, was a stocky, dour, square-headed Tibetan, a man of few words. Neither warm nor fuzzy, he was a million miles away from the Western fantasy of the wisdom-spouting, Yoda-like sage. I would soon come to appreciate that Khenpo Yonden was a shrewd operator. Although he didn't exactly drip with gratitude, he was more than willing to work with KhamAid on our construction skills training program, which had great potential to benefit his people.

The program had two parts. First, we would make some alterations in the roof of the main chanting hall to stop water from leaking in. Second, we would put up a new building from scratch to teach workers techniques for durable and quake-resistant construction.

But what should we build? During a spring planning trip, we put the question to Senggé's leaders. At first, they said they wanted a dormitory on the site of some old ruins, but a couple of days later, they changed their minds and asked for a building that would be both dormitory and kitchen.

I had always been delighted by monastery kitchens: the bathtub-sized cauldrons sitting atop mammoth stoves, the outsize ladles, and the stonking quantities of butter. Building a kitchen would be a fun project.

However, a few weeks later, they had changed their minds again. They still wanted a kitchen-dormitory, but they had moved it to a different site and made it bigger. Wu emailed a scan of their rough sketch to me. I responded that it was too big and that we couldn't afford it. After much more discussion and coaxing, Khenpo Yonden reluctantly agreed that we would add onto the existing kitchen to enlarge it.

To find teachers, we went to Ta'u County, where the houses were exceptionally strong, and asked friends there to recommend masters of stone masonry and carpentry. For a roofer, we looked to Chatreng County, where the people were experts in earthen construction. The technical aspects of the program would be overseen by a Tibetan-American named Tenzing Chadotsang, a fresh graduate of Columbia University's program in historic preservation. We hired a local college student named Norbu to be KhamAid's site manager.

## Preparations

As the year of the female Wood-Bird (2005) opened, we laid careful plans for the construction skills training at Senggé Monastery, doing everything by the book. We contacted the Kandze Prefecture Cultural Relics Bureau, which told us that Senggé was not listed as a historic monument, so we did not need any special permissions. (They advised us, however, that if we found any artifacts, we would have to stop digging, protect the site, and inform the government.) We sourced materials, paying cutting fees to have trees felled in a nearby forest, and arranged to have the timber hauled to Senggé in time for it to cure.

Mr. Wu and our new program assistant, Norbu, contacted the people in Dorakarmo to tell them that we would be inviting their people to get trained through our program, reassuring them that people would receive wages for the hard work they would do while they were in training. The Dorakarmo leader replied that there were four sub-villages within Dorakarmo, so he wanted us to select equal numbers of people from each to avoid conflict.

These words were a shot across the bow that we would have to take the utmost care with local politics. If the sub-villages of Dorakarmo started feuding, we'd be caught in the middle, and the program could collapse. We learned that a festival would be taking place in mid-July, attended by the four chiefs, representatives from each family, and many leading monks. At that time, we could explain the program and invite the chiefs to recommend candidates.

In meetings with the monastery's leaders, Mr. Wu repeatedly emphasized that our funds were limited and that we couldn't get the project done without help from the monks to control our costs. Khenpo Yonden agreed to find trainees for the program at a rate of twenty yuan per day for men and fifteen yuan per day for women, a bit below the prevailing wage at that time. However, he pointed out that digging the foundation was arduous work and did not involve much training. He said that, during the excavation phase, we should pay a higher wage of twenty-five yuan per day. We agreed to this.

Then Khenpo Yonden told us that adding on to their existing kitchen simply wouldn't do. They wanted us to demolish it so that it could be made bigger. That would require extensive site work and a lot more money. We took another look at our budget and stretched it to the limit so we could give them what they wanted. In the end, there was a meeting of the minds on all major points. To help with the project costs, the khenpo promised he would ask the local people to provide sixteen free worker-days as an offering to the monastery, that he would arrange for six earth-moving baskets, four hoes, and two spikes to be provided. The monastery would also supply firewood to the work crew, and the monks would help us do whatever shopping we might need for the project.

Mr. Wu knew that it would be difficult for outsiders to choose the trainees from Dorakarmo's population of roughly a thousand people, so he asked each sub-village leader to recommend five people to the program. Because Pasu Village was so close to Senggé, we also invited them to send people, too.

And so the stage was set, ready for the action to start.

## Shaolin Monks and a Rumble in Lhagang

Another of KhamAid's assigned tasks on the USAID grant was the *preservation of traditional fine arts and practices*. To fulfill this objective, we were planning to launch a handicraft project. Frankly, if we wanted to find artists, Lhagang was perhaps not the best place to look. The people there were either fully nomadic, or had only recently transitioned to a sedentary lifestyle, so they had limited materials and tools available to them and little opportunity to set up and develop workshops. Also, they had no exposure to outside ideas that might have inspired their creativity.

The culture, too, did not bend toward the artistic, for Lhagang society had more than a passing resemblance to America's nineteenth-

century Wild West. Despite the aversion of Lhagang people to taking life, fights were routine.[72] Anthropologist Gillian Tan, who completed a long-term ethnographic study of the people of Dorakarmo,
writes, "argument[s] over caterpillar fungus boundaries, accusations
of cheating in a sales transaction, even a misinterpreted gaze from
another young man could result in a swift jab, demonstrating that the
long knives carried on the left hips of Khampa men were not merely
ornamental."[73]

Sometimes, these fights set off extended and deadly feuds, as the
avenging of one killing led to another in an unending cycle of blood-
letting. The police dared not interfere, and feuding parties were resis-
tant even to the influence of tulkus.

In 1991, when I had first visited the town, Lhagang seemed like a
time-warp to the pre-industrial past. People got around on horseback.
The town had only a handful of streets, all unpaved but richly ornamented with yak- and horse-dung. Now, fourteen years later, Lhagang
was modernizing. Streets and sidewalks were paved, and there were
more of them. One could easily make a long-distance telephone call,
and there was excellent mobile coverage. A fleet of unlicensed "black"
taxis waited in the town square to take you almost anywhere. Many
drokpa had traded in their horses for motorbikes. Yaks and dung,
however, remained plentiful.

On the edge of town, the ornate and impressive Lhagang
Monastery sat beside a plain. In the distance was a dazzling view of

---

72  In 2006, I asked a young male in another part of Dartsendo County if knife
    fights were very common. He said, "It's not really a problem." Then I asked if
    many people got killed in fights, and he replied, "Oh, yes, all the time!"

73  Gillian G. Tan, *In the Circle of White Stones: Moving through the Seasons with
    Nomads of Eastern Tibet,* University of Washington Press, 2017, p. 75.

Mount Zhara Lhatse, a mammoth wedge of earth lifted like an offering to the abode of gods and snow. Between the monastery and the mountain was a good-sized pasture that was home to a colossal stupa built by a local tulku. Virtually all buildings in Lhagang had traditional stone walls, trapezoidal window treatments, and flat roofs, so there was no mistaking it for anything but a Tibetan town. At 3,900 meters above sea level, the weather was Tibetan, too. Visitors were assailed by altitude sickness, and residents weathered a moody succession of rain, snow, hail, and swirling dust.

Despite my years of bumbling about rural Tibet, I'd never seen any saleable objects lying around, ready to be plunked onto store shelves and snapped up by shoppers.[74] The things Tibetans manufactured fell into two broad categories: (1) heavily ornamented ritual objects used in Buddhist practice; and (2) everyday goods such as chubas and tsampa bags that Tibetans needed but weren't useful elsewhere.

We wanted something new: objects that appealed to people who weren't Tibetan and probably weren't even Buddhist. To help us identify marketable crafts, I recruited five freshly minted business school graduates from the Kellogg School of Management at Northwestern University.[75] They were highly trained business people, very practical and results-oriented. Perhaps they could solve the riddle.

Even before they arrived in Sichuan, the five MBAs were busy. They looked around Beijing, Shanghai, Lhasa, Chengdu, and Dartsendo to identify potential products, and learn about customer

74 Dropenling Handicraft Development Center, located in Lhasa and Gyeltang, was bankrolled by foreign aid. With few exceptions, their wares were specially developed for the tourist market.

75 The five came to KhamAid through the auspices of the Kellogg Corps, a volunteer program. They paid for all of their own travel, lodging, and food.

demand, sourcing, and prices. They researched startup costs and interviewed leading handicraft producers to explore alternative business structures. They talked to NGO personnel to assess what resources and capabilities might exist at our project site.

After the usual long road journey from Chengdu, the five Kellogg volunteers, plus translators and KhamAid staff, reached Lhagang. We checked into a small hotel near Lhagang Monastery, a far cry from the five-star luxury these MBAs would enjoy when they returned to their illustrious careers back in America. "Our room, next to the bathroom, stank of shit," blogged volunteer Cherie Yu. "There was only one shower for the hotel, which trickled and ran hot and cold on me. I was a dirty girl, to be sure."

That evening, I was standing on the sidewalk with the handicraft team considering where to eat dinner when we heard a giant commotion coming up Lhagang's main street. It sounded like a high school marching band stuffed through a meat grinder, amplified on a very bad sound system. All heads turned, straining for a glimpse of the source.

Then came a most peculiar and unexpected sight: about a hundred Han men and boys wearing red, yellow, and blue silk pajamas, marching up the highway in neat columns. Aged ten to thirty, many of them wore colored capes, which made them look heroic or preposterous depending on your point of view. The strangers looked like an army of invading plastic toys against the rain-soaked Lhagang streets and local people in their dark chubas. An ancient truck crawled along with them, carrying a youth who heralded their arrival through a staticky megaphone.

What was going on? Was the People's Liberation Army re-invading Tibet?

A passing marcher handed me a playbill mimeographed on rice paper. It told me that the invaders were not soldiers but monks— Shaolin monks from the famous kung fu school at Shaolin Monastery in faraway Henan Province.

The Shaolin Monastery, like every other house of worship in China, had been beaten down during the Cultural Revolution, but later it had bounced back and become a national shrine to China's enduring myth of the heroic warrior-priest. The monastery had pushed Buddhism into the background and rebranded itself as a vessel for sustaining China's venerated tradition of Shaolin Kung Fu. It received hordes of visitors and regularly sent troupes overseas to entertain audiences with their acrobatic stunts.

Like a traveling circus, Shaolin monks roamed through China as itinerant performers. I had never heard of any visiting Kham. The playbill said that the monks would be performing that same evening, giving the place and time.

Wow! I was so-o-o excited! A martial arts performance! *Yeah!*

After dinner, the KhamAid team found its way to the big black Shaolin tent pitched in an alley off Lhagang's main drag. We bought tickets. I went inside with four others, while the rest lingered outside, seeking a toilet to use before the show's start.

Inside the tent, rows of wooden planks striped the damp ground. These were the spectator seats, and they were unreserved. At one end of the tent stood a raised stage. The place was full of excited townspeople, mostly women and children, packed shoulder to shoulder. Outside, a loudspeaker blared, trying to entice passersby to buy tickets. Inside, monks bustled about the stage in a preparatory sort of way.

We had been sitting for a while, when suddenly, from outside the tent, there came a great noise. It was a chorus of Khampa whoops, a sound I knew well from the horse races at summer festivals in Kham. Everyone in the tent stood up. Murmurs moved in a spiral fashion around the tent, at last reaching us clueless foreigners. Evidently, a fight was going on outside.

What was happening, unbeknown to me and others in the tent, was that the Lhagang Township Chief was at the gate asking to be admitted free of charge. Not your typical polished cadre school graduate, the chief looked and dressed pretty much like every other Lhagang male. He was explaining to the gate-monk that he should be admitted for free because he had very generously excused them from "registering" (paying a fee) to perform in Lhagang.

The Shaolin monk said, "We don't register."

The chief said something like, "In my town, you do."

The monk offered that they would register tomorrow. Maybe.

The chief pressed a finger to the monk's forehead in a sort of threatening benediction. That's when the fight started. The monk took a swipe at the chief; several Shaolin monks grabbed the chief to pull him out of the queue, back toward the street.

I didn't know any of this, but I was very curious. Nevertheless, it seemed both inadvisable for reasons of safety and impossible for reasons of crowds to push my way out of the tent to take a look. Anyway, we had good seats and didn't want to lose them. The whoops quickly died away. Everyone sat down.

Outside, meanwhile, a tussle was going on as Shaolin monks struggled to oust the angry chief. Outnumbered and (apparently) unarmed, he couldn't resist them, but on his way toward the exit, he reached out and smacked the monks' loudspeaker. The blaring noise suddenly stopped.

Khampas began whooping again, daring the Shaolin monks to

retaliate. Inside the tent, people again rose from their seats. We outsiders had no idea what was up, but we rose with them. Then the whoops died away. We sat back down.

Outside, the wrath of the Lhagang townspeople had ebbed, but not for long. A few of them started heaving rocks at the tent, a declaration of all-out war. Shaolin monks began buzzing out like angry hornets. "Beat him to death!" they shouted in Chinese as they ran into the street.

We heard the whoops outside rise again to a crescendo. Everyone stood up again. We didn't notice the rocks hitting the tent and had no idea what was happening. I was getting annoyed. Where was the show? Was this whooping thing going to go on all night?

Then some Lhagang women came into the tent and began pulling people out the door. The word was quickly passed around in Tibetan that, under a barrage of rocks, the tent might come down at any moment. People started heading for the exits.

But we foreigners couldn't understand what they were saying. We stood frozen like deer in the headlights, utterly befuddled.

A local girl came into the tent. "Get out! Get out!" she shouted in Chinese. She started pulling us to the stage door in the front. Several of us Chinese-speakers were trying to frame inquiries along the lines of "What the heck. . .?" but the girl didn't want to hear it. She pushed and pulled and prodded us until we were standing in the alley outside.

Now under the night sky, we were in a cul-de-sac with no exit. The tent blocked the way we had come. "Hide!" said the girl.

Was this life or was it cinema? There was nowhere to hide. The yard where we stood was very dark and hemmed in by stone fortifications. The girl was both urgent and protective. She drove us backward until we were, literally, against the wall.

Pressed into a corner, we huddled like yaks awaiting slaughter. The tent was empty, but over the top floated an eerie, otherworldly roar. It seemed to emanate from Lhagang's main street. We shifted around nervously, ears perked skyward, trying to decide if the sound was getting louder. Where was this danger that the girl was talking about? Was it coming our way?

"Climb up!" said the girl, pointing to the wall behind us.

"You're kidding," we said.

Outside, on Lhagang's main street, rocks were flying. Cherie Yu relates, "A youngish monk, maybe twenty or thirty, came rushing back with a red, bleeding patch on his forehead. As we made our way out from the entrance area, [another volunteer] and I were both hit with rocks. One hit me squarely in the legs. Chaos was breaking out."

At first, the Shaolin monks had the upper hand. They surrounded the Lhagang Township Chief and pummeled him about his face and neck. But the Khampas weren't going to sit back and take this for long. A pitched battle was about to commence. Cherie Yu relates: "Suddenly, we saw [KhamAid staff member] Norbu. 'Get out of here,' he said. We took off down the street toward the hotel."

Meanwhile, back in the maze of stone walls, my companions and I had no clue what was happening. The girl told us to climb. Protests were to no avail, so climb we did, up to the top of the crumbly pile of stones; then, we dropped down into a narrow chasm on the far side.

Blindly, I put my hands out in front of me and touched another stone wall a short distance away. We could only go sideways. Tremulously, I put one foot beside the other, feeling my way in the dark. Glurg-glurg sounds came from below. Something bumped my shin: a board slung over the murk.

"I think," said someone, "that this is a toilet."

Indeed.

Now feeling even more like yaks bound for slaughter, we staggered sideways, then up, then forward. "Keep going" implored the girl. We stepped into a small shed, a dead end. Someone closed and bolted a door behind us. It was pitch dark. Again, we were trapped.

What was going on? It felt like we had fallen into a black hole.

Suddenly a portal opened. The darkness gave way to a faint glimmering, leading us to a yard beyond. Stars shone overhead, but there was little other light. We stumbled forward. Through the yard, then a left turn, and we were faced with the glad sight of an opening to the street. It was still Lhagang. People milled around aimlessly: men, women, shopkeepers, and tourists. No Shaolin monks in sight.

Eventually, we found the rest of our team. Injuries were attended to. Boots were cleaned. Then we repaired to a local watering hole and ordered beers all around.

The fight was over, and the Shaolin monks had scuttled like rats into the night. But where could they have gone? The next town was 28 kilometers (17 miles) away. We did hear that some Shaolin monks—the toughest ones, no doubt—stayed behind to protect their tent.

By morning, both the monks and their tent had vanished.

But our misadventures in Lhagang had only just begun.

## Handicrap

The morning after the Shaolin drama, the Kellogg volunteers got busy gathering market data to inform our handicraft project. From interviews and direct counts, they would learn the following:

- Number of tourist arrivals during July: about 5,000
- Tourist origin: 86% domestic Chinese, 14% international
- Duration of the average tourist visit: less than two hours

- Shops run by Han Chinese: 30
- Shops run by Tibetans: 3

The numbers told the story: Tibetans in Lhagang faced stiff competition, and furthermore had only a brief window of time in which to make a sale. But what goods would they pitch? Virtually everything sold in the souvenir shops was what the Kellogg team derisively termed "handicrap"—cheap, inauthentic items that reflected someone's Shangri-La fantasy of Tibet but were mass-produced in factories elsewhere. Display cases offered up costume jewelry, hippie accessories like bags and shawls, stuffed toy yaks, fake antiques, kitschy wall hangings, and mass-printed pictures of Buddhist deities.

This junk was what kept thirty Han businesses afloat, but it was extraterrestrial to Tibet. And even if Tibetans wanted to get into handicrap, it was not easy for them to source the goods, which came from far away.

We believed that real Tibetan-made crafts would be a refreshing and authentic alternative to the handicrap that choked Lhagang shops. Based on their research, the Kellogg team totted up the pros and cons of twelve basic categories of goods: woven products, sewn products, metalworking, jewelry, furniture, carpets, painting, leather goods, stone carving, paper products, pottery, and wood carving. Most of these were not made in Lhagang currently, so people would need training.

On the outskirts of Lhagang was a "New Nomad Village" of forty herder families who had settled there in 2003-2004 under the township government's policy of "planning and construction of small cities and towns." The government built the houses, and each household received a subsidy of 3,000 to 5,000 yuan to move in.

Word was that the newly settled herders were struggling both socially and economically, for the existing Lhagang residents looked down on them and resented the competition for jobs. We thought that they might be interested in learning handicraft skills, so I took some team members, and we walked over.

We knocked on doors until we had spoken to half a dozen residents. One was Ongmo, age thirty-eight. Ongmo's husband made money hauling goods on his *tuolaji* tractor; the couple also bought and sold floor coverings and furniture. Business was good because many newly settled herders were furnishing their homes. For a while, people had gobs of cash from the government subsidies and the sale of excess livestock, but after that was spent, many of Ongmo's neighbors could only eke out a precarious living gathering caterpillar fungus and doing unskilled construction work at fifteen to twenty yuan per day.

"For me, the situation is not too bad," she told us. "I can bear to live like this. But many people around here, they have no livestock, they have no job, and they have no skills. They would be very willing to learn something practical."

KhamAid was looking to teach them something practical, but what? Lots of people wanted to learn decorative painting, a high-status profession on account of its connection to Buddhism. Fewer people wanted to learn carpentry: it was hard work, took years to master, and suffered from stiff competition from migrants from outside.

Yet in Ongmo and a few others, we saw glimmers of entrepreneurial spirit. We just needed to fan the flame.

## A Crafty Abbot

Just ten kilometers (6.7 miles) away from Lhagang as the crow flies, logs were starting to arrive at Senggé Monastery. Even with the bigger kitchen we had agreed to, there were too many logs. Then we learned that the abbot, Khenpo Yonden, wasn't happy with our agreement. He thought the building would be too small, so he had made a new drawing of a larger building, told the excavators to dig a bigger hole, and ordered more logs. I was very annoyed, but I didn't want to make a stink now and derail everything. I figured that later we'd find a few spare dollars somewhere, or skimp on the interior finishing, or both.

On launch day, we gathered in the yard in front of Senggé's main chanting hall. Rain had been falling, but now the sun glimmered on the wet grass, promising a splendid summer day. The trainers were all there: one each in carpentry, masonry, and stone-cutting, and two in clay work. We had a group of students from Dorakarmo and Pasu, and a full complement of KhamAid staff, including our Tibetan-American consultant Tenzing Chadotsang and two foreign volunteers.

A group of Winrock observers, among them an executive from their Arkansas headquarters, arrived just in time, having hiked up the valley after their car got stuck in the mud. I was anxious that everything go smoothly, so the Winrock people would be pleased and want us as a partner on future grants.

When everyone had assembled, a monk brought a plank for us honorable experts to sit on to keep our derrières dry. The trainees, about twenty of them, sat on the grass in a semicircle around us.

Behind us was a big, fresh hole in the ground waiting for the new foundation.

I had asked KhamAid's occasional consultant, Doka, to act as master of ceremonies at this kickoff. He was a forceful middle-aged man from Kandze County who spoke Tibetan well and understood the macho Khampa culture. Standing before the trainees, he introduced everyone on the KhamAid team. He explained what our program was about, saying, "If we just wanted to build a building, we could hire some Han workers, pay the money, and get it done. But that's not our purpose. We're here to teach you new skills. We want to show you how to make buildings that are stronger, safe against rainstorms and earthquakes, and that are still Tibetan."

Doka explained how an earthquake in 1973 had killed hundreds of people in Ta'u County. Afterward, Ta'u people learned a lesson and became experts in quake-resistant construction, which was why our carpentry and masonry teachers were from that area. He explained that the Chatreng teachers had special techniques for making roofs out of *arga*, which is hardened clay. We had also invited a Han man from Dartsendo to teach stone-cutting skills, which had vanished among the indigenous population of Lhagang.

Then Doka frowned, paused for dramatic effect, and threw down the gauntlet. "If any of you is not willing to work *and* learn," he said slowly, locking eyeballs with each of them in turn, "you should leave right now."

Long silence. The trainees, nomads from Dorakarmo village and farmers from Pasu, stared back at us. Nobody moved.

It was a very fine moment, and the Winrock people were duly impressed. These clever KhamAid people clearly had it all under control.

Our Tibetan-American architect, Tenzing Chadotsang, didn't speak Doka's dialect, but he nevertheless got the gist of the speech. He nudged me and said, "He forgot to say that one of our purposes is to protect the monastery." I touched Doka's arm and reminded him to mention this very key point. He quickly explained to the trainees how we would also retrofit the monastery's roof to make it stronger and more rain-resistant.

With that addendum, the speeches were over. Students and

teachers got up and began forming groups. The Winrock folks left for the long trek down the valley to their waiting car.

Moments after they were gone, our luck turned south.

## Conflict

The work was just getting underway when I noticed a heated discussion between two of the Dorakarmo trainees and KhamAid's man, Doka. The latter called Mr. Wu, Norbu, and me over for a quick conference in the shade of the Dukhang portico.

"The trainees want thirty yuan a day," Doka said, speaking in Chinese, which most of the trainees did not understand.

"I thought we agreed to twenty."

"They said that the people who dug the hole got twenty-five, and they were just unskilled laborers, so the carpenters and masons, who are skilled workers, should get thirty."

The so-called carpenters and masons had only rudimentary skills judging by the stone hovels in Dorakarmo, but now was not a good time to bring this up.

"Who's going to pay the difference?" I asked. "Will the monastery pay?"

"Kham Aid Foundation," said Doka. His voice was calm, but I could see he was exasperated.

"No way. That's not in the budget. And anyway, the Pasu people agreed to twenty-five yuan a day. We can't pay different wages to different people for the same work."

"The Pasu people have gone home."

I looked around and saw that he was right: there was no one from Pasu in sight; they had all picked up and left.

"Why'd they go home? What happened?"

"The Dorakarmo guys threatened to beat them up," said Norbu.

"They want the jobs for themselves," Doka explained.

We called over Khenpo Yonden and reminded him of his promise to find laborers at low rates. The khenpo didn't deny it, but he argued that KhamAid had already raised the wages for the excavation, and if we reduced the wages now, he couldn't find any workers for the program.

"He wants the Dorakarmo people to make more money," Mr. Wu said to me in English.

"I will arrange the very best workers," Khenpo Yonden said earnestly. "They will do double the work of the others."

We knew that "the very best workers" would likely be the khenpo's relatives and friends, but there was no arguing that point. We had to pay the higher wage or risk total failure. Checkmate.

I wondered where the money would come from, but that was a problem I would solve later. We had a program to run.

The carpentry and masonry instructors began explaining to their students the first steps of preparing materials for construction. The clay experts from Chatreng headed out looking for suitable clay with which to remake the temple roof. Before long, our architecture expert, Tenzing Chadotsang, came to me and pointed at a spot about a quarter-mile away. "They found some clay up there. The monks said it's no good, but they don't know the technique."

Soon, the stonemason from Ta'u was showing his trainees how to dry-lay rocks in the foundation trenches. The stone-cutter was teaching his students how to identify various grades of steel and how tools are tempered and carbonized. The carpenter and his students got to work stripping bark from the logs that would form the kitchen's columns and beams.

While all this was going on, one volunteer, a photographer from Singapore, snapped away with his camera. Another volunteer, an

American, took notes on the techniques which would later be compiled into a manual.

On Day Two, we added fifteen women to our crew. Under the tutelage of the Chatreng clay experts, they began removing bad clay from the temple roof and carrying good clay over from the digging site. They would soon prepare it, layer it onto the roof and harden it with a thorough trampling. "With *arga*, every time it snows," one of the teachers explained, "you must sweep the snow off the roof right away before it melts. If you do that, the roof will last five years."

Five years was better than the clay roofs normally found in the Lhagang area, which had to be patched with additional clay throughout the monsoon season. After a few seasons of patching, the roofs became overloaded, risking collapse. The wise homeowner removed his roof every few years and relaid it from scratch. Yet inevitably, some water would leak through and rot the timbers beneath, hastening the day when the house would cave in. While many traditional Tibetan stone houses looked old, few lasted more than a couple of decades because it was so hard to keep their roofs watertight.

Because of the rain problem, Chinese-style tile roofs had lately become popular in Kham, and Han crews were getting rich going from village to village, slapping new roofs on Tibetan houses.[76] I hoped to halt that trend.

By now, everyone in the project was working well together, as if our earlier disagreements had never happened. "The first step is to create good cooperation by being kind to each other," said the sixty-six-year-old masonry instructor, who was like a father to us all. "We must all share our ideas like we are one family."

---

76 Many people find tile roofs aesthetically unsuitable for Tibetan buildings. Some towns, including Lhagang and Sadé, have banned them.

In time, the Dorakarmo nomads would even allow Pasu people to return and work with them side by side. Communication was not easy; our translator, who was versed in multiple Tibetan dialects as well as English and Chinese, was in great demand.

The architect Tenzing Chadotsang spent the first days on top of the Dukhang figuring out why the roof was leaking. Not only was the clay of poor quality, but the roof did not drain properly toward the exit holes in the parapets, allowing water to pool. The same area also collected prodigious amounts of runoff from the upper roof, far more than the existing gutter could handle. Whenever it rained, the Dukhang roof became a pond, and water seeped down into the building below.

To remedy the problem, Tenzing Chadotsang designed a new gutter that was larger and deeper. In hindsight, it was an obvious fix, but somehow the monks had not thought of it. A smithy in Rangaka hammered together the new gutters from sheet metal. Once installed, they worked like a charm, sending rivers of monsoon rain to a quick exit.

To feed our elite team of experts, our site manager Norbu hired a cook. She turned out to be a delicate young woman in a pink sunhat, slender as a reed, with waist-length hair. We Americans marveled at her ability to hike up and down the mountain in towering platform shoes. She was immaculate, too, without even a speck of dirt on her— no small achievement in the middle of mud season. Her name was Kelsang Chutso. By coincidence, I happened to know her husband Ngawang, the owner of a tea house in Rangaka.

A month before, Ngawang had told me he was seeking a loan to expand his cafe. KhamAid didn't have a loan program, so I advised him to try other aid organizations that offered seed money.

Kelsang Chutso's cooking was excellent, and morale soared. She also caught the eye of the photographer, whose name was Sai Man

Lim. Lim haled from Singapore but lived in Beijing, one of the hordes of free-spirited young expatriates freelancing at one thing or another. He was a short, skinny guy with an acne-scarred complexion, but that didn't stop him from flirting with the cook, nor did the revelation that she was a married woman.

At the site of the future kitchen, lessons were proceeding apace. The stone-cutter was showing his four students how to split a boulder and dress the two halves into blocks. Meanwhile, the masonry students filled up the trenches with large, carefully placed stones, making the broadest, deepest foundation ever seen in Lhagang. Carpentry students began the painstaking process of preparing logs to be knitted into a web of columns and beams.

Two days later, more labor unrest reared up. "When we started digging the foundation," the group chief reported angrily, "we were told that the wage would be twenty-five yuan per person per day. But when the work was done, we only got twenty yuan per day."

This was alarming. Cheating Tibetan workers out of their promised wages was hardly what KhamAid stood for. Mr. Wu, who handled the expense reporting, dug out the receipt showing how much cash KhamAid's site manager, Norbu, had paid to the monastery for distribution to the workers. He handed the receipt to the monastery leader, Khenpo Yonden.

"This is my name," said the khenpo, staring at the handwritten note, "but I didn't sign this."

"I'll call Norbu," Wu said. "He will know who signed it."

Mr. Wu stumped off to a far corner of the monastery grounds where there was a weak mobile phone signal. Ten minutes later, he was back. "Norbu says that when he turned over the money, Khenpo Yonden wasn't at the monastery. Another monk signed for him."

"Who?"

"A chubby monk," Wu replied. "Norbu didn't remember the name."

The chubby monk turned out to be the monastery's discipline-master, but he denied that the signature was his. Later, Khenpo Yonden would say that he was almost certain that no Senggé monk had "such nice handwriting." He didn't pursue the matter, and without his assistance, we could do nothing more, so we let it drop.

Meanwhile, the workers believed that KhamAid's site manager Norbu had stolen their money. They also thought he was hiring too many of his pals for project jobs. Norbu's friends cut and hauled our timber; they cooked meals for the trainee canteen; they provided vehicles to carry our stone and fetch our foodstuffs from town. Not only did Norbu hire his friends and relatives, but some complained he was paying them above the going rate, and this at the same time as the Dorakarmo workers were shorted and we were insisting that we could not afford the big kitchen that Khenpo Yonden wanted.

Anger was simmering through the project, but I didn't realize it. I thought the missing money would be found, and it would be smooth sailing from here on out, so I headed back to Chengdu and caught a flight home, where I was scheduled to attend four days of intensive martial arts training.

## Hostage

After I left for California, our Singaporean photographer, Sai Man Lim, grew even bolder in his flirting with the cook. He talked about her constantly to other team members, saying how beautiful she was. People teased Sai Man about his great new "love." No one took it seriously.

A few days later, the foreign team's work was almost complete, and they began preparations to leave. The teachers would stay, and construction would continue under Norbu's oversight. To mark the foreigners' departure, Norbu organized a celebration restaurant dinner.

The cook's work was finished, too, so she also came to join the party. After dinner, instead of sending her home to her husband, Sai Man took her to his hotel room.

The next day the KhamAid team went up to Senggé to tie up a few loose ends before heading back to Dartsendo. When they descended to Pasu Village, however, they found a couple of vehicles blocking the road. From one emerged the cook's husband, Ngawang. He had several roughneck friends with him. It was an ambush.

There was an angry discussion, in which the husband, Ngawang, threatened to kill Sai Man. Mr. Wu and I both being absent, the Tibetan-American architect was in charge of the KhamAid team. He kept his cool and attempted to negotiate with Ngawang, going back and forth between vehicles. Ngawang's gang wanted to take Sai Man to their village, but the American side refused to surrender him. They insisted that everyone return to Rangaka. At last, Ngawang agreed.

Tensely, the KhamAid team rode in their minivan for an hour, while Ngawang's vehicles followed. By this time, it was late afternoon. They went to the hotel where the team had been staying, the scene of the crime. Mr. Wu met them there, having been summoned from Dartsendo by telephone. "I was never so glad," one team member later recalled, "to see a skinny short guy with glasses."

In the intervening hours, Mr. Wu had placed calls to California but failed to reach me, for I was not at home, and my mobile was switched off. He left a message with a volunteer in the office. He also called the Public Security Bureau, but they declined to get involved.

Ngawang was demanding 60,000 yuan, about $7,500, as ransom to let Sai Man off the hook for committing adultery with his wife.

True, Ngawang did not have Lim physically captive, but that did not matter. On the wild and sometimes lawless high plateau, there was scant protection for someone with a death threat against them. Mr. Wu was worried: unlike us foreigners who could escape to our faraway countries, he lived in Dartsendo with his wife and young daughter. They were the real hostages, for they had nowhere to hide. Refusing to pay was not an option.

Meanwhile, as all of this was going on, our site manager Norbu was silent. Was he caught in the middle? Or had he helped to set up the ambush?

Mr. Wu went to work in the best Chinese fashion to haggle the ransom to a lower amount. The final price: 42,000 yuan. None of the KhamAid team had that much cash on them, so the entire crew, extortionists and victims, got into vehicles the next morning and traveled over the mountains for three hours to Dartsendo.

There, discussions continued at KhamAid's office until Mr. Wu left for the bank to fetch the money. Sai Man was holed up in an inner room, downloading his project photos to a KhamAid computer. Outside the door, Ngawang and his gang stood watch.

"I did something really bad, and you will probably hear about it from Pam," Sai Man texted to a mutual friend in Beijing. "I'm so sorry to have let you down. Please do forgive me."

Meanwhile, in California, the office volunteer was trying desperately to reach me. He finally drove up the coast to the training site, found me, and told me what was going on. Immediately, I called Mr. Wu in Dartsendo. By this time, they had already struck a deal and signed a letter recording the settlement terms.

I asked Wu to put Ngawang on the phone. In my best Chinese, I apologized humbly and profusely to Ngawang for the trouble Sai Man had caused. Then I got Wu back on the phone and gave him directions on damage control. KhamAid would *not* take responsibility for our volunteer's careless, immoral act. I wanted Ngawang to know that Sai Man would pay the 42,000 yuan, not KhamAid, although KhamAid would lend him the money temporarily. If anyone asked, Wu was to say this was the photographer's business, not ours. I also told Wu to confiscate Lim's cameras as collateral until he paid back the loan.[77]

Ngawang got his money, but the story was far from over. Did anyone else in Lhagang know what had happened? Would other NGO workers now be targeted for extortion?

Because of this potential threat, I called Winrock's Chief of Party and told him everything. I asked him to inform his staff and let us know if they heard any harbingers of more trouble.

Later, I would revise KhamAid's policies and procedures regarding foreign volunteers. We started collecting next-of-kin data, and we revised our fieldworker's agreement to add a new rule prohibiting them from having affairs with married Chinese nationals.

Days went by, and no one else was kidnapped, nor did the incident turn up in the ever-spinning local rumor mill. Having gotten their money, Ngawang and his gang were lying low.

Work continued at the monastery, managed by Norbu. I considered firing him, but there was no proof he'd done anything wrong, and it seemed unwise to provoke more trouble on top of what had already happened. As planned, he left us at summer's end and returned to university.

The dust from the Sai Man Lim disaster had barely settled when another problem cropped up.

---

77 Mr. Lim eventually repaid a little more than half of the total. We kept the cameras and later sold them to an amateur photographer who was much bemused by their colorful history.

## More Conflict

The next big crisis was the monastery roof. When the team had been at Senggé, there had been torrential rains that made it impossible to put an *arga* roof on the temple as planned, because *arga* needed dry weather to harden. "It would be a waste of time and money," our architect reported. "I had a long conversation with the khenpo before I left, and we agreed to do a layer of clay over the work. This clay was a fine layer of black soil which they had identified." The two agreed that KhamAid would pay for two truckloads of the black soil to use for water-proofing and for laborers to layer it on top of the work already done. But did they really do it? We assumed so, but never followed up because it made no sense for the monastery to leave their temple unprotected.

A week later, Mr. Wu met with Khenpo Yonden. The khenpo told him that the roof of the main temple was leaking, and the floors below were wet. This was seriously bad news. Our partners at Winrock were alarmed, for a problem with KhamAid's project at Senggé would reflect badly on them and endanger the success of the entire joint program. Ethan Goldings, Winrock's Chief of Party, wrote a pointed email: "Did the monastery agree to the idea of experimenting with the new roof technique on the monastery central prayer hall?" he asked. "Was the work carried out according to your instructions?"

The Tibetan-American architect, Tenzing Chadotsang, and the Chatreng clay specialists had returned to their distant homes, so we had no onsite expert to evaluate and fix the problem. I was in California, which left Mr. Wu alone on the front line. I learned that the Senggé monks were now claiming that we had done the roof work against their wishes. This was a lie, but we had no paper trail to prove it because, during the time our team was working on the roof, for a full ten days, all the monastery leaders were unaccountably absent, and could not be reached by phone. We had intended to write up a contract, but it seemed pointless if there were no senior monks present to sign it. Nevertheless, everything had been discussed with Khenpo Yonden beforehand. The monks continued to unlock the temple for us every day. We had an oral agreement and there was no reason to doubt it.

The leaking roof was a crisis we had to deal with—and fast. I authorized Mr. Wu to buy tarps, order truckloads of clay, hire workers—do whatever it took to get those leaks plugged. He got it done within a few days. Things were quieter after that, but the respite didn't last long.

Before I had left the monastery, I worked out a budget for the remaining construction on the new kitchen. Considering work completed since then, we still had about US$3,000 remaining to spend. One unknown factor, however, was the number of worker days needed—a number I repeatedly underestimated because the workers weren't inclined to hurry and give up their high-paying jobs. Also, everything that the monastery had priced for us was costing much more than the monks had said. Timber, labor—everything had gone up.

"Did Kham Aid agree to complete the building?" Ethan Goldings asked me in an email.

"I certainly wanted to complete the building and told them so," I replied. "I thought we would be able to do it, right up until we started having trouble with the Dorakarmo workers. Then I realized we would have to stop when the outer structure was complete, and not do the interior finishing. But the problems accelerated, and with each succeeding wave of extortion, completion of the structure appeared to be an increasingly expensive and distant goal."

Our instructors were in the middle: their salaries came from KhamAid, but the building could go nowhere else but in Khenpo Yonden's trenches. Plus, they were living on the monastery grounds and couldn't ignore the monks' wishes. Khenpo Yonden knew that the project was critical to us foreigners, and he didn't seem to care about our goodwill.

Well, if Khenpo Yonden was playing hardball, I would have to do the same. The only leverage I had was to pull the plug on the project altogether, to walk away and leave the kitchen half-built.

I crafted a message for Mr. Wu to deliver to the Senggé leaders.

"The purpose of our program is training," it began. "Since we have already accomplished that, and the sponsor is satisfied, we don't need to finish the building. Please tell them I'm very sorry about this. Our original plan was to finish the building. However, so many unexpected circumstances have come up, now it is impossible."

This was a drastic and desperate move. As I waited for Khenpo Yonden's reply, I couldn't help but think back with nostalgia on the repairs we had done at Pewar Monastery ten years before. We had removed Pewar's roof, replaced its timber columns, and separated paintings from its damaged walls. Then we rebuilt everything and put the murals back. Sure, there had been challenges, but nothing like what we were experiencing now. At Pewar, everyone had been honest, from the highest monk to the lowest laborer. No funds were embezzled at Pewar, and we experienced no threats, extortion, or attempted kidnappings.

Mr. Wu was understandably reluctant to go to Senggé alone and break the bad news to Khenpo Yonden. So instead, he phoned Dorje Tashi Rinpoche, a local Lhagang tulku. Not only was Dorje Tashi Rinpoche a high religious authority, he had many relatives in Dorakarmo and at Senggé Monastery. I had known Dorje Tashi for five or six years, and we had a good relationship. Would he mediate this mess?

# Chess Moves

The incarnate lama Dorje Tashi Rinpoche agreed to see Mr. Wu and discuss our problem at Senggé, so Wu traveled to Lhagang, calling at the tulku's residence within the buildings of the Golden Stupa just outside the town. Built on a pasture below a stunning view of sacred Mount Zhara Lhatse, the Golden Stupa was an opulent complex of gold-roofed concrete buildings surrounded by one hundred and eight smaller stupas. Dorje Tashi Rinpoche was a keenly intelligent and charismatic man in his early forties. Besides his religious activities, he was bankrolling a charity school in Lhagang for needy children and was planning to build an even bigger school in Dorakarmo.

I can picture the lonely figure of Mr. Wu wearing a dark business suit (his usual attire), bowed and weary, picking his way through mud and yak-pies under stormy monsoon skies to the Golden Stupa's giant gate. Once admitted to Dorje Tashi Rinpoche's audience room, the first thing Wu did (after accepting a cup of tea) was to hand him a written statement that he had prepared, explaining everything that had happened.

Dorje Tashi Rinpoche read the statement and sighed. The tulku was a veteran of local politics. He understood very well what we were up against.

"How can we withdraw our people from the monastery?" Wu asked.

"KhamAid is the program sponsor, so you have a right to stop the program," he replied. "But…" The tulku trailed off for a moment, perhaps searching for a polite way to express his meaning. "You know that herdsmen sometimes have a bad temper."

His meaning was clear: if we stopped construction, there would be trouble.

"I understand your feelings," the tulku continued. "When I started my school, I, too, had a lot of trouble. Anyway, I would like to help you. I will call Khenpo Yonden and the chiefs of the four villages of Dorakarmo together and help you negotiate. Both parties should abide by their agreement. What did the agreement say?"

This was a sticky point. "We had an agreement, but it wasn't written down," Wu admitted. "We had a drawing that both sides agreed to, but then the monastery changed it and told the excavators to dig a bigger hole. Then the monastery leaders disappeared. We couldn't reach them on the phone, so we never had a chance to work out a written contract."

"In that case, I will do my best to ask the monastery to honor the oral agreement."

Wu explained that his boss (me) had decided to walk away from the construction. If we weren't going to walk away, then he needed to clear it with me first. He took his leave of Dorje Tashi and went to a Lhagang guest house. When he phoned me that evening, I told him okay, let's give mediation a try.

The next day Wu returned to the Golden Stupa. The tulku Dorje Tashi Rinpoche first presented him with a formal apology, on behalf of Dorakarmo's people, for the problems we were having. Then he said, "I have considered the situation carefully, and I see two ways forward. The first is, both sides live up to their original agreement. If Pam doesn't want to do that, then the second way is this: KhamAid can state its terms, and the monastery can take or leave them. In that case, I can do nothing more for you. You are on your own."

That the Rinpoche was ready to use his influence was a big step forward, but what was the original agreement? Our partners at Winrock offered to hold a conference, facilitated by their staff, and both sides would air their views about what we had agreed to. The tulku decided he would take a back seat and let Winrock play the role of peacemaker. I was frustrated at being seven thousand miles away in California, but our budget didn't permit an extra trip to Sichuan, so I could only wait anxiously for Mr. Wu's report.

The meeting lasted five hours. A few misunderstandings were cleared up: for one thing, we learned that a rumor was circulating that KhamAid was going to spend two million yuan (US$244,000) on the Senggé project. Two million yuan! Wu set the record straight for the people present, but I doubted that the rumor would disappear so easily in the world outside.

Meanwhile, over the weeks of sleepless nights and nonstop heartburn, I was coming to realize that, even though KhamAid had expertise in historic conservation, putting up a *new* building was a project best managed by locals. It was stupid, I realized, for KhamAid to wrangle with Dorakarmo herders over wages. We were way out of our league. We needed to stop micromanaging the project, and we needed the monastery to take responsibility for cost overruns so that they would be motivated to write an accurate budget and be conscientious managers.

In business terms, we needed to change from a cost-reimbursable contract to a firm-fixed-price one. But what would the price be? No matter how cleverly the monks managed the project, KhamAid couldn't pay enough to finish the kitchen because we were just too far in the hole. The project needed a bailout.

I contacted Winrock's Chief of Party Ethan Goldings to propose that they make a direct grant to Senggé Monastery to finish the project. Construction skills training, I said, would lead to income generation, which had always been Winrock's area of responsibility under our three-way partnership. If the monastery managed the project, incentives would align, and it would be much more efficient. The current KhamAid-led management model was just building the monks' capacity for manipulating foreign NGOs.

Our partners slowly came around. At first, Winrock wanted a contract with Senggé that would spell out every detail of the building, from its size and construction to the richness of the interior decoration, and would include blueprints. I advised that we should avoid the quagmire of agreeing on the exact design beforehand, and we should especially avoid trying to hold them to a detailed budget. After all, things change. Prices go up and down. The Senggé monks, including the khenpo, had not even completed primary school, and most were illiterate, even in Tibetan. "Can you visualize them fiddling with their calculators to try to decide if they've missed a budget target by 15%," I asked, "and writing a memo to you asking for permission to change?"

And the blueprint idea was a pipe dream. None of the local people on the project could read blueprints, not even our instructors.

After much discussion, Winrock agreed to work with Senggé on a bailout grant that would make up the shortfall. Quid pro quo: KhamAid would put in another US$5,200. It was much more than I wanted, but now it was looking like a bargain. I drafted a contract for Senggé specifying the terms of our payment. It didn't say much about the building but defined in detail what we expected the trainees to learn.

Construction resumed two weeks later, and when our contribution was spent, we handed the baton to Winrock, who wanted to administer their part of the project without our involvement. Mr. Wu and I were delighted to step aside.

## A Girl Meets Her Sponsor

While I was stuck in project management hell, Richard Harlan, the retired engineer who was sponsoring Metok Tso's studies, was on one of his long perambulations around Kham. From time to time, he would visit schools that his sponsored kids attended. Now he was headed out to Batang to meet Metok Tso.

Batang was in Sichuan's far west, next to the TAR border, but that was no obstacle to Richard. Although he didn't speak Chinese or Tibetan, he rarely failed to reach a place once he set his mind to it. Strangers were always helping him. "Age is venerated, so I am blessed by that," he wrote in a letter to friends. "I get the royal treatment everywhere I go."

From Dartsendo, Harlan rode a public bus and reached Batang in two days, descending from the barren highlands into a bustling town in the throes of Indian summer. "Standing in front of my hotel the following morning," he wrote, "I saw kids in school colors passing by, so I joined the stream to see where it would go."

The children led Harlan to a campus, but it turned out to be the wrong school. He was directed to a second campus. "As before, the kids were friendly, and I began asking for Metok Tso."

At first, Richard feared he must be mangling her name because no one seemed to understand what he was talking about. But then two teenage girls approached him. One of them said, "I'm Metok Tso, the girl you sponsor."

The other girl was her best friend, Rinchen Dolma. It was time for their first-period class, English. So they took Harlan with them.

All heads turned when Harlan appeared in the doorway. The kids had been jabbering away, socializing, but now all conversation stopped. Everyone stared at the tall, gray-haired American who had suddenly beamed into their world. There was a nanosecond of stunned silence, broken by a chirpy "Hello!" from one of the boys. A wave of nervous giggles swept the room, then more children began calling out, "Hello!" and "Okay!" and "What's your name?" to peals of laughter.

There was no teacher around. When the bell rang, Richard seized the moment: he stepped to the front of the class and began addressing the students, an extemporaneous speech about his travels around Kham.

In places like Batang, English teachers rarely, if ever, taught the English *language*. To them, English was an algorithm, a cipher that was coded and decoded using abstruse rules. They taught students to pass tests, not to communicate. I doubt that Metok Tso's classmates understood what their American visitor was saying. Anyway, they were probably too busy taking in his tall, big-nosed strangeness to pay attention to his words.

Metok Tso was different. She was intensely curious and loved challenges. For her, Richard Harlan was a gift straight from heaven who could help her realize the burning ambition that was secretly in her heart.

Richard Harlan's debut at the school made for a great entrée to Batang. He found the town to be "an easygoing, laid back place; horses and donkeys on the main drag, pigs in front of the hotel, a lively disco, and many sidewalk tea shops." The girls took him to a club where he saw costumed Tibetan dancers and he watched the girls themselves dance. Richard learned that Metok Tso loved to dance.

He stayed four days in Batang, and during that time, he had many conversations with Metok Tso. She started calling him "Grandpa." Afterward, they took up an internet correspondence in English, something no other student in our program even attempted. Metok Tso's written English was flawed, but she didn't care; she was determined to drink deeply from the fascinating world outside.

Richard Harlan would visit Metok Tso once or twice more in Batang, and his visits would stoke her ambition to master English as a tool of liberation. "You can do anything," Metok Tso would often say, "if you want it badly enough."

"It's not true," Richard once challenged her. "You can't do anything just by working hard; you have to have some talent and intelligence to start with."

"That doesn't matter, Grandpa. It's how hard you work."

And she *did* work hard, studying her English textbooks and watching whatever English TV she could find, preparing for a faraway future which she was determined to realize.

## Ancient Homes

After the morass at Senggé Monastery, I thought I was sick of architecture, but then we received astonishing news: the government would now permit us to expand our USAID work out of Lhagang into an area about four times as big. Not only that, but rumor had it that there were genuinely old buildings in a township called Sadé, which lay within the enlarged program area. The weather was getting cold, so I wasted no time in heading out to take a look.

Using Winrock's car and driver, I traveled with Winrock and KhamAid staff three hours south along the Lingchu Chamo River. Just before the entrance to Sadé town was a turnoff to a steel frame bridge surfaced with rotting, splintery planks. Once over the fast-flowing torrents, we headed up a switchback track to a dirt path scraped into the wall of the gorge. The path snaked for three kilometers upstream to a farming village called Wayö.

Driving into the heart of the settlement, we were confronted with a massive and ancient citadel of stone, with two great entryways cut into the front facade. The four-story house looked primeval: its walls were uneven, and its windows were tiny, their frames cracked, weathered, and utterly bare of decoration, a stark contrast to the technicolor adornment on modern Tibetan homes.

Out of one door emerged an exceptionally tall and striking Khampa. About forty years old, the man had a long red tassel and an enormous ivory ring woven into the complicated follicular embellishment encircling his head. His name was Pema Penlo. He was expecting us, because Minyak Choekyi Gyaltsen (a.k.a. Minyak Rinpoche), a highly respected local tulku, had arranged for us to come. Pema Penlo ushered us inside.

The room we entered was dark as pitch, though I could smell the usual barnyard perfumes of dung, urine, and hay. When my eyes adjusted, I saw columns and beams glazed with the grime of the ages. Pema Penlo showed us to a notched-log ladder, and we climbed to the second level, also mostly empty and dark.

Along the way, Pema Penlo pointed out the distinctive features of his house. Its walls were a meter thick at the base, double the thickness of modern walls. For defense against attackers, each of the doors was surmounted by a narrow slot through which occupants could launch spears or stones. The house had no windows at ground level, and the second-floor windows were only just big enough for archers to shoot through.

The columns and beams of the house were made from enormous fine-grained timbers. Pema Penlo pointed out the nibbled surfaces, which showed that the wood was adze-hewn, not saw-cut. Looking up at the ceiling, we saw horizontal beams trebled and resting on boat-shaped capitals, far more substantial than those of modern houses in the region. The place had a grand, brooding, medieval character, and was clearly built to protect householders from the hostile world outside.

It was only when we scaled another ladder to the third floor that we entered a room where the family lived, but it was unlike any other Tibetan home I had seen. Instead of cooking on an iron or clay stove, this family had an open fire set on a low dirt platform at the center of the living space. There was no chimney; instead, the smoke free-floated to a hole in the roof. The walls and ceiling were tarred with centuries of soot. The place looked more like a cave than a home. Most strikingly, someone had used tsampa flour to daub ranks of Buddhist symbols on the ink-black walls. The bold and luminous figures evoked Tibet's mystic, animist past.

Pema Penlo showed us their ancient chapel, a windowless chamber that looked more like a storeroom than like a temple, adorned with printed pictures of deities. Another ladder took us up again to the first roof, which had open-air verandas arranged on three sides. This roof and the one above it had been carefully maintained, I noted, with clay patched and timbers refreshed.

Then Pema Penlo introduced us to his cousin, Pema Tsecheng, who lived in the other half of the duplex. Pema Tsecheng took us through his home, which was as well preserved as the one we had just seen. Then we returned to Pema Penlo's and sat by the fire while his wife served tea and the two cousins talked about their spectacular home.

Pema Penlo was a mesmerizing character: not just his appearance, but his deep voice and arresting gaze. "Minyak Rinpoche told me to take care of this house," he said, unrolling the Sichuan-hua in a dignified cadence. "Many times, I wanted to take the stones and timber from the house and use them to build a new home. But Rinpoche said I shouldn't. He prophesied that the house would feed my family. We've been waiting eighteen years for his prophecy to come true."

"Many people have come here," he added bitterly. "They took a lot of photos and measured my house. Then they left. They didn't come back, and they didn't do anything to help."

The house was a historic treasure, but I didn't envy the families who lived in it. Apart from electrical wires, they had no modern conveniences. Most families in Kham by now had plank stairways, not ladders. The house had no latrine, not even a long-drop toilet. The water they used for drinking, cooking, and washing was lugged up in buckets to the third floor. And the chapel was dark and dismal compared to the bright, elaborately decorated places of worship attached to most modern homes in the region.

I knew instantly that Pema Penlo's house was a rare find. Fires, earthquakes, and armed conflict have taken a toll on Tibet's historic structures, and most "ancient" buildings have been extensively if not completely rebuilt. Yet the house was not unique—remarkably, there were three other historic houses in the same village! After leaving the Pema House (as we began calling it), we looked at the other three. Each had its points, but the Pema House was easily the finest, a living relic of Kham's long-ago past.

I was not alone in my interest: a few others had already discovered Wayö's historic homes, but so far, they had done nothing but photograph them. None could bring enough cash to the table for a real project. Yet it would take more than money to preserve the houses; it would take political skills. Not only did I need to consider the house owners, various government bureaus, our partner, Winrock, and our USAID donor, but I could also do nothing without the blessing of the powerful tulku Minyak Rinpoche, a man I did not know, but who was tremendously influential in Sadé. Putting all of these stars into alignment would not be easy. As I flew home for the winter holiday, I was already plotting my next moves.

## Redemption in Dorakarmo

Early in the year of the male Fire-Dog (2006), the snow-covered rangelands of Lhagang dazzled under morning's eastern blaze. I was headed out to Dorakarmo Village in Winrock's car, which wallowed in sloppy tracks pressed into the ice-skinned mud. After several months at sea level, my frontal lobe shimmered with the metallic pain of an oncoming high-altitude headache, and my eyelids weighed heavily against the brightness outside.

Crammed in with me were Mr. Wu, three Winrock staff, and my erstwhile arch-nemesis, Khenpo Yonden, the abbot of Senggé Monastery and cause of intense stress the previous summer and fall. No longer the taciturn fellow I remembered, today the khenpo was downright loquacious. "The training was very useful," he said. "I'm rebuilding my home, and I hired some of the people who were trained. The government is giving 4,000 yuan per family, so many people are building houses. They are asking me if I know any good carpenters who can do the design and tell them how much wood they need. If there hadn't been the training, we would have to go to Rangaka to find builders."

The khenpo continued matter-of-factly: "Houses need to be earthquake safe. When herders built houses by themselves, the houses lasted only one or two years."

I could hardly believe my ears. *He gets it. He understands.*

We dropped onto a broad spread of rangeland encircled by mountains. In the middle of the snow-swathed pasture, a new village was taking shape. Wu and I jumped out to have a look.

"This is Khenpo Yonden's house," explained one of the Winrock folks, indicating a solid, two-story home with a rectangular footprint. On the south wall were its main entry and nine windows, all well-made with solid headers holding up carefully fitted stones. The house was modest by farmer standards but palatial for a drokpa area and easily the nicest in Dorakarmo. Half a dozen masons were on the roof, working on finishing touches.

Nearby were some sawhorses and tools, a few boards, and lots of wood debris. A wind-burnt carpenter was getting ready to saw a plank to make a window frame. He measured carefully and snapped a black powder line to mark the cut. Further on, we found another trainee sieving dirt, taking out the pebbles and lumps to make smooth, sticky mortar. On the house itself, a stonemason had set up taut strings to guide the flat of the walls; another mason was using a plumb line to check the fall. All of these techniques had been unknown in Dorakarmo a year earlier.

In a tent, Mr. Wu and I sat down with Tupten, the lead carpenter, who seemed at first disconcerted to find himself being interviewed by two outlanders. "We are practicing the skills we learned at Senggé Monastery," he said. "The khenpo's house has the highest walls in the village. I'm using the new carpentry skills, especially for the joists, to build it. It is a safe and strong house. We'll finish in about five more days."

We learned that the crew building the khenpo's home included two carpenters and six stonemasons from our program. Among them were people from Pasu, the folks who had been driven away by the Dorakarmo students on the first day of training. The khenpo explained that he had wanted to hire more of our trainees, but they charged so much now that he couldn't afford them, so the crew was partly composed of newbies.

Khenpo Yonden also told us that several program graduates had formed their own crews. They were now building houses elsewhere, where they were teaching their skills to a new generation of trainees.

All the way back to the office, Mr. Wu and I were giddy, and it wasn't the elevation. Against all odds, from the depths of misunderstandings and conflict, our program soared to improbable and dazzling success.

## A Sick Student

After four years as the volunteer director of KhamAid's education programs, Dana Isherwood had decided to step down. Her replacement was a thirty-year-old Australian named Kara Jenkinson. Kara was a great hire: she had lived in Beijing for four years, was fluent in Mandarin, and was sharp as a tack. Her pretty face, light brown hair, and lithe figure made people automatically warm to her. She knew the schools because she had already accompanied Dana on several trips.

Kara couldn't work for free, so we converted the job to a paid position and by now Kara had been in place for more than a year. While I was looking at Khenpo Yonden's house in Dorakarmo, Kara was in Derong County on a routine visit to check on our sponsored girls. She had just left the county middle school and was walking along the town's main boulevard when she spotted a young woman she knew: Lhamo Dolkar. By her side was a middle-aged man who would turn out to be her uncle. The two were walking very slowly.

Lhamo was wearing a sweatshirt and loose, dark trousers. At nineteen, she was small for her age and fragile-looking, with a heart-shaped face and high cheekbones. The name "Lhamo" means *goddess,* and "Dolkar" is a feminine manifestation of compassion. She was supposed to be at nursing school on the other side of the prefecture, not here in her hometown. Kara hailed her.

As Lhamo approached, Kara saw that her face was red and blotchy. Kara knew that for years Lhamo had been dogged by a mysterious illness that came and went. Kara asked if she was again ill.

Lhamo didn't reply, but her eyes shifted downward. Kara followed her glance and saw that Lhamo's feet were swollen and bulging out of her shoes. Kara gasped.

Lhamo hiked up her trousers to reveal skin dotted with black welts. In her letters, Lhamo had mentioned "sore legs," but gave no details. Now Kara saw the symptoms for herself.

"Awful!" said Kara. "How long has it been like this?"

"Since school started," said Lhamo. "Usually it goes away after a while, but this time it kept getting worse. My feet were so swollen I couldn't walk. I had a bad fever, and I missed six weeks of classes. I couldn't leave the dorm, and my classmates had to bring me food."

Lhamo was enrolled at the Kandze Health School, a place that had plenty of doctors. "Did you ask your teachers for help?" Kara asked.

"I did, but the teachers couldn't figure it out. They said I had to go home and rest."

Later, when I heard this story, I was appalled. Lhamo Dolkar was at a *medical* school! Her teachers should be experts, or at least capable of looking up information in books.

So, when the semester ended, Lhamo had come home to rest, but even after the month-long holiday, she was still too ill to return to school. She remained at home, a farmhouse belonging to her uncle. Her father had died years earlier, leaving the family destitute and forcing Lhamo, her mother, and brother to move in with the uncle's family. Lhamo had been their hope and pride, but now she was an invalid and a burden. Would she ever return to school and get a certificate? It looked doubtful.

Derong County, home to both Lhamo and our star Metok Tso, is riven by a deep river gorge. The county town lies at a mere 2,800 meters (9,200 feet) above sea level; it's nirvana compared to the wind-scraped highlands of Sershul and Litang, and it has good arable land. Yet because of its isolation, Derong was a difficult place to live. For a long time, it had been the only county in Kandze Prefecture without scheduled bus service from Dartsendo, which was 644 kilometers (400 miles) and four high passes away. Unless they were born in

Derong, officials didn't want to work there and left as soon as possible. The economy was undeveloped, and public services were mediocre.

It didn't have to be that way. The boomtown of Gyeltang, which the government had recently renamed "Shangri-La," was just 160 kilometers (87 miles) south and connected to Derong by a good paved road. But Gyeltang was in a different province: Yunnan. To use Gyeltang public services, people like Lhamo had to pay nonresident rates. This was one more reason that Derong, despite its natural advantages, remained deeply poor.

Lhamo had been an average student in a below-average middle school. It was only thanks to our scholarship program that she could aspire to be more than a farmer. A British couple living in Kuala Lumpur were her sponsors. Her training was supposed to prepare her for a government health care job—if she didn't die first.

Kara could see that Lhamo was in pain, yet the girl showed no self-pity. Her quiet dignity moved Kara, who could hardly comprehend how this young person could be so strong when there was so little cause for hope. Out here in Derong, she was unlikely to get competent care. Traveling to a larger town with a decent hospital was out of reach for families like hers. Among Lhamo's people, death was not a rare event or a remote possibility; it was a familiar if unwelcome specter that visited regularly.

KhamAid was not a health care provider, and it was problematic for us to get involved in the medical travails of individuals. The ill cling desperately to any shred of hope offered, no matter how tenuous. They may imagine that you, the rich foreigner, have miracle cures at your command. The cost of helping can bankrupt a small outfit like KhamAid. And once you start, the needs are limitless.

In Kham at that time, government workers got health insurance, but most others had to pay cash for care.[78] Lhamo probably had the fatalism that is common among people who see a lot of death from a young age. Doesn't the very first tenet of Buddhism tell us that existence is inseparable from suffering?

If Kara had been practical, she would have shaken her head, expressed her sympathy, and passed on, meanwhile making a mental note to get Lhamo's tuition back from the school and inform her sponsors that she was dropping out. But Kara was personally invested in each one of KhamAid's students. She wasn't one to walk away.

"Can I speak with your mother?" Kara said, knowing she was entering perilous terrain, but unable to stop herself.

Twenty minutes by taxi later, Lhamo, her uncle, and Kara reached the house, a modest two-story Tibetan home of mud-plastered stone set on a hillside. Kara followed Lhamo up a ladder from the ground floor stables to the family's main living area, dominated by a wood-burning stove. Lhamo's mother and aunt were there, as were her brother and two young cousins. The family exhorted the guest to take the most comfortable seat while the women churned fresh butter tea and set out *droju* (fritters) and candy for her to eat.

It wasn't until Kara was halfway through her second bowl of tea, and the usual queries about the difficulty of her journey had been exhaustively answered, that it became socially correct to bring up the reason for her visit.

Lhamo's uncle did the talking. Her illness had begun a few years

---

78 A short time later, the New Cooperative Medical Scheme (*Xinxing Nongcun Hezuo Yiliao Baoxian Zhidu*) was introduced in Kandze Prefecture. For a cost of ten yuan per person per year, it allowed rural people to access in-patient care at deeply subsidized rates. When I saw it rolled out in Wayö, residents were eager to join, but the rules were complicated and the system difficult to navigate, especially for non-Chinese speakers.

earlier, at first just a mild nuisance—fatigue, achy joints, rashes that came and went. Then the fatigue became deeper and longer-lasting, the rashes became sores, and her legs swelled. Lhamo's mother had scraped up her small savings and taken her to the county hospital. It was a small facility, and its doctors had limited training. Could they figure out what was wrong?

They had many diseases to choose from, not just the usual developing-world scourges like hepatitis and tuberculosis, but some that were unique to the Tibetan plateau. One was Kashin-Beck, or "Big Bone" disease, which stiffened joints, slowed bone growth, and stunted children. Another was *Echinococcus*, a parasitic disease found in herding areas and spread by dog feces. Another parasite, a tapeworm called *Taenia saginata*, enters the human digestive tract when meat is eaten raw, a common custom in Tibet.

Tibet has had a high rate of sexually transmitted diseases, notably syphilis, and at this time, the rate of HIV/AIDS was small but growing. Stories from our staff suggest that herders tended to be promiscuous, placing them at greater risk. Farmers, however, were more conservative. Lhamo was in her mid-teens when her symptoms first appeared, and probably not sexually active.

Against all the odds, the doctors in Derong correctly diagnosed Lhamo's illness as lupus, a disease in which the body's immune system mistakenly attacks healthy tissue. This part was right; the rest was a disaster. The doctor didn't know the standard of care for lupus and had prescribed antibiotics. Lhamo took them, and for a while, she seemed to improve, so she returned to school and continued her education.

That was three years earlier; now she was very ill. The Derong doctors had said that an allergic reaction to the antibiotics was the cause of Lhamo's condition, and they instructed her to come in daily for an intravenous drip. So, every day Lhamo had been going faithfully to a storefront medical clinic where they stuck a needle in her arm and dripped in a cocktail of glucose, vitamin B, and more antibiotics.

It was evident to Kara that the cocktail wasn't working, and that Lhamo needed better care. As a resident of Kandze Prefecture, she would normally have been referred to a hospital in Dartsendo, but that was three days' travel away. The big Gyeltang hospital was only six hours south, but Lhamo wasn't a resident, so treatment there would be costly.

Needless to say, Kara wasn't authorized to use KhamAid money to pay for Lhamo's care. But the girl plainly needed to go to Gyeltang. Kara pulled out the pouch she wore under her shirt and extracted one thousand yuan. It was her own money, her emergency fund. She handed it to Lhamo's uncle.

Kara had to leave the next morning, but Lhamo promised to stay in touch.

A few days later, her uncle used Kara's money to purchase three bus tickets: one each for Lhamo and himself, and the third for a family friend, an elderly lady who was like a godmother to Lhamo.

The road from Derong to Gyeltang followed the Ding Chu as it poured through southwest Tibet toward its confluence with the Yangtze. Where the two rivers merged, a suspension bridge took the travelers over the water into Yunnan Province. From there, they climbed steadily to the sprawling city of Gyeltang on a plain at 3,276 meters (10,800 feet) elevation and ringed by mountains.

A day or two later, Lhamo phoned Kara from the hospital to tell her that they were examining her and running tests. The doctors wanted to observe Lhamo's condition for forty days. That was typical. Hospitals boosted their revenue by stretching out patient stays, and families were unlikely to object. Hospitals didn't provide meals, so families had to stay nearby to bring food. Even a minor procedure could quickly exhaust a family's savings. In a city like Gyeltang, a thousand yuan doesn't last long.

The doctors agreed that Lhamo had systematic lupus erythematosus, or SLE, but they didn't have a laboratory that could determine its severity. They prescribed some medicines, including prednisone, a steroid, but it was all guesswork. They told Lhamo that lupus had no cure and that it would eventually be fatal.

Lhamo and her family took the death sentence without blinking. They didn't ask about their options. They had no medical knowledge and were unused to questioning authority. Lhamo stayed at the hospital until the money ran out. Then they went home.

## Advance Work

The village of Wayö, where I was hoping to launch a project to preserve the Pema House and other historic homes, lay within the Minyak kingdom, one of the many quasi-independent polities of Kham's feudal past. The Minyak reached a peak about nine centuries ago, ruling an area that encompassed all of Dartsendo and Ta'u Counties and portions of five others. The kingdom had its own language and traditions, distinct from the rest of Kham. The name "Dartsendo" is said to derive from Minyak words "dar," meaning *silk*, and "rtsi," meaning *medicine,* both items that were traded between Tibetans and Chinese.[79]

Minyak Rinpoche cast a long shadow in the region. Not only was he an incarnate lama; he was a trained and qualified architect, one of Tibet's few proponents of conserving old and damaged monu-

---

79  Minyak Gonpo [Mi-nyag nMgon-po], "Mi-nyag according to Tibetan history and an analysis of some Mi-nyag naming conventions," trans. Stephen Aldridge, *Krung-go'i bod-ljongs*, Vol. 5, (1998), pp. 21–23.

ments instead of rebuilding or replacing them. He lived and worked in Lhasa, but now he was on a (lunar) New Year holiday and staying in a private home a short distance from the Sadé Township seat. I borrowed Winrock's vehicle and driver to take Mr. Wu and me over there for an audience.

The tulku's hosts greeted us warmly and brought us to a small sitting room where Minyak Rinpoche was waiting. He was middle-aged, shortish, and bespectacled, with crew-cut hair—the epitome of a pragmatic, problem-solving engineer but for his lama's robes. After tea had been served, he wasted no time in getting to the point. "Fifteen years ago, I started encouraging the two cousins to protect their house," he told us in Chinese. "I told them their house is not just their family's affair; it's the affair of the whole Minyak people. But their relatives and friends said to them, 'It's dangerous; the house will collapse on you. Why do you continue to live there?' "

Minyak Rinpoche's life spanned two very different spheres. His early years had been spent at Guwa Monastery, not far from Sadé. When the Cultural Revolution began, instead of returning to his natal home like most monks, he went to Lhasa, where he learned the builder's trade. He married and had a daughter. Now he lived a double life: in Minyak, he was a revered religious leader, while in Lhasa, he was a respected professional, employed as director at the Tibet Ancient Architecture Design and Research Institute. His career was long and illustrious: he had helped repair Tibet's most celebrated historic sites, including the Potala Palace and the Jokhang Temple.

Minyak Rinpoche was well aware that homes like the Pema House were uncomfortable to live in. He also knew that if the owners demolished them and recycled the stones, they would save about a third of the cost of a new home. But unlike many others, he also understood the preciousness of authentic architectural heritage. Minyak Rinpoche had urged people not to tear down their historic homes. So far, many had listened.

"Just as in Lhasa," he said, "in Minyak, there are many contradictions. Private interest is always in conflict with public interest." He was referring to individual needs for habitable dwellings against the public's need to understand and enjoy their heritage. However, in Minyak, the public was resource-poor. "One hundred and thirty million yuan was allocated to the Potala," he said sadly, "but I can't get even ten thousand for here."

*KhamAid can get ten thousand yuan*, I thought. *In fact, for the right project, I can get a whole lot more.* Repairing Pema Penlo's house was certainly the right project, and if not his, then perhaps one of the other ancient homes in Wayö. Two of them had wall paintings possibly dating from the homes' original construction, and there were more paintings in the village's small temple, which was also several centuries old.

I suddenly burned with a desire to reprise the role I had played ten years earlier when I led the repair of Pewar Monastery and the conservation of its ancient Buddhist murals. At Pewar, we had done good work, but the scope was narrow: pure conservation. Now, I wanted to pursue integrated community development, to stitch together programs comprising all gates of the development mandala. But there were two impediments. First, I was a newcomer here. Minyak Rinpoche had roots in the region and titanic influence; he wanted to lead his own projects or at least have a substantial say in anything that was done.

The other challenge was the people of Wayö. I would need them to be active partners, to invest at least sweat equity and perhaps some cash, too, for KhamAid couldn't afford another money pit like Senggé Monastery.

# The Greenhouses Go Under

Ever since the 2004 windstorm, our greenhouse owners in Nyarong had been working hard. Using money contributed by the county government, the women had repaired the damage. The next spring, they had planted anew. However, as the weather warmed, many vegetables became infested with worms. The blemished produce did not fetch good prices at the Nyarong market, but the women did not want to use pesticides because it violated their Buddhist beliefs.

By the end of the 2004 growing season, each family netted 3,780 yuan for the year. It was far less than we had hoped, but it was still more than they could have earned growing wheat or barley on the land. The trainer's two-year contract had ended, and his departure left the women on their own. Despite the many setbacks and soaring costs, the county government had put up money to build two more greenhouses, and the Women's Federation had picked two more families to join. The program grew.

In the spring of 2006, another violent windstorm struck. When Mr. Wu arrived, he saw that the women had sown wheat in one less-damaged greenhouse, but only a few stalks were visible; the rest had been eaten by livestock. The other greenhouses were too badly damaged to grow anything at all. The women had given up. The project had failed.

The Agriculture Bureau performed repairs and improvements to the greenhouses and found some skilled farmers from outside the area to lease them from the owners and to operate them. Some of the women took jobs working in the greenhouses, adding wages to the rent they received. We didn't achieve our goal of creating rural entrepreneurs, but at least the families' finances had improved, and they had more vegetables.

The greenhouse venture taught me painful lessons about doing business on the Tibetan plateau. Besides the bitter winters and people's lack of technical knowledge, a business owner had to adapt to rapid changes in the marketplace as China developed. That was why, of all of KhamAid's program areas, increasing income was the most difficult. Yet the construction skills training at Senggé had been so impactful that I would not give up on job training. Our handicraft program had great potential to be our next big breakthrough.

# Part V

# Governance

*Men will always lose the battle*
*against cholera and bureaucracy.*
— Tibetan proverb

Most everyone prefers to be governed by their own kind and resents a government of aliens, so the details of *how* governance is performed matter less than the question of *by whom*. That's why, when the Nationalists wrenched control of western Sichuan from the Manchu emperor, they enlisted the cooperation of certain kings, clan chieftains, tulkus, and monastery abbots, and took care not to diminish them in the people's eyes. The Chakla king, for example, continued to wield limited authority in Dartsendo and surrounding areas; the Chinese also used him as a sort of envoy to regions further west.[80]

With this strategy, the Nationalists were able to secure population centers in western Sichuan with a small number of thinly spread troops. The spaces between remained the domain of nomads who were devoutly religious but otherwise ungovernable and recognized no temporal authority but their own. The Nationalists attempted, with limited success, to reduce banditry and keep order, yet they did nothing to reduce the economic inequality created by the concentration of resources in the hands of wealthy families and monasteries. An American missionary described

---

80  Ultimately, the King of Chakla fell from favor, was arrested, and died trying to escape. Louis Margrath King, *China in Turmoil: Studies in Personality* (Houghton Mifflin Company, 1927), pp. 96–110.

China's main activities on the Tibetan frontier as "collecting taxes, robbing, oppressing, confiscating, and allowing her representatives to burn, loot, and steal."[81]

When the Communists took control in 1949, they tried to emulate the Nationalist strategy of co-opting influential individuals by appointing them into paid positions in the new government. This was, by itself, not a bad thing, but then the Communists enlisted these newly anointed bureaucrats to carry out propaganda for their "democratic reforms" and to press-gang ordinary Tibetans as laborers on government projects.[82] These actions, plus many others, brought about the Khampa Rebellion.

Before and since the uprising, the Communist Party has never stopped working to bolster its legitimacy by training native-born Tibetans as officials and Party members. They have made substantial improvements in the mechanics of governance: reducing taxes and ending demands for unpaid labor, bringing in public services such as schools and clinics that were previously lacking, and improving public safety by cracking down on the robber bands that were roaming unchecked. Yet these improvements cannot erase the stark truth that Tibetans have lost authority over their traditional lands, and that Tibet's Buddhism, the treasure they hold most dear, has been deposed from its place at the center of public life. It survives only by the Party's good graces.

---

81  Eric Teichman, *Travels of a Consular Officer in Eastern Tibet* (Cambridge at the University Press, 1922). p. 228.

82  Jamyang Norbu, *Warriors of Tibet: The Story of Aten and the Khampas Fighting for the Freedom of their Country* (London: Wisdom Publications, 1986), pp. 80–82.

In addition, the new Communist ruling class has inaugurated an era of graft equal to or surpassing their predecessors'. There are no statistics on corruption, yet the stories are legion: Displaced farmers receiving only a pittance for their ancestral land. Mediocre students admitted to top schools. Choice jobs for sale. Arbitrary arrest and broken justice. Hordes of sticky-fingered technocrats and the ubiquitous red envelopes. The shrugging of shoulders: *mei banfa*, what can anyone do?

There was nothing KhamAid could do to fight ineffective government—that was far beyond our power. Yet governance is a critical gate of the development mandala. So, when an opportunity suggested itself, we pushed aside one or two small pebbles out of the millions blocking the path.

## Corruption

A couple of months after her visit to Derong, Kara Jenkinson went to Ta'u Number One Middle School to check on more of our sponsored students. This time she brought someone with her: John Giszczak, an American. He was a new KhamAid hire, a fresh university graduate, serving as Kara's understudy on this trip.

"So, all of our students are in school today? All sixteen?" Kara asked pleasantly in Chinese.

"They're all here," said Deputy Headmaster Liao with an ingratiating smile. He was a plump man in his mid-forties and wore a dark business suit. "They're in class now," he added.

"We'd like to see the students," said John, also in Chinese. "We want to chat with them, find out how they're doing. And we need to take photos for their sponsors."

John and Kara sat with Liao and two other officials in the school's VIP reception room. The room resembled a cheap Las Vegas smoking lounge, with three overstuffed fake-leather sofas arranged in an open rectangle, a heavy glass coffee table, and a ceiling caked in layers of molding and strung with a cheesy chandelier.

"No problem, no problem. We'll arrange it for this afternoon," said Liao. Like most officials, he had a velvet tongue and was well versed in the kabuki theatre of official visits. He and one of his side-kicks, a bureaucrat named Loden, smirked at Kara and John in the oily, fawning manner of government officials with something to hide.

Kara knew the look; she had seen it before. John was new, but even he could see that these people were fishy. It was written all over their faces.

"Great," said Kara briskly. "We'll go over the financials now; then we'll visit with the students." She looked down at her notes, frowning. "How much money did the school get from KhamAid this semester?"

"Chuju, can you answer the foreign guest's question?" said Liao, turning to one of his colleagues.

Chuju was a dour and sulky-looking woman in a dark Tibetan dress adorned with a traditional apron of striped wool. She opened her briefcase and began hunting through sheaves of paper bearing Chinese glyphs. "We received 24,010 yuan," she said finally. "The wire arrived on March 4th."

"And how much for each student?"

Chuju punched a calculator, then said, "707 yuan each."

John and Kara exchanged glances. The numbers, so far, were correct. The conversation was going according to plan. The trap was being laid.

KhamAid had a long history with the Ta'u County Number One

Middle School. We had begun sponsoring girls there six years before, partnering with the local Women's Federation, who identified the needy students for us, paid their tuitions on our behalf, and kept an eye on them. In 2002, I had introduced the school headmaster to a couple of adventurous Americans, and they had become English teachers there. For foreigners to live, let alone teach, in Ta'u was highly irregular, but the headmaster Tsewang Chimé not only pulled it off, he boasted about it, basking in the prestige that foreign teachers lent his school. They stayed for two years, dramatically improving the quality of English instruction and occasionally answering emailed questions about our kids.

The school had about eight hundred students, of whom three hundred boarded in dormitories on campus. Academically, it wasn't bad, at least not by local standards. The previous year, its students had scored second highest in Kandze Prefecture on the ninth-grade exit exam. It had a spacious campus of perhaps a dozen acres dotted with buildings, including several multi-story blocks housing classrooms.

Thanks to our good relations with the Women's Federation, our program in Ta'u had run smoothly until 2003 when our Federation contacts were rotated en masse to jobs elsewhere in the government. A new Women's Federation chair had come in named Deng Shuhua. Kara detested her. "Very domineering, bossy and overbearing," she had written in an email. Deng had long, oily hair pulled back in a ponytail, and she looked Tibetan, although Kara never asked her nationality.

For a while, we sidestepped Deng by relying on the two American teachers to keep us informed about our kids, but then the teachers departed, leaving Deng and her minions as our only link to the girls between KhamAid visits.

The more Kara got to know Deng, the more she distrusted her. Deng had the biggest, most handsome Tibetan house in Ta'u, built from immense trees harvested somewhere over the mountains. People gossiped that Deng had gone on extravagant junkets to Thailand and Myanmar. No one dared to speculate out loud where she got the money; in fact, people quivered with fear when Deng's name was mentioned. Deng was always slick and attentive toward Kara, perpetually urging her to start more programs in Ta'u. Kara figured that Deng only wanted more KhamAid programs, so there would be more money for her to skim.

Deng seemed like such a blatant crook that we dumped the Ta'u Women's Federation as our partner and started sending tuition money directly to the school. But now Kara suspected that the school was also stealing. There was no longer anyone in Ta'u we trusted, yet our students were in the school's clutches with one more year left to graduate. It was a nightmare.

Kara and John were determined to find out what the school was doing with the students' tuition money. "So, you got our wire transfer," Kara said, setting her notebook down on the table and leaning forward. "Good! And exactly how was the money spent?"

Deputy Headmaster Liao cleared his throat, glanced around the room, and reached into his pocket for a pack of cigarettes. He offered the two visitors a smoke, a Chinese sacrament of hospitality. They both shook their heads no. Liao stuck one in his mouth and lit it up. Loden followed his boss's lead and lit up his own. The woman, Chuju, abstained.

Outside they heard the musical sounds of children reciting in their classrooms, an *a cappella* chorus that echoed down the corridors and into the room where John, Kara, and the officials sat amid clouds of cigarette smoke.

The deputy headmaster crossed and uncrossed his legs. "Four hundred yuan went for book fees," he said finally, "and we gave 307 yuan in cash to each student."

"The cash," added Loden, "was so that they could buy food in the cafeteria." Loden was a minor functionary at the school, a skinny guy in his late twenties. He dragged hard on his cigarette and then politely turned his head so the poisons squirting between his brown canines wouldn't hit their guests in the face.

"I see," said Kara, an experienced China hand inured to cigarette smoke. "Paid in one lump sum? Or in installments?"

"In a lump sum," Chuju piped up. The other two nodded.

When?" asked Giszczak.

"It was April—," said Liao.

"It was at the start of the semester—," interrupted Loden.

"It was a couple of days ago," corrected Chuju.

"And 400 yuan was for book fees?"

"Yes."

"You're sure?"

"Absolutely sure," said Liao. "Absolutely."

"All of the *other* students here, the ones we're *not* sponsoring, pay this same amount?"

"Oh yes," said Liao. "They all pay the same."

"All the same," echoed Loden.

"And when our sponsored students received the cash, did they sign for it?"

"Of course," said the deputy headmaster.

"Absolutely," said Loden.

"Well, actually," broke in Chuju, the accountant, "we paid it to the students in installments. The first one was 310 yuan—"

"That can't be right," said John.

"It must have been 100 yuan every other week—," said Loden.

"It was two installments—," said Chuju.

"It was 307 yuan at the beginning of the semester," said Liao firmly, cutting off his staff. "Exactly that."

"Could you write that down for us?"

"No problem, no problem," said Liao. He nodded at Chuju, who took a sheet of paper from her briefcase, laid it on the coffee table, and began penning careful Chinese strokes: columns headed *xingming* (student name), *shufei* (book fee), *shenghuofei* (living expenses), and *youji* (sum). Then she wrote the sixteen names, and beside each of them wrote the figures 400, 307, and 707. She handed the result to John.

"Could you sign it and stamp it, please?"

"Of course," replied Liao. Chuju proceeded to add her name and the date. Then she got out the school's chop, inked it with vermillion, and stamped the bottom of the paper. The document was now official.

Time to spring the trap.

Back in Dartsendo, Kara and John had met with prefecture-level education officials, where they heard about a new law governing fees. When the two had seen the text of the law on an official's computer screen, they knew this was information they would need out in the field, but when they asked the official to print it for them, the official blanched and quickly shut off his screen. "I can't print this," he had spluttered, "It's *the law!*"

The two foreigners had thought it hilarious that Chinese law was treated as a state secret. As it turned out, they didn't need the printout because key provisions were posted on signboards in schools.

Now Kara looked Deputy Headmaster Liao dead in the eye, and she was no longer smiling. "Are you aware," she said, "of the Sichuan Province Eight Rules of Standardized Education Fee Collection Project?" Her easy-going Aussie manner had melted away, replaced by courteous rage.

There was a visible recoil. "What?" coughed Liao. All three officials were shifting in their seats, suddenly flushed.

"It's written on the notice-board in the corridor downstairs," John said helpfully. "The one that says *Public Announcement Regarding the Collection of Fees* at the top."

Kara consulted her notes. "It says that each student should pay no more than 275 yuan. That's 155 yuan for textbooks, twenty yuan for supplies, and 110 yuan for boarding fees."

The three officials began talking at once, a Niagara of conflicting bullshit so swift and turbulent that Kara and John could not follow it. When it was over, the officials were clinging to the mathematically untenable stance that the 400 yuan purportedly spent on school fees was somehow less than the 275-yuan legal maximum.

"But our kids are *poor*," objected John, as soon as he could get a word in. "The notice-board says that poor children shouldn't pay any school fees at all."[83]

"Their room and board should be subsidized," said Kara.

"They should be paying only twenty yuan for book fees," said John. "*Twenty* yuan. *Not* four hundred." He struggled to stay in his seat. He wanted to leap up, grab the closest official by the throat, and throttle him.

To catch low-grade yokels lying was like shooting fish in a ketchup bottle. The three were tongue-tied and flummoxed; nevertheless, they tried gamely to knit an explanation out of their tangled fabrications. To do that, they had to ignore what they had said earlier and the pay-

---

83  The government implemented *Liangmian Yibu* ("Two Exemptions and One Subsidy") program first on a test basis in 1998 in a few rural Chinese counties, then gradually expanded it. The program arrived in Kandze Prefecture in 2006. Its goals were to remove economic barriers to education and compel all children to complete school through grade 9.

ment record Chuju had just certified. Words came out in a torrent, lies piled atop lies, a deepening pool of skullduggery and slime.

Kara and John listened in disbelief. The officials were venal and corrupt, but they were also laughably obvious about it. It would have been funny if children's futures hadn't been at stake.

Eventually, the three circled to a new story: that 87 yuan of each 707-yuan payment had gone to school fees, and the rest was given to the students in two installments of 310 yuan each, one at the beginning of May and one near the end. Kara and John didn't believe this either, nor did they believe the document that was hurriedly produced to support it, but they had squeezed all they could out of the three sweating bureaucrats. It was time to talk to the students themselves.

But now the pair discovered another lie. Not all the sixteen children were in class that day, as the officials had claimed. Three were absent. They had dropped out of school, and the reason was that their boarding fees—KhamAid's money—had been stolen.

The girls' families, two of whom were dirt-poor farmers from inaccessible mountain fastnesses at the county's farthest reaches, had been paying the dormitory fees themselves. Their money gave out, and the girls left school just a few months short of their graduation from grade nine.

This was our worst nightmare come true. Children had dropped out of school; not only were we unaware of it, we had allowed corrupt officials to victimize them. We had failed those three girls, and we had let down the people sponsoring them.

When the thirteen students were brought out, Kara kept them occupied while John pulled aside a couple and asked them separately about the missing three. Both answered with the same words: "I'm not very clear about their situation." It seemed to Kara and John that school officials had told the girls to lie.

But the thirteen students also said each of them had gotten 620 yuan, split into two installments. "It was impossible for us to tell if they were lying or not," John wrote in his report. "But we both had a gut feeling that they had received something."

Having run out of questions to ask the thirteen students, Kara and John turned their attention to their missing classmates. Here, they had an ace up their sleeve. They went back to Liao and threatened to report him to the Kandze Prefecture Disciplinary Bureau. This was a threat with teeth. For several years, Beijing had been campaigning against school corruption, running hotlines so that parents could report suspicious charges. In the first seven months of 2003, the government had caught and punished more than a thousand officials.[84] I thought the system surely had more than a thousand villains. The true number must be a hundred times bigger. "Kill a chicken to scare a monkey," goes the Chinese proverb: sacking those thousand dirtbags was a warning to others that henceforth, they would have to be cleverer about their thefts.

A skilled politician, Liao didn't blink at the pair's threat. But later, he must have had a change of heart, because, that evening, a rather more humble Liao came looking for them at their hotel. He brought along his boss, Headmaster Tsewang Chimé, who rarely deigned to show his face to us. This was a good sign.

The two officials apologized for what they called "Chuju's boasting." They wanted to make amends. Kara and John said that the important thing was for this to remain an adult matter; the children should not be involved. They asked the officials to return the money paid for the three students. The next day the cash duly appeared, a stack of crisp pink hundreds.

---

84  *China Daily,* "Crackdown on illegal fees for schooling." Sept. 4, 2003.

How did we get to this point? At the inception of KhamAid's scholarship program, our partnerships were suffused with purpose, genuine goodwill, and mutual trust. The program ran well with only a little monitoring. But time passed, and the officials we knew were transferred to other jobs and replaced by strangers. Every year we had to forge new relationships. If I had to lay odds, I'd put money on there being at least two contemptible scoundrels in China for every honest public servant. It is one thing to overcharge naïve foreigners, but to take away an innocent child's chance for an education, which *these same officials* were legally, professionally, and morally bound to provide? What kind of jackals were they?

By now, we'd been running our scholarship program for seven years. We'd had good partners once, but those days were over.

We were having problems in other counties, too. We began stepping up our oversight, visiting more often, and this drove up our costs. The scholarship program was starting to pull heavily from our rainy-day account of unrestricted donations. It wasn't just the corruption that gave us fits. There were constant logistical problems, exacerbated by cultural differences and our unrealistic expectations.

In the developed West, we don't expect fourteen-year-olds to drop out of school. It was different in Kham. With no jobs in the back country requiring even basic literacy, some parents didn't see the point of education. All they knew was, their kids came back unable to do farm work, yet suddenly choosy about what they wore and ate. In the view of many parents, four or five years in a classroom was plenty— just until boys could join a monastery and girls could herd livestock, gather medicinal plants, or farm.

Our girls dropped out because they or a family member fell ill, because they got married or were needed at home, or because menstruation was too messy and mortifying. One girl in our program ran away to a distant city and didn't tell anyone where she had gone (we found out years later). I wondered if teachers had molested any of the girls, but it was impossible to know. In any event, dropping out was normal; getting to grade 9 was unusual. And finishing grade 12? *That* was revolutionary.

There wasn't much I could do about kids leaving school. A problem that did rest directly on my shoulders was cash flow. By now, KhamAid was sponsoring 285 children at eighteen different schools. Every year, fees changed, schools changed, sponsors changed, and many kids had special circumstances. The work was growing ever more complicated. Qualified, capable people like Kara needed salaries they could live on. The program was hemorrhaging cash.

Advisors wanted me to shut down the program, but I couldn't bear to let down the children who were depending on us for help. Less nobly, I feared the anger of sponsors who would be crushed if we cut them off and allowed their girls to drop out. Nor would it be easy to phase the program out gradually due to fixed costs shared by many donors. Killing the program would be agonizing and expensive. And when all was said and done, I still believed in it. I refused to give up.

I argued that we should keep going, and in the end, I wore down the detractors. But we would have to restructure. And fast.

For starters, the government had recently lowered the cost of grades 7-9 to the point where it no longer made sense to sponsor them. So, we would phase out the junior middle school scholarships and apply sponsors' money to grades 10-12, for which there were no subsidies. To shut out sticky-fingered officials, we would stop wiring money and instead dispatch our staff to pay the fees in person at the beginning of each semester, just as if they were parents.

And Kara and John were determined to somehow reclaim those three lost girls.

## Picture Frames

One year after we completed our market research in Lhagang, we methodically went about setting up a handicraft training program. With the help of the report prepared by the volunteer MBAs, we selected what appeared to be a promising product: wooden picture frames painted with Tibetan designs. They were, I thought, just the thing to frame a tourist's vacation photo. After commissioning several prototypes, we had hit on an attractive and saleable design. We leased two floors of a building on Lhagang's main square, renovated them, and christened the place the Handicraft Training and Demonstration Center. We hired local experts to teach the woodworking and painting skills required to make the product.

Now came an important decision: whether to pay stipends to trainees. Other NGOs were paying wages to people to attend training, so that many in Lhagang had come to regard NGOs as just another *dri* to be milked. I was determined to break this regrettable precedent. Mr. Wu and a newly hired employee named Adrol went door to door in Lhagang's New Nomad Village to promote the program and recruit students.

On June 24th, the first day of class, staff and instructors gathered in the training center to wait for students to appear. A few people trickled in, but only one decided to stay. Adrol went over to the New Nomad Village again, but the residents now said they preferred to send their boys to a local charity school, not to job training.

It was all very discouraging. But we had come too far to give up.

Three more days of determined recruiting got us a total of eight students. Only one belonged to our target population of New Nomad

Village; the rest were from town or the grasslands, but we were none-theless glad to have them. Our woodworking instructor noticed right away that these unpaid students were much more interested in learn-ing than paid students in other programs. Our training center was alive with the sound of saws. It was music to our ears.

The class forged ahead, and before long, each student had pro-duced a picture frame. However, the frames didn't look good. The workmanship was clearly that of beginners; with time and practice, they would get better. After six weeks of slow but steady improvement, we decided to move ahead with the painting class, for which we had twelve students.

The students spent two weeks learning painting basics, such as how to compound the pigments, and they practiced drawing the shapes on paper. They made rapid progress and soon were ready to work on the picture frames themselves.

## The Test

Out in the western town of Batang, our star student, Metok Tso, was finishing twelfth grade, the last year of senior middle school. This is the year that's hell for ambitious students, for they face the notorious *gaokao*, or college entrance examination, held on two days in June si-multaneously throughout China. The exams are a watershed moment that decides a student's entire future: whether they will attend univer-sity—which practically guarantees a good job—or will return home in shame and defeat, sentenced to a lifetime of economic insecurity and physical labor.

With so much at stake, the *gaokao* is preceded by months of in-tense parental pressure and furious cramming. The workload is unbe-lievable. One Dartsendo student I knew headed out to school at six each morning and didn't return home until eleven at night, Monday through Friday, and Saturday was a half-day. This went on throughout her entire twelfth-grade year.

In 2006, 9.5 million children in China were taking the exam to compete for 5.3 million slots in colleges and universities.[85] Despite lowered standards for ethnic minorities, Metok Tso was at a disadvantage because of the poor quality of her school and her rural background. She was competing against minority kids with two educated parents, lots of encouragement at home, much better schools, and perhaps even tutors and cram programs.

To make matters worse, in the months before the exam, Metok Tso had been ill and unable to concentrate. She didn't think she could pass, but she had nothing to lose by trying. When the big day arrived, she went to the testing hall with zero expectations.

Until this time, we at KhamAid knew that Metok Tso had personality, but we didn't realize that she was also smart. Very smart. She passed the exam and was the only one in her class of forty to be admitted to university. Later, she would attribute her *gaokao* success to a complete lack of nerves because she was so certain she would fail. "She laughed about it," Richard Harlan would recall, "She said, 'those other kids just study, study, study. I just stay relaxed.' "

She would attend Southwest University for Nationalities (SWUN), a school in south Chengdu serving Tibetans, Yi, and other minorities. It had an enrollment of more than 20,000 students among its eighteen colleges, and offered degrees in a range of academic fields, including Tibetan language and culture. It wasn't Beijing University, but it would be an enormous step up for a country girl from Sichuan's far west.

---

85　Edward Wong, "Test That Can Determine the Course of Life in China Gets a Closer Examination," *New York Times*, June 30, 2012.

# Community Ties

*Hunters in the snowy heights are of the same mind.*
*Passengers in a skin boat are of the same heart.*
— Tibetan proverb

Community ties are the mortar of civilization. In Tibet, as elsewhere, agrarian people unite to care for land and livestock, to celebrate marriages, to raise children, and to defend against interlopers. Yet the Communist "reforms," introduced in the late 1950s, exploded the social order in communities throughout China by yanking resources and status away from those who had long held them and handing them to people from the lowest strata.

However, wealth transfer was perhaps not nearly as damaging as Communist efforts to make ordinary people despise the former elite. The most destructive and terrifying tool used by the Communists for this purpose was a Machiavellian ritual known as *thamzing* in Tibetan, or "struggle session." Communist cadres targeted landowners, intellectuals, religious leaders, and dissidents, arresting and interrogating them in front of their entire communities to humiliate them and force their confessions to crimes against socialism and the state. The sessions often devolved into torture and sometimes executions.

Two decades of thamzing caused countless suicides. They fractured families and destroyed social cohesion and trust. But after the death of Mao in 1976, as memories faded and new generations emerged, the wounds slowly healed. In contemporary Tibet, thousands of communities endure, cemented by shared languages and histories. The young may feel the tug of faraway places, yet few wander far or for long.[86] Caterpillar fungus is a compelling economic reason to stay at home; another is the difficulty of finding employment outside Tibet due to weak language skills, job experience, and social networks, as well as outright discrimination by non-Tibetan employers.

Another reason—and certainly not least—is people's attachment to the land itself: the alchemy of blood and sweat and soil, the miracle of growth, crops feeding generation after generation in an unceasing cycle. As KhamAid's work in Wayö Village unfolded, I would come to know its people, their land, and their collective abiding strength.

## The Life and Times of Wayö Village

Minyak Gangkar, at 7,556 meters (24,790 feet), is the highest peak on the eastern Tibetan plateau—a mountain so treacherous that it has slain almost as many climbers as it has suffered to reach the summit. The ice-clad, wind-flayed peak is a source of glacial melt that sends glittering threads rushing downhill, one of them passing through Wayö Village before entwining with the Lingchu Charmo River, the region's lifeblood. Perched just above the white-water torrent, Wayö and its ancient houses rest on a tongue of alluvium, the core of the community occupying about half a square kilometer of gently terraced fields.

---

86  In 2018, about one in forty-two Tibetans was living in exile, with the remainder residing in China. This ratio is based on a Central Tibetan Administration estimate of 150,000 Tibetans belonging to the Tibetan diaspora and a 2010 Chinese census count of 6.2 million.

As seen from Wayö, Minyak Gangkar's foothills obscure the mountain itself and throw cold shadows on the fields until midmorning. Yet by afternoon, the sun beats hard, drawing up the heads of grain and burnishing the faces of farmers. Situated at only 3,250 meters (10,000 feet) above sea level and sheltered from the highland winds, Wayö's soil sprouts wheat and pulse in addition to highland barley, the staple grain of Tibet.

From a project management perspective, Wayö's location was not inconvenient. From KhamAid's field office in Dartsendo, we'd motor six hours, first west over Gyu La, then south on national highway 215 to the Sadé Township seat. The seat was a small but useful town with half a dozen restaurants, a couple of tea houses, four rustic guest houses, a primary school, a square where "black" taxis gathered, and shops carrying all manner of supplies. Travelers passed through on their way to Gyezur County to the south, and traders came in late summer to buy mushrooms.

In the summertime, tourists passed through Sadé on their way to hiking trails on Minyak Gongkar's lower flanks. Some also came to see the valley's extraordinary stone towers, some more than 20 meters (70 feet) tall, built by the Minyak people in ancient times.[87]

Farming was Wayö's economic base. During the timber boom, a few residents had invested in trucks to haul logs, but the 1998 logging ban put an end to that income. Under the *Tuigeng Huanlin* (Grain for Green) program, Wayö people had surrendered 72% of their less-productive agricultural land so that it could revert to forest, leaving an average of only 5 *mu* (.33 hectares) per family. In exchange, families

---

87 Wood samples taken from the two stone towers nearest to Sadé have been dated by Frederique Darragon at A.D. 1030-1290 and A.D. 1170-1280 (personal communication).

were paid 240 yuan per *mu* per year so that they could replace their lost crop with purchased food.

Despite the loss of farmland, residents were increasingly prosperous thanks to the caterpillar fungus bonanza. Many built new houses. In the mid-2000s, the community got mobile phone coverage, and roads were improved, making it easier to sell the fungus they gathered and to access goods from outside. Their standard of living improved, and a couple of families even sent their sons to university.

One leading citizen of Wayö Village was the party secretary, a man named Tsedo. Tsedo didn't look like a Communist Party official: no slicked-back hair, no blue suit, no Mao cap with a red star pinned to it. Instead, his long hair was done up in the traditional Khampa red tassel, and I usually saw him in dark trousers and a dust-streaked sweater, as if he had just stepped away from the fields. Tsedo had a square jaw and a sun-creased face; he was as tall as his neighbor Pema Penlo, and even more imposing thanks to his broad shoulders.

Wayö Village also had a headman, but Secretary Tsedo wielded far more influence. One resident told us privately they thought Tsedo was a wise leader, in touch with his people, and he always tried to help them when they were in need. I later learned that the community had elected Tsedo to his position in a balloting process held every three years. He was laid back and self-effacing, as if his appointment as Party Secretary was just a paperwork snafu that would likely be cleared up soon. His Chinese was rustic, but his people listened well whenever he spoke to them in Minyak, their native tongue.

Tsedo's household owned a medium-sized herd of about twenty cows, including some *dzo*, the yak-cow hybrid preferred for milking and plowing. They also had sheep, goats, and three horses. Tsedo's family didn't have the nicest house in Wayö, nor the largest herds, but their land was considered prime: it included good pasture, fields for growing barley, and a bit of forest. The family's greatest assets were its young people: a son at university and Tsedo's daughter and her husband at home. Strong workers were vitally necessary to keep a farm going and maximize cash income from collecting caterpillar fungus.

Tsedo was a good politician. He knew how to make money, but he also knew that if he was too greedy, people would criticize his family. So, he got some profit from KhamAid by lodging and feeding our teams at his home, but he also provided many free services to us, skillfully balancing his short-term profit with his long-term need for village harmony and support.

Tsedo's son would probably not return after graduating from university, so Tsedo's daughter and son-in-law looked set to inherit the farm. In keeping with Tsedo's stature, the son-in-law, Ahmee, was tall, handsome, and smart, a good catch for any girl and an excellent prospect for safeguarding the family's future.

At this time, Wayö Village had 245 residents divided among forty-five households, of which twelve had been officially designated as poor by the government and were, therefore, eligible for special assistance. Families were permitted to have three children, but some had fewer. Overall, Wayö's population was stable or slightly shrinking, unlike most rural Han villages, which were being hollowed out as working-age adults left in search of jobs. One Wayö girl had become a nun and gone to India; other girls married out of the village; some young men also left to seek their fortunes elsewhere. I did not hear of any sons becoming monks, although surely there were a few.

One source of vexation in Wayö was having to send children three kilometers away to the Sadé Township seat to attend primary school. A few years previously, Wayö had had its own school, but the government had closed it as part of its policy of consolidation. While people valued education, they didn't like sending their children so far away and feared the outside world would pollute the souls of their children. As a result, many kept their children at home.

A problem that the residents didn't notice, but we did, was that their farming techniques were old-fashioned and inefficient. They planted, tilled, and harvested crops as their grandfathers and great-grandfathers had done: by hand and using *dzo*-pulled plows. They ground their barley with a water-driven millstone. The only "modern" machine in the entire agricultural cycle was a gasoline-powered blower used for winnowing.

Wayö farmers did not use chemical fertilizer, take measures to control pests, or plant scientifically improved varieties of grain.[88] The small scale and illiquidity of family landholdings made it difficult for them to consolidate, commercialize, or modernize their methods.[89] Their livestock went almost entirely to domestic consumption. They paid little attention to breeding or feed balance, and so the quality of their animal products was low.

Hygiene and sanitation in the village were poor. The residents had no organized system of trash disposal, and litter was rife. Most of the newer houses had long-drop toilets, which were convenient for householders but created open sewage flows on the ground. During the daytime, livestock roamed freely and left manure everywhere. At

---

88  Emily Yeh states that, in late 2000, farmers in TAR were required to purchase a set quota of chemical fertilizer. I have never heard of such a requirement in Kandze Prefecture. *Taming Tibet: Landscape Transformation and the Gift of Chinese Development* (Cornell University Press, 2013), p. 183.

89  Much of the socio-economic data on Wayö Village presented here was collected by Zhao Jun, an agricultural economist from the University of Saskatchewan, who interviewed thirteen randomly chosen Wayö families in the spring of 2007.

night, most families kept their animals close by, creating opportunities for diseases to spread. The nearest clinic was in Sadé, but people were dissatisfied with the care offered there.

There were no showers in Wayö, so people bathed infrequently. They didn't use solar energy or biogas to heat water; they used wood-burning stoves, which contributed to deforestation of the surrounding area.

Wayö people's Buddhist beliefs led them to eschew pesticides and forgo raising poultry, innovations that might have improved yields, diversified their income, and added protein to their diets. Owing to bitter memories of forced collectivization in the 1950s, they were averse to any kind of land sharing. Except for caterpillar fungus and wild matsutake mushrooms, everything they grew or made was for local use.

As long as caterpillar fungus demand stayed strong, Wayö would be prosperous. But only a few families, those with children in high school or college, had a backup plan if the fungus market failed. Few had more than a primary school education. Easy fungus money left them disinterested in other kinds of business. One family owned a microvan that they hired out, but these days taxi services were a buyer's market, and the van generated little income.

What *did* protect Wayö families was strong social cohesion based on generations of living together and few ways to leave. Social rewards for cooperation were great, and sanctions for defecting were strong. Wealthy families helped poor ones, and people commonly lent each other cash or grain in times of need. Belying the heavy fortifications of the ancient houses, residents told us there was no crime in Wayö, and most families didn't even keep dogs.

Yet there were many potential sources of friction in the community. Animals got into other people's fields and pastures. Tsedo regularly requisitioned labor for communal projects such as road building that brought unequal benefits. Brothers sometimes married into shared-wife arrangements to prevent land from being divided. Yet despite these and other reasons for conflict, Wayö's people generally got along.

## Gaining Trust

When I returned to Wayö eight months after my first visit, Pema Penlo's words still rung in my ears: *Many people have come here. They took a lot of photos and measured my house. Then they left. They didn't come back, and they didn't do anything to help.*

I was determined not to let the community down. But before I could do anything, I had to win their trust.

The key, I decided, would be wiring.

At this time, anyone from a developed country who visited a rural house in Kham was bound to be startled by the unskillful electrical arrangements. In this respect, Wayö was typical. Whether indoors or out, materials were of the lowest quality and looked like they had been installed by a 12-year-old with a hammer and a kitchen knife. Cables were draped everywhere like Christmas tinsel and held up by bent nails. Fuses were unheard of. When they needed to connect something, they twisted bare wires together and left them completely exposed.

An ounce of prevention: I didn't want any house in Wayö to end up like the charred ruins I'd seen around Kham, or Wayö children to be electrocuted by the bare wires that hung easily within reach. So, when I brought a team of architect-conservators to Wayö, we carried with us a special consultant: a Han electrician from Dartsendo. He would be our wedge for the entire Wayö program.

Wayö's electricity, we learned, came from a tiny hydropower station that had been running for more than twenty years under poor maintenance. It provided power to several townships and was desperately overloaded. The valley was slated to get a new station in a few years as part of a national push to dam rivers in the Yangtze watershed and send their energy to China's ballooning cities. While the new dams would be terrible for people whose homes would be submerged, it would benefit villages like Wayö that were badly underpowered.[90]

Wayö residents were lucky to have electricity—many people didn't—but it was woefully inadequate. Chinese households normally run on 220 volts AC, but in Wayö, the voltage varied unpredictably throughout the day, sometimes dipping as low as 40 volts. Conventional wiring was impossible. Customers had to combine two positive wires and one neutral wire to boost the voltage sufficiently to operate lights and recharge mobile phones. The current was inadequate for major appliances like electric stoves and heaters. With any other arrangement, small appliances wouldn't work either. Some families didn't even have a neutral wire.

Wayö already had an electrician, a man named Dzandoi, but he had been trained in outdoor wiring only. Moreover, many residents did their own work and didn't consult him. Everywhere in Wayö, indoors and out, the wiring was in chaos. We paired Dzandoi with our electrician, and the two of them went through the four ancient houses ripping down derelict wiring with its crumbly cloth insulation and replacing it with pretty color-coated wire mounted neatly with plastic clips. They installed junction boxes, switches, outlets, and fuses, none of which had existed in Wayö before. Dzandoi got a crash course in how to do it right, and the ancient houses became models of electrical correctness for the village.

We also gave a fire extinguisher to the families in each ancient

---

90  A major dam was planned for the Lingchu Charmo River, but the project was later canceled.

house, and trained the women on how to use them.[91] We told the families that these gifts were unconditional because we wanted the houses safe against fire.

The strategy worked, and the families began to warm to us, allowing our architect team to crawl all over their homes with cameras, sketchbooks, and measuring tape. But documenting the houses was just the first step. Not only did we want to help Wayö preserve its unusual architectural heritage, we also hoped they could parlay these assets into income. To do this, I would need to do some major social engineering and expose residents to radical new ideas.

The immediate problem, however, was stability. How long would the houses continue to stand? Would the owners let us fix them? And after the repairs, would owners allow their homes to become part of a master plan for cultural tourism? If we could make *that* chemistry work, could we then withdraw into the background so that the residents would truly own the project themselves?

Our wiring improvements had built a measure of trust. The local government was throwing up no roadblocks. On the contrary, they were pleased because Wayö had been named as one of twenty-five pilot villages in Dartsendo County to participate in the New Socialist Construction Program. Under this program, Wayö would receive an 800,000-yuan grant for new infrastructure, including an access road and a pipe to carry spring water.[92] As a cultural tourism site, Wayö would shine even brighter, and make the township officials look good.

---

91   Structure fires are a recurring problem, especially in monasteries. Later, KhamAid helped a local Tibetan organization get a grant to put on a fire prevention training program that was attended by monks from twenty-nine monasteries.

92   The village was expected to raise 200,000 yuan themselves and to contribute labor.

All of that mattered, but we would be nowhere without support from the residents themselves. I asked Secretary Tsedo to assemble the elders and the owners of the ancient houses for a meeting. They came to his home that very afternoon.

My stomach was full of butterflies as the men dragged up stools and cushions into a circle. They were illiterate farmers with calloused hands and stained shirts, but they held the fate of my project in their hands. To them, of course, the future of their community was a matter of extreme importance. They looked very serious.

As soon as Tsedo's wife had poured tea for everyone, we got started. After making introductions, I handed the floor over to my chief consultant, a genial British conservation architect named John Sanday. His manner was open, respectful, and direct. "My name's John, and I've been doing this work in Nepal for thirty-five years," he said pleasantly. "I've been asked by KhamAid to come here and put together a program for the conservation of these marvelous ancient houses."

There was a pause while our translator rendered Sanday's words into the Minyak language. Then he talked about the project's next steps: investigating the buildings' structural condition, developing a work program, training local people to do new repair techniques. He continued for some minutes, with pauses for translation, while the elders nodded and murmured "Ah-leh" and "Oh-oh," which assured us that they were listening and that they understood.

Then it was my turn to speak. I told them how we believed their houses were important, not just to Tibetans, but to history and humankind. KhamAid stood ready to help the community preserve them. But there was a catch. Legally, ethically, we could not use USAID funds to do a project that would enrich only the house owners. The entire village would have to benefit. That meant that owners who got our help would have to share any resulting tourism income with the rest of the village.

The men looked grave and thoughtful but gave no reply, nor did they ask any questions. I told them there was no need to decide today, but if they wanted to work with KhamAid, that they should let me know, and the sooner, the better.

Then, one by one, owners of the ancient houses expressed their views. To a man, they all praised Minyak Rinpoche and said that, for his sake, they had done their best to preserve the old homes. But their words also betrayed growing impatience. "When I was building my new house," one man said, "I wanted to take the stones from my old house, but Rinpoche said not to, so I borrowed fifty thousand yuan from my wife's family. I'm still in debt."

Another owner was one of the richest men in Wayö. He had already remodeled his house extensively. He said, "I'm not sure about a new house and giving my old house to the public. My only hope is to stay in my old house." He added politely, "If you could do some repairs, it would be very kind of you."

Then Pema Penlo began to speak. His voice was subdued, but his words were bitter: "Others have scolded us, laughed at us, and teased us because we've stayed in our old house. We've suffered enough."

His words must have touched a chord, for there were murmurs of "*Re, re, re*" (yes, yes, yes) from several others in the room.

When Party Secretary Tsedo opened his mouth, the murmuring stopped. The men even stopped slurping their tea. Everyone listened intently to hear what Tsedo had to say.

"If not for Minyak Rinpoche, we would have destroyed the buildings long ago," Secretary Tsedo began, his manner earnest and direct. "Many foreigners have come here; they took lots of photos and notes, but in the end, they went away and didn't do anything. Today you are here, and this is like sunshine in our hearts."

Secretary Tsedo continued, "If you can provide a benefit to the village and especially the people who own the old houses, we will welcome you very warmly." To underscore this message, he repeated it using Minyak's honorific language.

"I'm very touched that you came here," he continued, and added, "I apologize for the bad condition of the road. And I'm sorry we didn't prepare any special foods for you."

I had to smile at this. It was so delightfully typical for Tibetan hosts to fret about the rough conditions, oblivious to the stunning ecstasy of their landscape, the radiance of their spiritual practices, and the many other intangibles that pulled like a tractor beam drawing me and countless others to Tibet.

As the meeting broke up, I exchanged notes with my team. We agreed that getting Secretary Tsedo's public endorsement was a big win. But Secretary Tsedo's praise alone wouldn't be enough to get us a willing partner. Make no mistake: anyone who allowed us to repair their house would be taking an enormous leap of faith.

In the days that followed, one by one, the house owners gave us their answers. One home was in bad shape and partly vacant; nevertheless, its owners declined our help. I wondered if they weren't secretly waiting for their house to fall down so they could take the stones and build a new one. The roof was collapsing, and it wouldn't be long.

The wealthy man also declined to work with us. That was okay because he could take care of his own house.

I was disappointed to learn that the two owners of the Pema House, the grandest and best-preserved historic home in Wayö, also declined our help. This was not a disaster, however, because Sanday had determined that their house was stable and would stand for a long while, even if nothing was done.

The fourth and last owner was Dendrup Gyantse, who was 66 years old. Dendrup's family was one of the poorest in Wayö. He had lost both of his sons: one had died young, and another had gone to Chengdu and hadn't come back. Dendrup and his wife Tsewang Drolma were raising their young granddaughter alone. For years, the family had consisted of the tiny girl and two senior citizens who could do little heavy work. They could not possibly gather enough caterpillar fungus to support themselves, nor could they run a farm or maintain their giant old house.

Poverty notwithstanding, Dendrup was much respected in the village. He was a devout man with a prodigious memory who could recite family trees going back ten generations. Lately, his family's prospects had been improving because his granddaughter was now about seventeen and had recently wed, and her husband had joined the household. The young couple wanted a new house, but the cost was far beyond their means. Yet the old house had serious problems. To keep a roof over his family's heads, Dendrup would have to work with KhamAid.

When we left Wayö, we had what we needed. Dendrup agreed to our condition for repairing his house: villagers could use it as a Minyak heritage center for five years. Our most urgent task was to fix a wall that was badly bowed. Now I had to line up resources and bring the team back to do the necessary work while we still had forward momentum—and before the wall collapsed.

# Our Girls Overcome

When Kara Jenkinson got the bad news about the nineteen-year-old student's incurable lupus, she didn't take it lying down. She got busy networking in Beijing to find doctors she could talk to. They told her that while lupus had no known cure, the symptoms could be controlled, and most sufferers can live something like a normal life. But Lhamo Dolkar would need expert help.

8/1/2006

Dear Friends,

Since many of you have been asking how the situation with Lhamo Dolkar, the 19-year-old Tibetan girl sponsored by KhamAid Foundation, is proceeding, I thought I would write and update you all.

Lhamo Dolkar, her "grandmother" (not a biological grandmother, but a close family friend), and her uncle arrived in Chengdu on Saturday morning, while I arrived late Sunday night after taking an almost nonstop 14-hour bus ride from Ta'u. I felt so exhausted after the eventful trip, during which we witnessed fistfights over who should pass first over a landslide and had Chinese songs expressing their love for Chairman Mao and Tiananmen Square blasted into our ears for hours on end, that I swapped my much-anticipated Mexican dinner for two panadol and slept till 6:30 A.M., when I met Lhamo and her relatives in the lobby of the Traffic Hotel in Chengdu.

There were lots of hugs and tears with the family being extremely emotional that she had this chance to see medical experts in Chengdu.

Poor Lhamo was very unwell when I first saw her. She could barely walk unassisted, most of her skin was discoloured, and her joints swollen and painful. As the day wore on, her fever increased, and she had headaches and stomach pain. Despite this, she was constantly sweet and good-natured, more interested in hearing about her sponsors and former and current KhamAid employees (that's you, John and Dana) than in talking about her own situation. She hasn't complained once, despite being in serious pain.

We didn't think registering at the hospital would be difficult with Lhamo speaking Sichuanese and Mandarin, and myself also speaking Mandarin. However, after queuing to register for an hour and a half, the man at the counter started firing questions at us that neither of us could understand. After much impatience on his part, we finally realized he was asking Lhamo what sickness she had! And here I was thinking that that was what they were supposed to be telling us!!

Anyway, we were allocated an appointment with a doctor in the Clinical Immunology Department that afternoon, who pleasingly was very patient (though in the beginning directed all questions to me as she thought that neither Lhamo nor her relatives spoke any Chinese!). I have to say that at the hospital we do make quite a sight. While Lhamo is dressed in western clothes, her grandmother is dressed in traditional Tibetan dress and shirt with red thread woven into her plaits. Lhamo's uncle, while wearing the traditional male chuba, also has a large knife attached to his waist! The four of us make an interesting team.

Yesterday, Lhamo completed all the blood and urine tests, and today we picked up three of the four results. One test showed significant problems with her kidney, so we were immediately referred to a kidney specialist. The kidney department happily seems to give preferential treatment for Tibetans accompanied by foreigners, and much interest was aroused in our case. The kidney doctor was extremely kind and seemed to accept that Lhamo was my "sister" (she calls me "sister" in any case). Despite the masses of people waiting, they got us in immediately to see a doctor who had trained at Harvard. He didn't even charge us for the consultation and instructed us to see him again on Friday when the remaining test results come through.

Both doctors today and yesterday have stressed to Lhamo that she must not stop taking her prednisone (lupus medication) as if this occurs she will immediately be as ill as she was yesterday, or worse. Yesterday afternoon, she started taking prednisone again, and today was already markedly improved in her energy levels. This information is already a great start as her doctor in Derong (her hometown) frequently instructed her to stop taking this medication.

That is as far as we have come now. After Thursday and Friday, we shall have much more information, and Lhamo will have been taught how to control the lupus as best as possible from her hometown and will have been provided with plenty of medication and doctors' phone numbers. If all goes well, she may even be able to return to school in September.

We are not getting our hopes up too much yet, though, but keep your fingers crossed for her!

Kara

From here, it was not all smooth sailing, but with Kara at her side, Lhamo got what she needed to control her lupus and return to school in the fall.

Meanwhile, John Giszczak and Kara together had tracked down the three Ta'u students whose scholarship funds had been stolen and gave them the money that the officials had repaid. All three girls returned to school to repeat the ninth grade, and we were relieved to find that administrators held no grudge against them.

At this time, Metok Tso entered the Southwest University for Nationalities, helped by her sponsor, Richard Harlan. She arrived with big ambitions, enrolling in the Department of Literature and Art. However, she was still suffering from the illness that had afflicted her the previous spring. Soon after classes started, she had a relapse and had to go home to rest.

It was a setback, but Metok Tso was never one to give up. After she was better, Harlan arranged for her to come to Dartsendo to receive tutoring in English from someone he knew there.

The changes we made to our scholarship program were helping to thwart corrupt officials. We did not recover all the money we had lost—some of it disappeared forever—but we kept the girls in school. By now, sixty-one were in senior middle school, and twenty-two had already graduated. Some of these young women took the civil service exam and landed government jobs. Others were going to college, helped by us or others.

The newcomer John Giszczak succeeded Kara Jenkinson as

KhamAid's Education Program Director, and in that role, he was perfecting the art of handling sleazy officials. His weapons: unfailing politeness, artful flattery, comprehensive policy knowledge, and slick sleight-of-hand: he would lay a pile of cash on the table, get them salivating, then, moments later, snatch the money away and stuff it into his bag, to be kept safe there until they agreed with whatever he had in mind.

## Repairs to an Ancient Home

After the fall harvest, we returned to Wayö to perform surgery on the ancient home belonging to the old man, Dendrup Gyantse. The south wall of his house had a dangerous bulge in the middle, which Sanday said resulted from seismic activity, the poor-quality clay used as mortar, and flawed masonry technique.

Walls in Wayö, as in many other parts of Kham, suffered from instability because the people could not afford the cost of rectangular stone blocks, so they used uncut stones despite their irregular shapes. To make a wall made of natural stones look good, masons would orient the stones with their biggest, flattest sides turned outward, toward one of the two faces. The rounder sides were hidden in the middle, creating an irregular interior space that builders filled up with pebbles and clay.

The rubble in the middle had little power to hold the wall together, so, over the centuries, the two faces of Dendrup's wall had come partially unglued. The wall had a void in the middle of it and a three-story vertical crack. We would have to work very carefully. Too much movement would send the wall crashing down, and with it the roof, and that would be the end of Dendrup's house.

To avoid this catastrophe, Sanday was going to teach our hired crew how to insert temporary shoring inside the house to hold up the

weight of the roof so that the damaged wall could be safely disman-
tled. This technique could be readily applied to the Pema House and
many others around the region.

As soon as we arrived, we let it be known that we needed construction workers. The prospect of paying jobs quickly brought in
folks from up and down the valley. Our foreman found it all too easy
to say yes. After all, it was someone else's money, wasn't it? In no time,
we had forty or fifty workers. Moreover, the unskilled laborers thought
they would get fifty-five yuan per day, much higher than the norm.

I was having flashbacks of the trouble we had had at Senggé
Monastery, but Secretary Tsedo saved my bacon; he sent home un-
needed workers and hammered out a compromise on wages for those
who remained. Crisis averted.

Normally, to insert columns as shoring, local workers would get
some logs, cut them a tiny bit too long, then bang them into place with
a sledgehammer, sending shock waves throughout the structure—not
a good idea in Dendrup's house, which was far too fragile. Instead,
John Sanday showed them how to nudge columns into place so that
the structure was undisturbed, a technique called "folding wedges."

## "Folding Wedges"

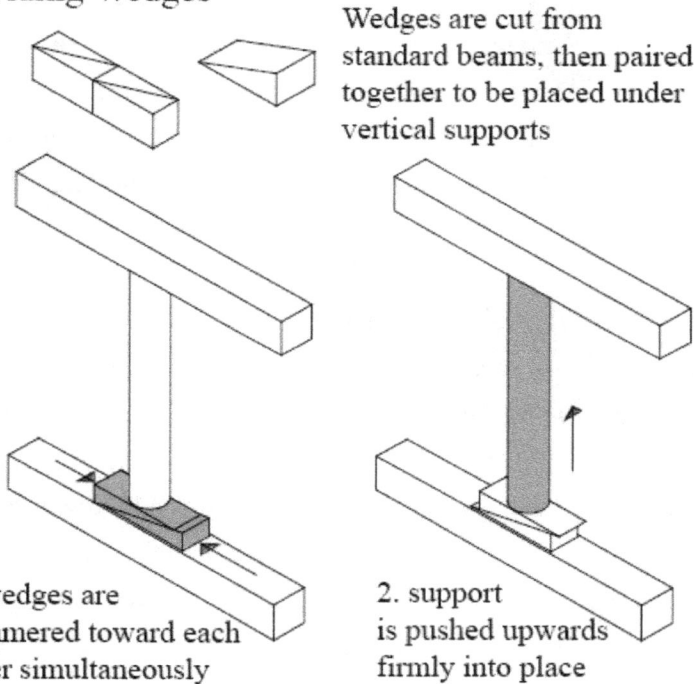

Wedges are cut from standard beams, then paired together to be placed under vertical supports

1. wedges are hammered toward each other simultaneously

2. support is pushed upwards firmly into place

After several hours of using this technique to shore up the first floor of Dendrup's house, we went upstairs to his living room for tsampa and cigarettes. The foreman remarked, "This is an excellent method that we have never learned before. We want to learn more. Can you stay for a month?"

Sanday could not stay for a month, but he was there for the next three days as the workers installed temporary shoring on every floor; then he was ready for them to remove the damaged section of the wall. Working from the roof, they first used their bare hands, then sledgehammers and crowbars to pry the stones loose. A hole opened and expanded.

The shoring worked. Defying gravity, the wall held together, and the roof stayed up. With Dendrup's home now exposed like a doll's house, Sanday showed them how to use jacks to level the sagging floors. Then the masons went to work, putting back the stones they had taken out, this time using better clay and orienting the longest stones to tie the two faces together. A few days later, the wall was whole again.

## Search for the Perfect Product

On the high grasslands of Lhagang, our carpentry and painting students had been practicing their skills throughout the summer. By September, they had produced about a dozen finished picture frames. We gathered them up and placed them in shops around Lhagang town to be sold on consignment. Now came the big test: would people buy them?

The answer was yes, they would—but the buyers were not tourists; they were KhamAid's friends and supporters. The Kellogg volunteers, now back in the United States, all wanted them, and we got some mail orders from our website. By autumn, the trainees had returned to school, and demand dried up, too. The picture frames seemed like a fizzle.

Now we had just nine more months on our USAID grant to find a product with long-lasting appeal. To get a quick win and meet USAID targets, we held training classes in tailoring, bootmaking, and painting—traditional skills that we hoped would equip local people to compete against copycats from outside.

Nevertheless, I was dissatisfied with Tibetans selling things to each other and remained hungry to find something that would attract outside money. A proposal for such a product came from an unexpected direction: a young, flaxen-haired former Peace Corps volunteer named Angela Lankford. In her quest to support herself while remaining in western Sichuan, Lankford had discovered a niche market for high-end Tibetan textiles. Not rugs; we had long ago dismissed the notion of trying to enter the highly mature and competitive rug market. In Lankford's travels around Kham, she had acquired a few antique blankets of exceptional beauty woven in Shamalong, a grasslands community in Lhagang Township. Made with a mixture of yak hair and homespun, hand-dyed wool, the blankets had an earthy appeal that excited American connoisseurs. Yet Tibetans were abandoning the craft because they had acquired a liking for the soft synthetic fabrics and bright chemical dyes found in factory-made blankets. If this trend continued, indigenous textile skills would soon vanish.

KhamAid entered into a partnership with Angela Lankford's business, the Khampa Nomad Artisans Cooperative, which she had started with her husband, a Lhagang herdsman. KhamAid would run a class to teach the disappearing art of working with yak hair, and the Cooperative would sell the blankets to its customers overseas.

In November, the training started with eight trainees and two teachers. It lasted for two months, during which the trainees, all women, produced four large blankets and four small ones. However, the blankets were not made to our specifications. "Even the most basic and clear requirement that the items be at least fifty percent yak hair was not met," Lankford wrote in a report. The trainees had found it too difficult to work with yak hair and had substituted wool. She knew her discerning customers would not buy these rather ordinary blankets.

The lesson we learned was this: developing artisan products is a long, painstaking process that is part business, part social science, and part art. The key was developing and maturing a terrific product. Herders could not do it, at least not by themselves in the beginning, because they did not understand outsiders' tastes. The women simply could not fathom why Americans would prefer rough yak hair over soft wool. Like many herders in Tibet, the women had little exposure to the arts outside their own insular world, and what is more, they belonged to a culture that valued the ability to make exact copies rather than express new ideas. Creativity would have to come from outside. We needed help.

## Market Linkages

At the start of the year of the Fire-Sow (2007), our USAID grant was almost gone; however, there was still time and money for one more hail-Mary pass. I posted an advertisement on KhamAid's website seeking a product developer. A few weeks later, I received a note from a stranger. "I am a handicrafts specialist," it began. "I have worked in a number of countries in West Africa for the past fifteen years."

West Africa? That had to be at least as challenging as Kham.

"For the last four years," the letter continued. "I founded and ran a highly successful crafts production, retail, and wholesale export business in Mali."

There was much more, but I was already sold.

Elaine Bellezza was a development professional who not only had a knack for product design but also understood how to work with native artisans and bring crafts to market on a large scale, providing consistent and long-lasting employment for a whole community. Her Malian artisans made household goods like table linen, bedspreads, and furniture. The products reflected African influence but were smart, contemporary, and eminently suitable for homes in America and Europe—the sorts of things you see in department stores and import shops.

To her, the failure of our picture frame enterprise was no surprise. "Training never inspires people except if it is directly linked to orders," she wrote in an email. "We do not want to 'train' people; we want to do more than that, and that means linking them to markets."

I spent hours on the phone with Elaine absorbing her way of doing business. She advised us to target buyers who were not Tibetan culture buffs or Tibetan Buddhists, but ordinary people who knew nothing about Tibet but were enchanted by the product's beauty and value.

The idea that folks might buy Tibetan products without caring where they came from was a revelation. That was a much bigger market, and it would mean employment for many more people. My problem was, I had been thinking too small. We should have started with a much bigger pot of money and at least three years to develop the project. Now, we had only enough time and money from our USAID grant for a last-ditch effort.

After the weather turned warm and caterpillar fungus season was over, I brought Elaine Bellezza to Kham where Mr. Wu took her to meet various artisans. She spent two weeks working her creative magic with them and fashioned half a dozen prototypes of totally new products.

Meanwhile, Mr. Wu and other field staff prepared for the second part of this eleventh-hour effort: a workshop on the handicraft business, to be held in Dartsendo. We notified everyone we knew, offering grants to people like teachers from Gyalten Rinpoche's school and residents of Wayö Village to cover the cost of travel. To our great satisfaction, many accepted, as well as others who had to pay their own way. The workshop opened with a motley crowd: product designers, university professors, aid workers, foreign entrepreneurs, Buddhist monks, and even a group of Dong nationality embroiderers from Guizhou Province.

In addition to Elaine as the crafts expert, we also had a new team of Kellogg Corps volunteers to teach business planning. And we had an army of translators so that all of these people could communicate.

The first sessions covered how to access the international market, the buyer's expectations, and the nuts and bolts of how sales are made, from producer to end consumer. Then, to great fanfare, Elaine unveiled her prototypes. They were unlike anything seen in Tibet before:

Pillow covers made of undyed yak hair interwoven with wool (traditional Tibetans would never use undyed cloth for decoration).

A mirror frame sparingly decorated with a lotus flower painted only at one corner (traditional Tibetan decorations are never sparing).

A table runner appliquéd with endless knot symbols tilted at irregular angles. (A Buddhist symbol tilted? Unheard of!)

"Even though we're not doing traditional-looking Tibetan *products*," Elaine explained to her baffled audience, "they are traditional *techniques.*" And then came the punchline: "The people who are doing the traditional techniques," she said, "*as long as they have an income, their techniques will not die.*"

She proceeded to critique her own prototypes, holding nothing back. "The painting is perfect," she said about one, "but the construction is bad. This product is not market-ready. It takes at least three remakes on your product before you have a product. Very rarely is it right the first time or second time."

The highlight of the workshop was one-on-one sessions in which artisans showed their products to Elaine and got her input. Later, after the workshop was over, participants completed opinion surveys: thirty-four out of thirty-four thought they learned something useful, and twenty-six out of thirty-four said they would pursue the handicrafts business afterward (five more said 'maybe').

We wanted the prototypes to remain accessible, so we gave them to a tea house in Dartsendo with the understanding that they would be on public display. Anyone could go into the tea house, study the prototypes, develop the designs, and market them.

That was it for our handicraft program. We had planted many seeds—training, designs, market linkages—but did any take root? Only time would tell.

## Integrated Community Development

When spring arrived, we returned to Wayö and performed more repairs on Dendrup's house, this time on the roof, introducing sheets of rubbery material between layers of clay to improve water resistance, a technique pioneered by Minyak Rinpoche. According to our agreement with Dendrup, in exchange for repairs to his house, Wayö Village would be able to use it as a cultural center and hostel for five years. KhamAid brought in a development expert to introduce the residents to the idea of organizing a cooperative tourism business. During the summer, we enlisted some tourists to help the residents learn hospitality skills.

However, the community needed more than tourists; they needed their abandoned schoolhouse reopened so children would not have to walk so far to school. So, I recruited more volunteers to renovate the derelict classroom and living quarters, and I secured a grant from NVIDIA Corporation to hire a teacher and buy supplies. In autumn, the school reopened with twenty-nine students.

A month later, I brought a group of American volunteers to spend a week at Wayö and help with the wall paintings conservation at the village's small temple and two of the ancient houses, work led by an Italian conservator and five assistants from Nepal. It was thrilling to watch the painted deities being cleaned of centuries of dust and dirt, their colors emerging and taking on new life.

Like the paintings, the outlines of Wayö's future were beginning to appear: children getting educated, the economy diversifying, and the village becoming a showcase for Minyak cultural heritage.

Meanwhile, the government was improving the community's access to water and electricity. Wayö's future looked bright indeed.

## Return to Palpung Monastery

My group of American volunteers spent a week at Wayö cleaning paintings. Then I brought them west to see the printworks at the Degé Parkhang, the most famous cultural heritage site in Kham. I had not been there in three years and was glad to see the site well cared for: new wooden columns in one of the chanting halls, improved drainage outside, and no sign of any tar or concrete, showing that the local officials had heeded our advice.

From the Parkhang roof, I took a moment to gaze up the valley toward Sögyal's grave and to remember our brief time together. Then it was back to work. Under crisp autumn skies and blazing sunshine, the volunteers and I motored out to Palpung Monastery, in Degé's back country. The monastery guesthouse I had jump-started eight years earlier had outgrown its original quarters and had been moved to a different part of the main temple. It was not Club Med, but the floors were cleaner and bedding fresher than I ever thought possible, and the views and atmosphere remained as spectacular as always.

At day's end, while the volunteers were snugged up with hot drinks around a stove, I went up to the rooftop to be alone with my memories of everything that had transpired at this place since my first visit sixteen years before. The long, broad roof floated like the deck of an aircraft carrier; beneath it, the temple purred, an engine of compassion for all sentient beings. From far below came the familiar sound of dogs calling to each other. The sun teetered on the horizon, and shadows were rising from the forest depths. Far in the distance, glistening whitecaps stood upon wave after wave of mountains. Stars, brighter here than perhaps anywhere on earth, fired in the indigo sky.

Suddenly, a young novice emerged from the darkness and beckoned me to follow. I trailed the narrow, red-robed figure as he led me into the highest part of the monastery, a complex of rooms set like a wheelhouse upon its broad clay roof. He led me inside, then along a balcony looking down on the lap of the giant seated statue of Maitreya Buddha in front of the main chanting hall, to a staircase around back. Behind the stairs was a small, hidden portal, a door that opened into the former *torkhang*, or tailoring room.

Inside this chamber, long retired and high above earthly cares, was Khenpo Tsering, the prickly abbot who, eight years earlier, had agreed to my absurd proposal to start a guest house at his monastery. He was frail and shrunken, but he still had the same proud back, tall like a tent pole cloaked in the folds of his robes. The pale orange glow of a hanging lightbulb showed me that his eyes were soft, and he was smiling.

Khenpo Tsering struggled to rise; the boy took his arm and helped the elderly monk to his feet, whereupon he seized both my hands in his. We stood there for perhaps a minute, unmoving and mute, and an odd feeling of joy suffused me. Then he released my hands and invited me to sit.

There was not much to say (my knowledge of Degé-ke had little improved in the intervening years), but Khenpo Tsering asked the boy to pour tea, which I happily accepted. Then his face lit up with a remembered thought. He pulled open a drawer and rummaged inside it until he found a small parcel wrapped in cloth. He unwound the fabric to expose a wristwatch of ordinary manufacture but clearly precious to him. Then he took my hand, pressed the watch into my palm, and closed my fingers around it: a gift.

## Looking Back—and Forward

Six years earlier, we had returned to the village called Oro and worked with residents to replant their burned forest, planting 20,000 spruce seedlings on the mountain. Every year since, I had stopped by to check on our trees. While the great majority—at least 75%—had died, those that remained were growing at about seven centimeters (three inches) a year, their blue crowns slowly lifting above the burnt stumps and shrubs. With the scattered small pines that had survived the fire, they were creating a healthy forest.

Ponru School, the nomad outpost on the Sershul grasslands that we renovated in 2004, had continued with its thirty-one enrolled children. Thanks to dispatches from the American NGO that funded it, I learned that most of the youngsters had completed the sixth grade, after which about half entered the county middle school. Ultimately, six would acquire enough education to become salaried professionals, and several more would become Buddhist monks. One would die, apparently of leukemia.

Although many of the Ponru children didn't earn diplomas, I hoped that their academic achievements would help them live better and spur the next generation to go further. By the standards of Tibet's herding areas, the Ponru School was a great success. Nevertheless, it saddened me that on the grasslands, the bar for success was set so low.

In all, 2007 had been a banner year for KhamAid. We wrapped up our three-year USAID grant and turned in a report boasting many success stories. We hosted successful workshops on handicrafts, cultural heritage, and fire prevention. Ninety-five scholarship students began the new academic year.

To the money left over from our failed greenhouse project in Nyarong, we added another $50,000 raised by one of the cyclists who had biked with me to Degé in 2001.[93] These funds had built green-houses at three schools in Sershul and five in Litang, with more to come. Now we knew to make the greenhouses out of stronger materials, resistant to Tibetan weather. Thanks to the teachers' efforts, most of these greenhouses were successful.

We also completed a second construction skills training program, this time working on a charity school in a different part of Lhagang township. That same year a KhamAid team brought fifty-six wheelchairs to disabled Tibetans and worked with the families to enhance their caregiving skills.

Besides repairing Dendrup's house in Wayö, we completed documentation of seven ancient buildings, with measured drawings, structural analysis, and full sets of photographs. We also put together a first-of-its-kind repair manual for traditional stone houses.

Most exciting of all, we discovered an entirely new historic site south of Sadé, in a place called Pusarong Upper Village. That village featured a small but phenomenal temple with 160 square meters (191 square yards) of vivid, beautifully preserved, black and red paintings, probably dating from the sixteenth century, the largest and most significant collection of murals known in Minyak to date.

KhamAid was evolving from a bootstrap charity doing opportunistic projects at random spots around Kham, to an organization that could plan and carry out complex, multifaceted efforts with measurable results. Our relations with the government seemed solid. These days I was doing less fieldwork, leaving most of it to Mr. Wu and other staff, and spending more time writing reports and putting numbers into spreadsheets. I missed the creative excitement of trekking in the

---

93  That was Mr. Martin Dunphy. Among his several fundraisers was a nine-day bike ride from Lijiang to Dartsendo in 2006.

backcountry and designing projects on the fly, but it was worth it because our impact was growing.

We had big plans for 2008. We would repair the roof at the temple in Pusarong and begin the conservation of its paintings. We would continue more work at Wayö. We would deliver more wheelchairs, add more young people to our scholarship roster, and build more school greenhouses. I was also getting ready to launch a new project to preserve and perpetuate the Minyak language. Our USAID grant was closing out, but we were hopeful that we would get another one and find matching funds to do even more good work for the people of Kham.

## The Prodigal Child Takes Wing

After a year to recover her health, the student Metok Tso went back to Southwest University for Nationalities and plunged in. She had no intention of hiding in the library; she was there to discover the world.

Her sponsor, Richard Harlan, continued to support her studies. To defray her expenses, she found part-time work tutoring other students in English.

One day Harlan was passing through Chengdu and stopped by to see her. She took him for a stroll around the campus, and they happened across a talent contest underway, an audition for a Chinese TV show of the same genre as *American Idol*. Harlan saw a stage, several judges, a gaggle of nervous contestants, and a much bigger crowd of onlookers waiting for the show to start.

Right then and there, Metok Tso decided to sign up. "She's fearless," Harlan later recalled, "and she loves to be the center of attention."

Metok Tso had to conjure up an act quickly, so she stepped to the side to get clear of the other people. A few minutes of singing to herself was all she needed. When they called her name, she mounted the stage seeming utterly at ease, joking with the judges before launching into her performance.

The judges liked it and advanced her to the next level.

The next competition was a few weeks later, but Metok Tso was away and did not go. "She doesn't care if she loses," Harlan later explained. "She just wants the experience, to meet people."

That was only the beginning. With the help of a teacher, Metok Tso created a music video starring herself and won the school's first prize for it. They sent her to represent SWUN in the national competition in Wuhan, where she took second place. She entered a school photography contest and took second place, and she entered a computer skills competition for all of Sichuan and took third. She piled up other honors and awards and raked in several thousand yuan of prize money.

Almost from the moment that Metok Tso set foot at SWUN, she had an admirer, one of the school's leading graduate students, a man from the Amdo grasslands, but she would not admit to Harlan that he was her boyfriend and called him "brother." Whenever Richard Harlan shared news with us, Metok Tso was always rocketing up to some new and fantastic height. There was no telling what her future would hold.

## A Terrible Year

At the start of the male Earth-Mouse year (2008), KhamAid was going gangbusters in Sichuan. However, trouble was brewing in Lhasa, a powder-keg of resentment forever on the brink of detonating. As it did most years, tension crested during March, the month that triggered memories of 1959 when the Chinese army shelled the palace of the Dalai Lama, the year of his secret flight out of Tibet, a journey from which he never returned. The year 1959 shattered Tibetan illusions of Chinese benevolence and marked the start of several decades of turmoil, bitterness, and suffering.

Every March since, when memories of the past threatened to flare into public protest, Chinese authorities tried to keep Lhasa calm by tightening security and clearing out foreign tourists, whom they viewed as instigators. For many years this strategy had worked: Lhasa had remained calm. Perhaps the Party's leaders believed that, after so much investment and economic progress, their Tibetan subjects were finally content.

Now, in 2008, the stakes were high, for this year China would host the Summer Olympics, and soon the torch relay would start. There was bound to be trouble, but the authorities failed to foresee how bad it would become.

On March 14th, a riot broke out. What seems to have triggered it was a peaceful demonstration in front of Ramoche Monastery that was dispersed by police, coupled with rumors that two monks had been beaten up by authorities.[94] But the exact cause quickly became irrelevant as rampaging mobs took to the streets, attacking Chinese businesses and looting and burning them.

Within hours, protests ignited in Gansu and Qinghai Provinces. In Sichuan, in Ngawa Prefecture, police clashed with monks, and several police vans were set ablaze. Reports indicated that one policeman and several demonstrators had been shot.

At first, the authorities reacted moderately, perhaps hoping to shield their Olympics from unpleasant headlines, but as the destruction intensified, police went into action, soon reinforced by several thousand troops of the People's Armed Security. Wearing helmets and carrying shields, they fanned out across Lhasa's main arteries and sealed off the Tibetan quarter. They fired tear gas, used cattle prods,

---

94  James Miles, "Trashing the Beijing Road," 3/19/2008 and "Lhasa Under Siege," 3/13/2008, *The Economist.*

and shot the occasional round to persuade the few youths still on the streets that it was time for the burning and looting to stop.

When the streets were quiet, the authorities began going house-to-house to hunt down and arrest those who had taken part in the riot. They hauled untold hundreds or thousands to jail. The Chinese did not declare martial law, but they may as well have done so, for Lhasa was locked down tight. In front of the holy Jokhang Temple, in a square usually thronged with Buddhist faithful, there were now only armored personnel carriers and swarms of police. Fearful residents cowered in their homes. Shops were closed, and street vendors stayed away. The city froze.

The Chinese government reported that about twenty died in the Lhasa unrest; the Tibetan government-in-exile said it was eighty. Several hundred people were wounded. As was their habit, the Chinese government blamed "the Dalai clique" for masterminding the violence.

KhamAid's staff were safe, but everyone was afraid. Police vans were parked in the middle of Chengdu's Tibetan district, ready to erupt with blue uniforms at the first sign of trouble. A Tibetan employee of KhamAid who lived in the city was afraid to leave his apartment, and Mr. Wu, who lived in Dartsendo, was afraid to go to the countryside. Across China's west, people who resided in mixed communities hunkered down, suddenly frightened of their neighbors.

Within days, authorities told us that KhamAid's teacher at the Wayö Primary School must leave. No matter that he had been trained and certified at a government-run teaching academy; if foreigners paid him, he had to go. All over Tibet, the government ordered foreign-funded schools to shut down; the students had to return home or enroll in government schools. Fortunately, the high school and college students KhamAid was sponsoring were allowed to continue their studies; however, our plans to build five more school greenhouses in Litang County had to be put on hold.

Tourism crashed. Foreign tourists were forbidden to visit Tibet Autonomous Region, and Chinese tourists, millions of whom had visited in recent years, were now afraid to go because they feared Tibetans might harm them. The 4.85 billion-yuan tourism sector in TAR vanished virtually overnight.[95] Although there had been no violence in Kandze Prefecture, locals told us that tourist arrivals there dropped by 60%.

Foreigners were also barred from visiting NGO project sites in Tibetan regions. KhamAid and other foreign organizations were permitted to continue only our existing, approved programs, and only if they did not involve teaching and were carried out by Chinese nationals.

Besides reining in tourism and foreign aid, the Chinese government responded to the crisis by doing what it always does: sending the Party's loyal foot soldiers, rank-and-file cadres, out to the townships for extended stays to mingle among the proletariat and persuade them to reject the Dalai Lama's "traitorous" views. A friend in the government confided to me that no one wanted this assignment. No matter what their ethnic background, officials were nervous about what might happen to them out there. The chasm between Tibetans and those who ruled them had opened up so wide that it was hard to see how it could ever be bridged. The cooperation of years past seemed a distant memory.

Stateside, I was embroiled in some drama of my own. I had hoped that we would win another USAID grant, but the 2006 election brought a Democratic majority to Congress that was not nearly so keen on sending taxpayer dollars to Tibet as their China-bashing

---

95  The figure is for 2007 and applies to Tibet Autonomous Region only. Source: www.tibetinfonet.net/content/update/172 accessed on 7/27/2012.

Republican predecessors had been. Without any major grants, KhamAid could no longer afford to pay me. The guiding and consulting work I had done in the past also vanished. What was worse, I had made a hasty and ill-considered marriage to a man I didn't know very well, a builder. Lured by California's high-flying real estate market, we had spent my inheritance on a house down payment and then, based on its anticipated rapid appreciation, had taken out a whopping home equity loan. We planned to enlarge the house, then resell at a profit.

So, now I had a husband to support, a remodeling project to finish, and enormous interest payments. This was no time to be unemployed. I applied for technical and nonprofit jobs, but my peculiar résumé—that of a scientist-turned-humanitarian—found no takers. The only offer I received was for an entry-level engineering job at the Hanford Nuclear Reservation in Washington State, cleaning up the radioactive mess left by the production of atomic weapons.

So, I went north. My husband remained in California. By day, I worked with radioactive waste, and by night, I hunched over a laptop, pushing KhamAid forward. I could not go to Kham, but I wanted KhamAid's work to continue. For the time being, however, we would have to lie low and wait for conditions to normalize.

Little did we realize, things were going to get worse.

On May 12th, at five o'clock in the morning, my husband phoned me to say turn on the TV. What I saw made my heart stop. Tenzin Gyaltsen, an American volunteer for KhamAid who was living in Chengdu at the time, tells what it was like:

> It took one second to register, EARTHQUAKE!!! Come on, I yell to my girlfriend. We stand in our doorway of the seventh-floor apartment for about a second or two, then frantically run down the stairs accompanied by all of our

Chinese neighbors. Sixth floor, fifth floor, fourth floor; then third floor it hits: the realization that the building may come down at any second. The plaster and concrete begin to buckle and shoot out in the staircase. The second floor has massive cracks in the walls. Barefoot and half-naked, we run down to the courtyard. Standing amongst hundreds of also half-naked Chinese, we realize that this quake is still happening: the longest quake I, a California native, have ever witnessed.

Chengdu was 80 kilometers (50 miles) away from the epicenter and got off lightly. The rupture, which took place on the Longmen fault, was one hundred times bigger than the 2001 quake at Gokar. It unleashed forces of unimaginable power. In some places, the earth jerked upward by as much as 12 meters (13.1 yards). In mountainous Beichuan County, the damage was apocalyptic: entire villages were erased by landslides or sucked into mammoth crevasses that opened beneath them. Elsewhere, the earth spat geysers of mud tens of meters tall.[96] Landslides blocked a river, creating a new lake that rose higher and deeper until the natural dam burst, giving way to an immense mass of water that pounded down the valley crushing everything in its path. Aftershocks continued for days, terrorizing survivors and wreaking more devastation.

The worst damage was in the north of Sichuan, in Ngawa Prefecture, home to about 160,000 Qiang people and 470,000 Tibetans, who together comprised nearly three-quarters of the registered population. In Ngawa's farming valleys, both Qiang and Tibetans commonly lived in

---

96  These descriptions, supported by photos, came from a Chinese photographer using the name "Chengdu Xinyang" who entered the region soon after the quake.

stone homes similar to those in Minyak and Gokar. As I knew only too well, this type of house quickly shakes apart.

At the moment the quake struck, KhamAid's greenhouse contractor was driving on a highway close to the epicenter. As the earth bucked and heaved, his minivan left the pavement and crashed. He came away with an injury to his leg, but he considered himself lucky. In Wenchuan County alone, some fifty thousand people were dead or injured, and more than seven thousand were missing. Many of the dead were children who were crushed when substandard school buildings collapsed on top of them.

Among the eighteen counties of Kandze Prefecture, Rongtrak took the hardest hits. Besides thousands of damaged houses and some tens of casualties, county officials reported that three ancient stone towers—similar to the ones in Minyak—were partially collapsed. Twenty-seven more towers were considered "very dangerous" and a direct threat to the people living beneath them.

Outside of Rongtrak, damage in the rest of Kandze Prefecture was slight. Our field office was unharmed, although impacted by power outages. The houses we had built or repaired at Lhagang and Wayö had fared well, perhaps helped by our shake-resistant innovations.[97] Pema Penlo's amazing ancient house still stood.

Back in the United States, between my radioactive waste duties, I put out bulletins by email. Our supporters responded, and donations began flowing in. I was not sure what we would do with them, but I knew we must do something. Aid organizations across China and the world were joining hands to help the communities flattened by the

---

97  Khenpo Yonden's house, which had been built by graduates of our Senggé Monastery training program, survived this earthquake and another one in 2014, but was later torn down to make way for Dorje Tashi Rinpoche's school.

magnitude 7.9 quake and the hundreds of thousands of people who were now injured or homeless.

In Chengdu, many cast aside their normal lives to join the massive relief effort. One American expatriate friend wrote, "Never in all of my eight years in Sichuan did I feel more at home than during those minutes, hours, and weeks after the quake tore a hole in the province and buried 80,000 people under rubble, metal, and dust. I took several trips into the disaster area. I attended poetry sessions and carried water up hills. I wrote stories and took pictures. I sobbed in my room, thinking of children crushed and wailing."[98]

The Dalai Lama expressed sadness at Sichuan's tragedy; however, the Tibetan government-in-exile was otherwise uninterested in the temblor. Their massively effective communication apparatus was silent. A couple of weeks after the quake struck, I attended the Himalayan Fair in Berkeley, California, where I set out a jar to collect donations for victims. Tibetans who stopped by had no idea that their brethren back home were affected by the quake, nor did the hordes of other fairgoers. The next newsletter published by the International Campaign for Tibet carried a map showing locations of political protests in Kakhog and Barkham but, in an ironic parallel to the selective coverage of the Chinese media, the newsletter said nothing about the twenty earthquake fatalities in those same counties, nor about Tibetans elsewhere who were injured or homeless. A calamity shared with Qiang and Han people was not in their Tibetan Independence playbook.

The Chinese media trumpeted heroic rescues of quake victims from obliterated Tibetan and Qiang villages, but otherwise had little to say about the quake's impact on minorities. Since the Lhasa riots,

---

98 Sascha Matuszak, "Flower Town: The rise and fall of a Sichuan village," http://theanthill.org/flower-town, accessed 5/18/2014.

everything Tibetan was über-sensitive. International aid for earthquake victims was piling into China, but it stopped at the edge of the Tibetan plateau, where the rescue operation was purely a Chinese effort.

To their credit, most ordinary Sichuan people looked beyond race and politics, uniting as one to respond to the disaster. "The moving stories and brave heroes coming from the earthquake," wrote one of our students, "have interwoven all of the world's hearts."

When KhamAid had accumulated about five thousand dollars in our earthquake relief fund, I asked Mr. Wu to put together a project in Rongtrak County, but county officials rebuffed us. No matter how desperate the need, they dared not accept American money. It took us several months to find a back door so that we could deliver help to one small, overlooked village, and then arrive at a formula for distributing aid that was regarded by residents as fair. We delivered cash grants in varying amounts to thirteen of the worst-hit families and distributed 4,500 kilograms of rice and wheat flour among all of the fifty-five households.

I thought the worst had already happened, but terrible year 2008 was not even half over. Now loomed the Games of the XXIX Olympiad, and with the frenetic preparations in the Chinese capital came a renewed crackdown on freedoms in Tibet. Government officials in Kham, extremely risk-averse even in the best of times, were now paralyzed for fear of career-wrecking missteps. They advised us to keep our heads very low. Most summers, we had fieldworkers streaming through our field office, but this summer, our office was like a morgue. We asked if we could send our wheelchairs to disaster-stricken areas, but the authorities said no.

Nevertheless, I remained hopeful that, after the Olympic frenzy was past and memories of the Lhasa riots had faded, 2009 would be better. I had big ideas for new KhamAid projects. The wall paintings at the temple in Pusarong Village badly needed help, first to repair the temple roof, and then to consolidate the walls so the paintings would endure.

The Pusarong images were unlike anything painted in Tibet today: black and white figures on a deep garnet-colored background, snarling wrathful deities and serene Buddhas. The temple was such an extraordinary find that a group of Buddhists in Ashland, Oregon, offered to put on a fundraising event to save it.

The event would be a Tibetan cultural festival, and it would be huge. Ashland was a perfect home for it: a community of people devoted to the arts, home to several Buddhist groups and countless other spiritual seekers. The organizers booked space, assembled an army of sixty-five volunteers to do everything from hanging prayer flags to reading stories to children. Slogging from door to door, they gathered donations from thirty-five individuals and businesses to bankroll the upfront costs. They rounded up goods to be raffled off, and businesses to rent booth space. They printed posters and papered the town with them.

Local newspapers and radio shows received press releases and duly informed the public. The magic day would be October 5th. The schedule included lama chanting, a film, a fashion show, a lecture on traditional *thanka* painting, music, dance, activities for children, and a raffle. I had been invited to give the keynote speech about our discovery at Pusarong.

Then the world flipped on its side.

Already, the world had been wobbling for some time: America's real estate bubble was starting to deflate, and investors were growing nervous. Then came an event that sounded a giant *crack!* across the thin ice holding up the American financial system: on September 15th, the world's fourth-largest financial services firm, Lehman Brothers, filed for bankruptcy. Confidence evaporated, and housing prices began to plummet. Like a nuclear chain reaction, a liquidity crisis rippled across the American financial system and quickly spread overseas.

I am not privy to the investment habits of residents of Ashland, Oregon, but from the effect of the crisis on our Tibetan cultural festival, I will guess that many of them were living on mortgage-backed securities. Just at the time we needed ticket sales to take off, they slowed to a crawl. When the day arrived, the place was not empty, but most of the people milling around were event volunteers. Hardly anyone purchased the books and paintings that we needed to fatten our bottom line. The event barely broke even, and the volunteers were crushed. It was as good as certain that they would never put forth such a heroic effort again.

Meanwhile, my personal finances went from shaky to disastrous. The value of my unfinished house dropped like a rock; I would ultimately sell it for far less than what I owed. My husband disappeared, paying not one penny of our shared debt. Within a year, I would be filing for both bankruptcy and divorce.

Ironically, I recalled the detractors who, over the years, had accused me of being in the pay of the Communist Party. If only! As the year drew to a close, KhamAid's receipts were way down, and 2009 would be worse.

While our income plunged, our expenses did not. Since 2004, the dollar had lost 19% of its value against the yuan, and matters were made worse by Chinese inflation: the government claimed it was only 5-6% a year, but outside analysts said the real rate was three times higher.[99] Our costs skyrocketed.

KhamAid's prospects were as gloomy as they had ever been. The

---

99   "China's Economy: An alternative view." *The Economist*, 3/15/2014, p. 70.

people we had hired for the USAID work saw the handwriting on the wall and left for other jobs. With only Mr. Wu still on the payroll, our reserve of unrestricted funds would last awhile, but what was the point of operating if we could not help people in Kham?

# Part VI

# Resilience

*Suffering is inseparable from existence.*
—The Buddha's First Noble Truth

"One of the most difficult things for us to accept is that there is no realm where there's only happiness and there's no suffering," writes Thich Nhat Hanh, the famous Buddhist teacher. "This doesn't mean that we should despair. Suffering can be transformed."[100]

The people of Tibet—and China—have weathered storms that we, in the ordered West, can hardly imagine. So, it is also true that they have practiced resilience, the power of which we can scarcely conceive. Consider these examples: Professor Palden Nyima at his university quietly advocating for Tibetan education and strengthening the role of science in Tibetan culture. Gyalten Rinpoche, the incarnate lama, overcoming the scars of the Cultural Revolution to build a school so that thousands of children could learn. The people of Degé setting out to replace 270,000 hand-carved printing blocks, re-carving them one by one. Minyak Rinpoche working not just to restore Lhasa's holy sites but also to protect and preserve the history of his homeland. Communities rebuilding after decades of violence, turmoil, and the horrors of thamzing.

And, of course, the young girl, Metok Tso, aspiring to overcome her rural origins and take on the world.

---

100 Thich Nhat Hanh, *No Mud, No Lotus: The Art of Transforming Suffering* (Parallax Press, 2014).

## At University

Now in the year of the Earth-Cow (2009), her third year at Southwest University for Nationalities, Metok Tso was embracing the college experience with an almost savage hunger. She joined the Association for Nationality Communications, where she met students from other ethnic backgrounds. "I love this group," she wrote in her résumé, "because it not only lets me meet many people, but it also improves my stages skills." She became the group's president.

She joined the Student Association of the Literature and Art Department and became its secretary. She also joined the Organization for Foreign Affairs and Bilateral Contact, a committee that hosted foreign exchange students and dignitaries. They tapped her language skills by making her into a translator. She also helped put on shows.

Having known the depths of poverty, she was vigilant with her money and stretched every yuan to the utmost. Her diligence was noticed, and the campus Committee on Student Life made her their treasurer.

In the fall of her third year, Metok Tso set an even higher goal: to study abroad. Her university had an exchange program with Konkuk University in Seoul, South Korea, but getting in was not easy. "It's very good, and many people want to go there," she wrote in an email to Richard Harlan, "but they fail the interviews."

The application process was just another contest, and Metok Tso excelled at contests. Money, however, was a problem. "Yes, I know it's very expensive for me, and I thought about it for a long time, but I still don't know exactly the way. But I don't want to give up that easily."

Her email closed with, "Don't worry, Grandpa! I heard that students who are good can get scholarships."

At the end of October, she learned that she had qualified for the final stage, which was three months of intensive language study, after which she would have to pass an interview in Korean. In the midst of this, she learned that she could only be issued a passport in her hometown, three days' travel away. In November, she made the long trip back home, said a quick hello to her mother, did the paperwork for her passport, and dashed back to Chengdu to resume her studies.

## Under the Radar

Meanwhile, conditions for foreign NGOs in Tibet remained dicey. Even the large, well-established groups were finding that they could not renew their licenses to operate as Chinese charities; they were forced to reinvent themselves as for-profit businesses. Their Chinese partners canceled or declined to renew cooperative agreements. KhamAid had never been licensed, and our partnering agreements were mostly informal, so we carried on, albeit more quietly than before, with no expatriate personnel in the field.

Despite these challenges, we scored some victories. Thanks to a grant from the National Geographic Society, we collaborated with an indigenous nonprofit, the Minyak Cultural and Environmental Service Group, on a Minyak language project, a significant effort.[101] A team of Minyak scholars invented a way to render Minyak sounds in Tibetan script. They recorded speech from all over the region, including songs and stories, and compiled it into a Minyak language textbook. They sought and received approval for the book to be used in a few area schools. They tested the draft in actual classrooms and trained eight teachers.

The project was going well until it came time to print the book in quantity; then, we hit a brick wall. Because of the current sensitivity of anything Tibetan, publishers shied away from the project. After

---

101 Minyak belongs to the Qiangic language group and is unrelated to Tibetan.

six months of searching, we finally struck a deal with the *Ganzi Bao*, a newspaper. The fruit of our labors was four hundred precious copies, three-quarters of which went to schools, the rest to libraries, scholars, and as gifts to officials who had helped the project. Spoken by about twelve thousand people, the Minyak language was considered useless when we started. Now, it was suddenly fashionable, and we were inundated with requests for our book.

Although our cultural heritage work at Wayö Village had foundered, we found a back door to get their little school reopened, and the government even sent a second teacher to help the one funded by KhamAid. The school operated for another year before the Education Bureau reversed itself and decided that Wayö children would have to attend the school in Sadé after all. At this turn of events, residents spoke up, pleading for their school to remain open. However, the Education Bureau wouldn't budge; they closed it anyway and blamed KhamAid for the community's intransigence. We were advised to steer clear of Sadé Township for a while.

The temple at Pusarong got some help thanks to grants from a private donor and the Global Heritage Fund; we used the money to replace the temple's disintegrating roof. Later, in partnership with the Palace Museum of Beijing, we would send a team of Chinese art historians to document its extraordinary murals.[102]

We fulfilled our promise to the people of Litang by building greenhouses at five more primary schools, giving hundreds of children fresh vegetables to diversify their diet. We released and distributed the

---

102 They published their work in 木雅地区明代藏传佛教经堂碉壁画 / 故宫博物院，四川省文物考古研究院合著；罗文华主编, (Ming dynasty Tibetan Buddhist murals in the Lhakhang Towers of Mi nyag district, Editor-in-Chief Luo Wenhua), 2012.

92 wheelchairs that were stranded when the riots broke out, sending them to Derong, Dabpa, and Chatreng counties.

Throughout this period, our sponsored students marched steadily through school. One fresh graduate sent money from her first paycheck to sponsor another student. Lhamo Dolkar, the student who had lupus, completed her nursing program and graduated in the summer of 2009. "My illness is now much better," she wrote in a letter to her sponsors. "I take several traditional Chinese medicines, and I am still taking Western medicine, too. So, you don't need to worry about me." Prednisone can have serious side effects if taken long term. After Lhamo graduated from school, we lost track of her for a while, but later learned she was working at a township clinic.

While KhamAid had some successes, life in Kham became harder. Because of the global financial crisis, demand for caterpillar fungus tumbled. In 2009, Tibetans were getting only six yuan per grub instead of the twenty-two yuan they had gotten the previous year. Demand for mushrooms also plunged. Tourism was whacked by a quadruple whammy: riots, earthquake, Olympics, and global recession. Although backpackers still trickled in, traffic was way down.

Since our first assessment of our midwife training program in 2004, we had trained thirty-nine more women, who benefitted from the lessons we'd learned: we cooperated with county health bureaus to ensure that they would have paid jobs after training. We would have continued the program but ran out of donor money. I tried but failed to find more; US$24,000 to train a class of twenty midwives was a high bar.

Yet there was one more thing we could do: perform another assessment and document our findings so that others could learn from them. Thanks to the growing mobile phone network, it was much easier to interview the women this time around: instead of taking long road trips, this time Mr. Wu could just telephone them. With the help of the Women's Federation, he was able to track down and interview sixty-five out of the seventy-nine midwives.

Our survey showed that forty-five of our original seventy-nine women were still providing health care services in some form, and thirty-four had quit. As for the health outcomes, we took our data with a grain of salt, because some women could not recall all of the patients they had seen, nor did they keep written records. Also, the women may have been pressured by officials to exaggerate their success. Based on the data he collected, Mr. Wu conservatively estimated that those forty-five midwives had seen approximately eight thousand patients for ailments such as headache, fever, cough, and diarrhea, especially in children and women. They had delivered about 2,800 babies[103] and sent nearly five hundred women with high-risk pregnancies to the hospital. If the women were telling the truth, they had saved hundreds of newborns who might have died without help from a trained healthcare worker.[104]

## Into the Blue

As the day of her Korean interview drew close, Metok Tso wrote to Richard less often, for she was cramming harder than she ever had in her life. The hard work paid off: she passed the interview and was one of twelve SWUN students chosen for the program. SWUN would pay tuition.

---

103 More than half of this number was due to just five Dabpa women, three stationed in township clinics and two working in county-level hospitals where births were frequent and doctors were present.

104 In 2006, we obtained some limited data for Kandze Prefecture as a whole, showing maternal mortality had decreased from 0.20833% in 2000 to 0.12228% in 2005, and infant mortality had decreased from 3.637% to 2.126% during the same period.

While her classmates and teachers left for a month-long holiday to celebrate the year of the Iron-Tiger (2010), Metok Tso stayed at school, living alone in the empty dormitory. She taught English by day and studied at night, taking time off only to get guitar lessons from a friend. "I told you, I do all of these things because I want be a great Tibetan woman and make you proud, and also so my mum can live a better life," she wrote to Richard Harlan, adding, "Especially my mum. She is very tired now. I know I can't reward her forever, but I will give her a better life at least."

Working odd jobs, Metok Tso saved furiously and accumulated enough money for the plane ticket to Seoul. She would need more for living expenses, but she figured she'd find work after she arrived.

"That's how she is," Richard would say later. "She steps out to the end of the board and jumps."

In late February, she landed in Seoul, a stranger in a vast alien metropolis nearly twice the size of Chengdu, and found her way to Konkuk University.

If she had plunged into her freshman year with passion, she now did so doubly at Seoul. "You know, this afternoon I had dance class," she wrote in an email to Richard, "and we had our mid-term test. I got 92 goals for cha-cha. I am in the first place in the class, and the professor loves me so much. She told everyone, 'she is a foreigner, and she doesn't even know our language, but she made it.'"

"Anyway, I'm really good here," her message concluded. "It's a new life, a new me, a new future!"

## Reckonings

On the morning of April 14th, 2010, everything changed again when a magnitude 6.9 earthquake hit Yülshül (Ch: Yushu) County.

When news broke, all I could think was: *not again!* The epicenter was in Qinghai Province, just tens of kilometers outside Kandze Prefecture—and KhamAid turf.

I told myself that we didn't have any resources in Qinghai, no government partners there, and no way to help. But the truth was: I was tired now, so very tired. Fourteen years of relentless struggle had worn me down, and now I was doing another full-time job in addition to managing the work in Kham. KhamAid would likely never pay a living wage, provide health insurance, paid time off, or a retirement plan. At fifty-one, I was too old to be penniless.

I had lost my father long before KhamAid started, but my loyal, stalwart mother had been my spiritual companion throughout the years. So many times, she had watched me disappear, waited weeks or months, not knowing if I was even alive. Now she had Alzheimer's disease, and it would be wrong to make her wait any more.

It was time to stop.

I told Mr. Wu, KhamAid's three directors, Doka, and a handful of others that I would resign at year's end. They were dismayed but eventually surrendered to the inevitable. Given the conditions of my job, there was no question of replacing me.

And so, with sadness and relief, I laid plans to shut us down.

While I worked on an orderly dissolution of the organization I had built, Metok Tso was in Seoul studying at Kongkuk University. When the Yülshül earthquake struck, she heard about it instantly. Her birthplace was hundreds of miles from the epicenter and completely undamaged; nevertheless, she was powerfully affected. For two days, she could not sleep. "Although now it's close to exams, I was more worried about the quake, I'm sorry!" she wrote to Richard Harlan. "I cried a lot and can't sleep. I really, really love my people, love Tibet."

She joined a candlelight vigil for quake victims, a mournful girl with a tangle of black hair in loose pigtails, hands pressed together in prayer. But praying was not enough; Metok Tso was determined to help. She decided to put on a show of Tibetan singing to raise money for the relief effort. She herself would be the star performer. Why not? She certainly knew how to sing. Immediately, she threw herself into the task.

"I was very, very busy, to tell you truth," she wrote two weeks later. "These twelve days, I was working all night except last night, because I have many things to do." She asked for and won school approval for her event, and rounded up friends to help her. The show was a success and elicited an outpouring of support for earthquake relief in Yülshül.

"To tell you good news," she wrote to Richard, "my story touched many people, and I was also spoken highly of by the school and the Chinese embassy in Korea."

The embassy knew a good thing when they saw it; they helped Metok Tso arrange benefits at other universities, even sending a car to ferry her around. She raised thousands of dollars for a relief fund set up by the Chinese government. The government would later claim to have spent a whopping $7.2 billion on the recovery effort, a sum that probably includes Metok Tso's contribution.

I was troubled that she entrusted the government with her precious funds, but when I asked her about it later, she only shrugged. Looking back, I wonder who was I to question her judgment? I'd made plenty of mistakes of my own. She acted when I did nothing. And she would certainly learn and grow.

## Farewell Tour

Before shutting down KhamAid, I had promises to keep, one of which was to deliver a load of 92 wheelchairs. Our wonderful friends at the Federation for Disabled Persons promised the higher-ups to take responsibility for us. Thanks to them, we would be the first foreign NGO officially permitted to enter western Sichuan since the riots two years before.

The director of KhamAid's wheelchair program was in charge; I was tagging along as an observer. We set out in a van with Mr. Wu, two other physiotherapists, and a mechanic, accompanied by a truck-load of chairs.

Our gracious hosts warned us that we must stick exactly to the approved plan, stay out of internet cafés, and avoid trouble of any kind. I found that public telephones no longer connected overseas, and mobile phones wouldn't connect either, although I could send text messages. The clock had turned back, and Tibet was curtained once more.

Stopped for the night in Dartsendo, I went to see my old friend Gyalten Rinpoche. Over bowls of noodles, he told me his school was now doing well, with 327 students and 28 teachers. Their vocational programs had grown to include auto mechanics and tailoring, and fifty-three of their primary school graduates had been admitted to the county middle school. He was raising funds to build a computer lab. His clinic was busy, too, with thirty or forty patients a day, and three doctors dispatched to various institutes for advanced studies.

The next morning, we left Dartsendo and headed west. As our little caravan trundled along, the wheelchair boxes started coming loose, so we stopped in Lhagang to secure them. Across the square, I saw a café in the space that used to be our training center. The café, I knew, belonged to a local man and his American wife, Angela Lankford, the entrepreneur who had helped me design the blanket-weaving training class a few years previously. I headed over to say hello.

Lankford was there and greeted me warmly. The café and shop had been open for two full seasons and were doing well. Along one wall were shelves of goods: Tibetan jackets, boots, hats, and religious paraphernalia—things I knew were "too Tibetan" for the mass market, although the café's Tibet-loving clientele did buy them.

Then, to my surprise, an old friend sprang up to meet me: a picture frame.

Where'd this come from? Was it one of our prototypes, still unsold four years later?

No, Angela told me; it's newly made. "People look at your website," she said, "and they write me an email saying where can I get a frame like this? So, I started [having local artisans make] them. And people buy them."

She spoke as if this was the simplest, most obvious thing in the world, not a resurrection of something long written off as dead, not a freaking miracle.

But there was more. Pillow covers made of yak-hair and wool. Three different designs. Leftover prototypes? Again, no.

"Same thing," said Angela. "I wholesale them in America, and I sell them here in this shop. And they were designed by [KhamAid's consultant] Elaine. I copied the design."

I asked her how much the artisans earn per pillow cover. Net of materials, she said, about twenty-five yuan. She had sold about a hundred so far.

It wasn't fabulous wealth. But it was *wonderful*.

Our cargo now secure, we drove to the next town, Bamé, and pulled up to a restaurant packed with animated diners. No sooner had we been seated than a woman came over to our table. "I recognize you," she said. "You are from KhamAid Foundation."

The woman introduced herself and explained that she used to work for the Ta'u County Women's Federation. Then she began to reel off the names of girls we had sponsored. "Yan Meiling—she's an official now, works in the Agriculture Bureau. Tamu Tsering—she's a teacher. Deshi Lhamo is at Nanchong University, and Chukyi Dolma is at SWUN..."

For me, moments like this made it all worthwhile.

## Bittersweetness

Over the next three days, we delivered wheelchairs to people in Drango and Kandze counties; then, a long day's drive over two high passes and lots of emptiness in between brought us to the Sershul County seat. Following Tibetan custom, county officials were waiting a few miles outside the town to greet us; they slathered us with khata that hung to our ankles and presented silver bowls of fiery *arak* for us to sip.

We learned that scores of rescue and relief folks were staying there, joined by the wealthier Yülshül residents fleeing the chaos of their obliterated town. All of the best hotels were full, as were the second-best hotels, so our hosts led us to a sketchy dive of questionable cleanliness. Just like the old days! The bathroom was a reeking, waterless chamber at the end of the hall. A jagged crack wrapped like a lasso around the walls of my room. At least the electricity worked. As I got busy plugging in gadgets to recharge them, a girl arrived carrying thermoses of hot water. She seemed much too young to be doing this job. Her hair was a ratty mess, and she had a haunted look in her eyes.

"How old are you?" I asked her in Chinese.

"Fourteen," she replied, which made her thirteen by Western counting.

"So young! Why aren't you in school?"

"I can't go to school; I'm not a Sershul person. I'm from Yülshül."

"*Aiya!* I'm so sorry. You're here because of the earthquake?"
She nodded.

"Is your family okay?"

At this question, she did not flinch, at least not visibly. Her face didn't change; her voice didn't quaver, but her hollow eyes drilled into me. "My two younger brothers died," she said flatly. "I'm in mourning. I took a vow to not wash my hair for thirty-two days."

She touched the dull, tangled mess cascading over her shoulders, handling it like something dead, and added, "It's been twenty-three so far."

"How did you get here?"

"My parents sent me. My aunt works at this hotel, and she took me in."

"Do you know where your parents are? Can you talk to them on the phone?"

"They lost their phone...*underneath*." Her face was all edges and shadows. "I've heard nothing since we separated."

"At night," she added, "I'm afraid to go to sleep."

What can you say to something like this? What can anyone offer to replace her dead brothers, reunite her family, and restore her shattered life? Before this trip, I had asked whether we could divert our team out to Yülshül, where our people might have helped those injured in the quake. But our chairs had already been promised to other places, and given the current tension, it was impossible to stray even one inch from our approved plan. At least we had brought along extra crutches and canes for a friend to carry over the border.

## The Next Generation

As we delivered our last wheelchair, one urgent task still preyed on my mind: to find another American charity to take on KhamAid's remaining twenty-five sponsored students and see them safely to graduation. Lately, I had been getting newsletters from a new organization called Tibetan Village Project led by a man named Tamdin Wangdu, born in TAR. His work impressed me, so I contacted him and arranged for a meeting.

Mr. Wu and Doka accompanied me to the Kandze Hotel in the heart of Chengdu's Tibetan district. Adjoining the lobby was a small teahouse where we met Tamdin Wangdu and two of his staff, the six of us pulling up giant rattan chairs to a tiny, glass-topped table. A server brought fragrant tea elegantly served in tall glasses.

The meeting, conducted in English, was cordial but businesslike. As Tamdin Wangdu talked about his lending program for Tibetan-owned businesses, he struck me as smart and careful enough to succeed in the precarious vocation of bringing aid to Tibet. And he was *Tibetan*. It was high time, I felt, for foreigners to step away and let Tibetans carry on the work themselves.

Although no promises were made at this meeting, my request resonated with Tamdin Wangdu because he, too, had benefitted from a scholarship and understood the transformative power of education. After further discussion, he agreed to adopt KhamAid's remaining students and their sponsors. Ultimately, all of our students would graduate under his care.

During that last summer, I asked Mr. Wu to look up our graduates and find out what they were doing. He tracked down twenty-two, of whom ten had become teachers, two were health care workers, one was in the local police department, and nine were entry-level officials.

Then there was Metok Tso. A month after her campaign for the

Yülshül earthquake, Chinese Premier Wen Jiabao arrived in Seoul to take part in a trilateral summit with the president of South Korea and the prime minister of Japan. On May 29th, Metok Tso wrote breathlessly to Richard Harlan: "Big news from me, I was very lucky to be chosen by the Chinese embassy from the seventy thousand Chinese students [in Seoul] to attend a very big meeting between China and Korea. I met Premier Wen and other leaders and also took pictures with them, so excited . . ."

Two weeks later, she and several other students were invited to the Chinese ambassador's residence to dine with him and his family. By now, however, she was more concerned about her university exams, which were looming, and earning enough money to survive in Seoul. She took several part-time jobs, tutoring Chinese and English by day, waitressing in the evening, then disk-jockeying at a club until the wee hours of the morning. For seven months, she kept up this marathon pace, sleeping only three or four hours each night, and managed to pay her expenses, help her mother, and sock away cash for future travel—for Metok Tso was determined to see the world.

"I am very much enjoying my life in Korea," she wrote in an email to Richard Harlan. "I will study hard, do not worry about that, because whatever I do, I always remember my dreams!"

## The Wisdom to Know the Difference

As I write this, China's leaders are crushing dissent ever more brutally. The country's explosion of new wealth has not quelled its people's desire for a greater voice in who rules them. China's 1.6 billion people seem to be inching toward yet another revolution.

Scores of Tibetans have committed suicide by setting themselves on fire as a form of protest. The 14th Dalai Lama, the world's greatest advocate for peace and compassion, seems helpless either to return home or to loosen China's grip on his people. When he passes from the scene, a lamp that has remained lit for more than half a century will be extinguished. The struggle to name his successor promises to be long and bitter.

If the Dalai Lama himself cannot rescue his country, if the fiery deaths of those impassioned innocents do not alter its fate, then what can an ordinary person do?

Easy. Turn away from unresolvable conflict, let go of what is hopeless, and embrace those things one can shape with one's own hands. Like this:

## Chimé

This day in April 2007 would be a special day for Chimé, the day she would take a trip to town in an old wheelbarrow.

It began like any ordinary day. Chimé woke from sleep on a heap of dirty, stinking bedding next to a pile of hay. There were no windows in the cowshed she slept in, but the bright white light slivering around the door told her it was morning.

At 8:30 am, her sister Jampa arrived as usual. Jampa wrapped Chimé's chuba tightly around her, tucking Chimé's stunted legs and bare feet inside the furry lining so they would stay warm. Then Jampa took hold of one long sleeve, bent low, and pulled Chimé up onto her back in one smooth, practiced movement. Staggering under Chimé's weight, Jampa carried her across the yard and into the small house, gently lowered her to a pile of straw on the wooden floor, then adjusted Chimé so that her twisted back rested securely in a corner.

Chimé and Jampa's father had passed away six years earlier, but Ama lived with them, as well as Jampa's husband and three children.

As she did every morning, Ama mixed tea, butter, and tsampa in a bowl, then pinched off lumps and fed them to Chimé one at a time.

So far, it was a very ordinary day, like every other day Chimé could remember going back the forty-two years of her life.

After they had eaten, Jampa took a damp towel and cleaned Chimé's face and hands. She poured warm water from the kettle into a basin and washed Chimé's hair, which was not too difficult because it had been cropped short. Jampa pulled off Chimé's old, dirty clothes, scrubbed her well, then put clean ones on her. The shirt was bright red, and the clean fabric felt nice on Chimé's skin. She beamed.

"Today you are getting a *lunyi*," said Jampa, using a Chinese word that Chimé didn't know. Jampa looked happy about it, so Chimé smiled back at her.

There was knock at the door, and Jampa opened it to find a stranger standing there, a young man who spoke with a strange accent, saying his name was Adrol. He had brought with him a foreigner, very tall and pale, who introduced himself in Chinese, saying his name was Bao Ke.

Adrol explained that Bao Ke was a journalist from Germany and that he wanted to hear about Chimé. Jampa was flustered—a foreigner at her door! She invited them to sit down and offered them tea, but they politely declined. Jampa's mother, husband, and children pulled up low stools to listen in.

The journalist Bao Ke had many questions, which Adrol translated. Jampa answered that Chimé had been born with a crooked spine, that her legs were deformed, and that she couldn't use her hands. Also, she had the mind of a child. Nobody knew why. Just karma.

Bao Ke was hairy and strange, but his eyes were kind. From her place on the floor, Chimé smiled at him and blurted out, "Ni hao!" (hello).

Bao Ke smiled back at her and answered, "Ni hao!" which made Chimé grin.

Why does Chimé sleep in the cowshed? Bao Ke asked. Jampa explained that Chimé could not tell them when she needed to go to the toilet, and the family didn't have the conditions to wash her bedding often—there was no running water in their one-room house. The only way they could manage was for Chimé to spend her days and nights on straw.

Bao Ke asked about their finances, and Jampa said she and her husband worked on road crews as often as she could, earning twenty to twenty-five yuan per day. They also got 2,000 yuan a year, paid by the Civil Affairs Bureau, for Chimé's care. It was hard for them to manage on so little. They couldn't afford to take Chimé to a doctor.

Who looks after Chimé when you're at work?

Jampa replied that her fifteen-year-old son Tashi looked after Chimé. As a result, he could not attend school.

"She never leaves this place," said Jampa. "A couple of times, when she was younger, I carried her to the temple. But now she is too heavy. I can carry her only from the cowshed to the house and back."

"How much does Chimé weigh?" asked Bao Ke.

"About forty kilos," said Jampa.

"I weigh four pounds!" called Chimé, and the family burst out laughing.

"Chimé is famous for her jokes," said Tashi.

Adrol looked at his mobile phone. "It's time to go. How will you take her there?"

"I borrowed a wheelbarrow from the neighbors," said Jampa.

Jampa again hoisted her sister, carried her outside, and set her down in a wheelbarrow parked in the yard, while Bao Ke snapped pictures. The wheelbarrow's inside was powdered with cement dust, but

Chimé didn't mind. Jampa and Ama helped Chimé get settled while she giggled, loving the attention.

Once Chimé was comfortable leaning up against the back of the wheelbarrow, Jampa pushed her out to the street. The group made a procession toward the center of town, Chimé in front. She gazed around, delighted at all of the novel sights. Although she had lived in the town all her life, she never saw it. There were so many buildings and people! She smiled and called out to people passing by.

A large crowd was milling around the plaza in front of the county government offices. Adrol led them to a table where a Han man in a blue windbreaker was leafing through a sheaf of papers. They gave Chimé's name, and the man penned a checkmark on one of his papers. He told them that they should wait with the other people until Chimé's name was called.

Jampa took Chimé where she was told, and they waited with the crowd in front of a long table. To one side was a parked truck, and next to it, a row of large cardboard boxes. Several foreigners were there fussing with the boxes, opening them, and pulling out metal contraptions with black vinyl seats. One of the foreigners had streaky golden hair. She seemed very beautiful to Chimé.

Presently some officials sat down at the table, and the foreigners sat down next to them. One official stood up and made some remarks. The crowd fell silent, a few nodding at the speaker but most staring at the foreigners.

The talking lasted a long time, and when it was done, the foreigners got up and went to their contraptions, and the man in the blue windbreaker picked up his sheaf of papers and called out, "Yonden! Seventy-six-year-old Yonden!" A man with a walking stick hobbled forward, and Blue Windbreaker pointed him toward a group of waiting foreigners.

"Lorong! Ten-year-old Lorong!" called Blue Windbreaker. A woman came forward carrying a young girl. "Please go over there," he told them.

Jampa was crestfallen that Chimé's name was not called, but then she saw Adrol looking at her, smiling as if to say *don't worry*. She settled down to wait.

When Chimé's turn arrived, the foreigners looked her over and measured her and talked among themselves before finally choosing one of the contraptions from the row. One foreigner stood on each side of her, and they lifted her and set her down on the seat.

No sooner was Chimé seated than she keeled over to one side, so the foreigners went to work cutting blocks of foam into cushions so that Chimé could sit upright. Chimé was bewildered by it all, but when the work was done, she found herself sitting taller and prouder than she ever had in her life. And she could roll! People took turns pushing her chair around the plaza while a grinning Chimé crowed with astonishment and delight.

Adrol came over and translated the foreigners' instructions on how to lock and unlock the brakes. He showed Jampa how to pull the chair up a flight of stairs and lower it back down. The foreigners cautioned her to watch out for sores on Chimé's behind from sitting too long, and they gave her extra blocks of foam.

Around two o'clock, the family headed home, Chimé's mother pushing the empty wheelbarrow. Chimé couldn't stop talking. Jampa was quiet but bursting with joy and relief, for her life would be so much easier now. Perhaps Tashi could even return to school.

"This is not a sewing machine," Chimé said, "it's a bicycle," and everybody laughed.

# Final Notes

# Epilogue

In the years since KhamAid closed, I have put my personal affairs in order while continuing to engage in Tibet's development through involvement with other NGOs. Although economic progress in Tibet has continued, it still has a long way to go; pockets of deep poverty remain. Freedoms are being further curtailed by the growing reach of China's surveillance apparatus, and foreign media are increasingly restricted and harassed. Yet I also see a few causes for hope: slow but steady improvements in several gates of the development mandala and growing numbers of Chinese embracing Buddhist teachings on compassion. As China, the United States, and the rest of the world move forward, I remain convinced that the most powerful force for progress is small deeds done by ordinary people. If this book inspires a few more of them, then it will have served its purpose.

# Gratitude

The events described in this book would not have happened without the donors, volunteers, staff, and institutional partners who made Kham Aid Foundation's work possible. KhamAid's privacy policy prohibits me from mentioning donors by name, but my gratitude to them is boundless and everlasting. Among staff, Wu Bangfu stands first and foremost, and alongside him his family, the unsung heroes of this story. Doka, Adrol, Meng Changshou and Xu Bin also deserve special mention for their contributions to KhamAid's mission. Dana Isherwood is a dynamo who ran our education program, served on our board, and raised funds.

On the home front, our heroes include the other directors: (at various times) Stephen Aldridge, Jonathan Bell, David Bleyle, Bridget Bray, Brandon Davito, Marion Fay, Ruth Hayward, Bill Isherwood,

Craig Jones, and Melinda Liu. Our officers included Esperanza Gemberling, Adrienne Harris, and several board members wearing multiple hats.

In addition to these folks, there were many others toiling in California and elsewhere on the unglamorous work of administration, publicity, and fundraising, among them Rebecca Edwards, Shirley Cooper, Erica Hayward, Jennifer Ho, Aimee Hunter, Julie Rogers, Hilary Stetson, and Karin Tang.

The valiant and resourceful directors of our field programs were Jonathan Bell, Bridget Bray, John Giszczak, Linda Griffin, Kara Jenkinson, Billie Karel, Eunice Shen, Shiyin Siou, Ute Wallenböck, as well as many Chinese nationals whose names I will omit considering that their involvement with a foreign NGO may not be convenient for their future career prospects.

Because the story of KhamAid's volunteer English teaching program didn't make it into this book, I want to acknowledge here the hard work and personal sacrifice of the many individuals who stayed in Kham for long periods and expanded the horizons of hundreds of young people. Ditto for the people who worked on our brief project at Dhetsang Monastery.

A hearty bravo to Martin Dunphy, cyclist and fundraiser extraordinaire. A tearful salute to David Bleyle, KhamAid's capable chairman during our latter years, and to Tenzin Gyaltsen, who volunteered on several programs, along the way introducing many a young Tibetan to beat-boxing.

It takes a village to produce a book. I want to thank the people who bravely waded through drafts and gave me their feedback: Barbara Pulling, Mark Lemke, Adrienne Harris, David Holmstrom, Cathy Suter, Jaya Chatterjee, and George Mason. Much appreciation to Wu Bangfu, Richard Harlan, and Gyalten Rinpoche for their help. *Domo arigato* to Karin Kempe for sharing her understanding of Zen. *Xiexie* to Henrik Bork for sharing Chimé's story with his readers and with me. *Tujijay* to Adrienne Harris for her consultations. Notwithstanding the efforts of my KhamAid village, if I have strayed from the facts, I bear that responsibility alone.

Most of all, I thank my husband Greg for his extraordinary love, patience, and support during the years I have spent climbing this mountain.

## On the Use of Pseudonyms

I have used some false names for a variety of reasons: ethical considerations governing NGO work, personal commitments made to individuals, and risk of reprisal. To protect identities, I have also altered some facts. Those affected include all of the scholarship and wheelchair recipients, as well as Kelsang Chutso, Sai Man Lim, Chokyi Yangchen, Ngawang, Thubten, Ajeh, and Chimé's family members. Others are identified by their real names.

## Places

The table that begins on the next page lists places mentioned in this book. The hierarchical system used within Sichuan Province from largest administrative entity to smallest is: prefecture (*zhou* 州); county (*xian* 县), district (*qu* 区), township (*xiang* 乡), and village (*cun* 村). The chief town in every county has its own name; however, for simplicity's sake, in this book, these towns are referred to by the name of their enclosing counties. Where the Tibetan script was not available, entries under "Original" are blank.

| Type | Tibetan name | Original | Alternate names | Chinese name |
|---|---|---|---|---|
| **Places in Kandze Tibetan Autonomous Prefecture, Sichuan Province** | | | | |
| **Prefecture** | **Kandze** | དཀར་མཛེས་བོད་ རིགས་རང་སྐྱོང་ཁུལ། | **Xikang, Jiangdong, Garzê** | **Ganzi Zangzu Zizhi Zhou 甘孜藏族自治州** |
| **County** | **Dartsendo** | དར་རྩེ་མདོ། | **Tachienlu, Dardo** | **Kangding 康定** |
| Town | Rangaka | ར་ཉ་ཨབར། | | Xinduqiao 新都桥 |
| Village | Wayö | ཝ་ཡོད། | Oyeu | Wayue 瓦约 |
| Township | Sadé | ས་བདེ། | | Shade 沙德 |
| Township | Lhagang | ལྷ་སྒང་། | | Tagong 塔公 |
| Village | Pasu | འཕགས་གསོས། | | Basang 拔桑 |
| Pass, River | Gyu la (Chu) | རྒྱུ་ལ་ཆུ། | | Zheduo Shan 折多山, 河 |
| Village | Dorakarmo | རྡོ་ར་དཀར་མོ། | Duola | Duori Agamo 多日阿嘎莫 |
| Monastery | Senggé | སེང་གེ་དགོན། | | Bajiao Si 八角寺 |
| Village | Gorima | གོངས་རི་མ། | | Gerima 各日马 |
| Township | Chakgé | ལྕགས་གད། | | Jiagenba 甲根坝 |
| Monastery | Guwa | འགུ་བ་དགོན། | Gewaka, Gurwa | Guwa 古瓦 |
| Village | Pusarong | ཕྱུ་ཉ་རོང་། | | Pusharong 普莎绒 |
| **County** | **Chakzam** | ལྕགས་ཟམ། | | **Luding 泸定** |
| Mountain | Minyak Gangkar | མི་ཉག་གངས་དཀར། | | Gongga Shan 贡嘎山 |
| **County** | **Rongtrak** | རོང་བྲག | | **Danba 丹巴** |
| **County** | **Serthar** | གསེར་ཐར། | **Sertar** | **Seda 色达** |
| **County** | **Ta'u** | རྟའུ། | **Dawu, Tawu** | **Daofu 道孚** |
| Township | Mazur | མ་ཟུར། | | Mazi 麻孜 |
| Town | Bamé | བ་སྨད། | Qianning | Bamei 八美 |

| | | | | |
|---|---|---|---|---|
| **County** | **Drango** | བྲག་འགོ། | | **Luhuo** 炉霍 |
| Township | Hre hor | ཧྲེ་ཧོར། | | Zhuwo 朱倭 |
| **County** | **Kandze** | དཀར་མཛེས། | **Garze** | **Ganzi** 甘孜 |
| Township | Rongpatsa | རོང་པ་ཚ། | | Rongbacha 绒坝岔 |
| Monastery | Dargye | དར་རྒྱས་དགོན། | | Dajin 大金 |
| **County** | **Degé** | སྡེ་དགེ་ | **Derge, Dêgê** | **Dege** 德格 |
| Township | Manigan-go | མ་ཎི་གད་མགོ། | Mani Gego | Manigange 马尼干戈 |
| Township, Monastery | Palpung | དཔལ་སྤུངས་དགོན། | Belpung, Pelpung | Babang 八邦寺 |
| Monastery | Pewar | དཔེ་ཝར་དགོན། | | Baiya 白垭寺 |
| Township | Khorlondo | འཁོར་ལོ་མདོ། | | Keluodong 柯洛洞 |
| Township, Monastery | Dzokchen | རྫོགས་ཆེན། | Dzogchen | Zhuqing 竹庆 |
| Lake | Yilung Lhatso | ཡིད་ལྷུང་ལྷ་མཚོ། | Yihun Lhatso | Xinluhai 新路海 |
| Mountain Range, Pass | Tro La | ཁྲོ་ལ། | Cho La | Que'er Shan 雀儿山 |
| Monastery | Gönchen | དགོན་ཆེན་དགོན། | | Genqing 更庆寺 |
| Cultural site | Parkhang | པར་ཁང་། | | Yinjing Yuan 印经院 |
| River | Ser Chu | གསེར་ཆུ། | | Sai'er Qu 赛尔曲 |
| **County** | **Sershul** | སེར་ཤུལ། | **Dzachuka** | **Shiqu** 石渠 |
| Monastery, School | Ponru | དཔོན་རི། | | Benri 本日 |
| Township | nJu-nyung | འཇུ་ཉུང་། | | Yiniu 宜牛 |
| **County** | **Nyarong** | ཉག་རོང་། | | **Xinlong** 新龙 |
| Township | Bangmé | བང་སྨད། | | Bomei 博美 |
| Township | Lharima | ལྷ་རི་མ། | | Larima 拉日马 |
| **County** | **Nyakchukha** | ཉག་ཆ་ཁ། | | **Yajiang** 雅江 |
| Village | Shanbeihou | | | Shanbeihou 山背后 |
| Village | Oro | | | Wolong Temple 卧龙寺 |
| Township | Gokar | མགོ་དཀར། | | Egu 恶古 |
| Township | Panyukrong | སྤ་སྐྱུག་རོང་། | | Bayirong 八依绒 |
| Township | Nyayülzhab | ཉ་ཡུལ་ཞབས། | | Yayihe 牙衣河 |
| Township | Posershö | སྤོ་སེར་ཤོད། | | Boshihe 波斯河 |
| **County** | **Litang** | ལི་ཐང་། | | **Litang** 理塘 |
| **County** | **Batang** | འབའ་ཐང་། | | **Batang** 巴塘 |

| County | Dabpa | འདབ་པ། | Dappa | Daocheng 稻城 |
|---|---|---|---|---|
| Nature Reserve | Nyingden | ཉིང་ དེན། | Aden, Konkaling | Yading 亚丁 |
| Monastery | Tronggu | | | Chonggu 冲古 |
| County | Chatreng | ཆ་ཕྲེང་། | Chantreng Chaktreng | Xiangcheng 乡城 |
| County | Pelyül | དཔལ་ཡུལ། | | Baiyu 白玉 |
| County | Gyezur | བརྒྱད་ཟུར། | | Jiulong 九龙 |
| County | Derong | སྡེ་རོང་། | | Derong 得荣 |

| Type | Tibetan name | Original | Alternate names | Chinese name |
|---|---|---|---|---|
| **Rivers in Kandze TAP** | | | | |
| River | Nyag Chu | ཉག་ཆུ། | Nyak Chhu | Yalong Jiang 雅砻江 |
| River | Dri Chu | འབྲི་ཆུ། | Dri Chhu, Yangtze River | Jinsha Jiang 金沙江 |
| River | Zi Chu | | | Xianshui He 鲜水河 |
| River | Tatu Chu | ཏ་ཏུའི་ཆུ། | | Dadu He 大渡河 |
| River | Ding Chu | ཐིངས་ཆུ། | | Dingqu He 定曲河 |
| **Other places within Sichuan Province** | | | | |
| Prefecture | Ngawa | ང་བ་བོད་རིགས་ ཆ ང་རིགས་རང་ སྐྱོང་ཁུལ། | | Aba Zangzu Qiangzu Zizhizhou 阿壩藏族羌族自治州 |
| County in Ngawa Pref. | Zungchu | ཟུང་ཆུ། | Sharkhog ཤར་ ཁོག | Songpan 松潘 |
| Nature Reserve in Ngawa Pref. | Zitsa Degu | གཟི་ཚ་སྡེ་དགུ། | | Jiuzhaigou 九寨沟 |
| **Places outside Sichuan Province** | | | | |
| Monastery in TAR | Samye | བསམ་ཡས་ལྷ་དགོན། | | Sangye Si 桑耶寺 |
| County in Yunnan | Gyeltang | རྒྱལ་ཐང་། | Shangri-la, Zhongdian | Xianggelila 香格里拉 |
| County in Qinghai | Yülshül | ཡུལ་ཤུལ། | Jyekundo སྐྱེ་རྒུ་མདོ། | Yushu 玉树县 |
| Town in Qinghai | Jyekundo | སྐྱེ་རྒུ་མདོ། | Jyegu, Gyêgu | Jiegu 结古 |

# Index

# About the Author

SEEKING A PATH TO THE highest places, Pamela Logan studied aerospace at Caltech and Stanford, worked at a couple of NASA laboratories, and taught college-level aeronautical engineering before setting aside her technical career to explore Asia. As science director at the China Exploration & Research Society, she led a wall paintings conservation project at a Buddhist monastery in the Tibetan region of Kham; she also helped search for Silk Road ruins using spaceborne imaging radar. In 1997, Logan launched Kham Aid Foundation, a nonprofit that she led for fourteen years doing development and humanitarian assistance projects on the eastern Tibetan plateau. She lives with her husband in Colorado.

www.ingramcontent.com/pod-product-compliance
Lightning Source LLC
Chambersburg PA
CBHW030234030426
42336CB00009B/99